THE POLITICS OF
PROVINCIALISM

———————>>)(((———————

The Democratic Party in Transition,
1918–1932

THE
POLITICS

OF

PROVINCIALISM

The Democratic Party in Transition,

1918–1932

—————⟫⟫⟪⟪—————

DAVID BURNER

—————⟫⟫⟪⟪—————

Alfred A. Knopf   New York   1968

To

SANDY and DIANE

ACKNOWLEDGMENTS

I am indebted for criticisms to Professors Richard Hofstadter, Walter Metzger, and William Leuchtenburg, all of Columbia University. Professor Hofstadter, critical yet patient and encouraging, was a model doctoral adviser; the rich content of one single-spaced, seven-page letter from Professor Metzger kept me working for the better part of a year; and Professor Leuchtenburg's help was invaluable in matters of bibliography and style. For criticism and favors I am obliged to Robert Burner, Robert Cross, Alden Vaughan, Marvin Weinbaum, Jordan Schwarz, David Ellis, Lowell Dyson, and to many helpful students and librarians; and I owe a special debt for the typing and editorial assistance of Marian Wilson. As Gilder Fellow at Columbia I was able to devote the year 1962–3 to research, and Oakland University later awarded me travel grants. I am especially pleased to thank Thomas West of Catholic University, whose keen sense of literary architecture and style has its imprint on every page of this book; the work has profited in every way from his generous help.

Stony Brook, New York   D . B .
June 1967

CONTENTS

PREFACE

In the years of Republican ascendancy from 1920 to 1932, the national Democratic party transformed itself from an institution largely rural in its orientation and leadership to one that embodied the aspirations of the American city dweller—and most notably, the urbanite of immigrant stock. Ever since the elections of 1894 and 1896, the party had looked to the country for its largest vote; even in the Wilson era the strength of the party in rural areas exceeded its strength in the cities. But in the congressional elections of the 1920's, the urban representation in the House began to take on a solidly Democratic cast; and since the cities were growing steadily, rapidly surpassing the countryside in population, the urban congressional victories signified that the city Democracy was destined to electoral predominance within the party. The nomination of Alfred E. Smith as presidential candidate in 1928 demonstrated the power that the city could wield in national Democratic politics.

Strife and bitterness accompanied the passage of Democratic power from country to city. The rural Democrats fought a strong rearguard action upon the grounds of nativism, prohibition, and Protestantism; often their efforts were directed less against the Republicans than against the urban Democratic faction. The conflict centered in the national conventions and in the presidential elections, where country Democrats, even when they did not cross political lines, gave only lukewarm support to their party. Each of the losing candidates in the twenties—James M. Cox, John W. Davis, and Alfred E. Smith—was in some way associated with the city or its political machines and therefore possessed little real appeal for the rural South and West. Yet in each of these presidential elections—if in that of 1924 the Democrats be credited with the La Follette supporters who voted for Democratic congressional candidates—the party gained additional urban strength. Had the city and country been able to cooperate by naming candidates acceptable to the whole party, the Democrats could have provided the Republicans with a more formidable opposition during the twenties. But a national coalition could not easily be constructed in a party so deeply split over emotionally charged issues.

The most prominent Democratic figures of the decade were not pawns in a greater battle between conflicting social factions, for their own persons and ideals represented too vitally the issues at stake. Informal, slangy, cigar-smoking, Governor Smith of New York was the personification of the city, its natives as well as its immigrants. The qualities of his speech, his gait and bearing, betokened an upbringing and way of life as yet new to American presidential politics. William Gibbs McAdoo, born in Georgia and raised in Tennessee, defended rural society against the encroachments of the city; he advanced prohibition and accepted support from the Klan. But McAdoo was also a New York businessman—he had secured financial backing for the first Hudson River tunnels; in his person the manner and outlook of the countryside found only partial expression. The champion of the country was the aging William Jennings Bryan, after whom McAdoo attempted to pattern his own political career. Bryan, the spokesman of fundamentalist religion and prohibition, remained until his death an influential figure in the Democratic party.

The programs of the Democratic leaders reflected their divergent loyalties. Bryan believed in the innate superiority of rural to urban America, and in the style as in much of the content of his reform he was an agrarian; Smith, who went so far as to exhibit a personal misunderstanding of the hinterland and a distaste for its ways, proposed reforms that were directed chiefly toward the urban population. Substantially more radical than the multitudes he enraptured, Bryan championed a galaxy of far-reaching reforms as emphatically in the twenties as at any other period in his life. The progressivism of Al Smith was somewhat more narrowly circumscribed; it limited its attention mostly to the kinds of change that would promote efficiency in government or lift some economic or legal burden from his working-class supporters. In the late twenties, as the city eclipsed the country in the Democratic party and as the immigrants began to vote in larger numbers, the evangelical reformism of Bryan and his followers among the small, unorganized farmers gave way to the self-interest of urban political pressure groups, both ethnic and economic.

It was to a large extent the Great Depression, against which the two factions of the Democracy could make common cause, that restored the party to health. But the restoration also demanded an individual who could somehow bridge the gap between the mores of city and country, and mold the party's program to a more encompassing and inspiring form. Franklin Delano Roosevelt of upstate New York was ideally suited to this task. Throughout the twenties he had maintained ties both with Tammany Hall and with the South and West; and one day, his craftsmanship as a mediator of divergent views and personalities would prove itself amidst the administrative and party tensions of the New Deal.

THE POLITICS OF PROVINCIALISM

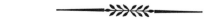

The Democratic Party in Transition,

1918–1932

CHAPTER I

Rural Traditions
and Urban Encroachments

In the decade following World War I, as the American city made continuing encroachments upon the countryside and an earlier, village way of life, the traditional and the younger Americas came into something approaching total conflict. One faction, the rural and nativist, had been long familiar to America in the politics of William Jennings Bryan; the other, the urban and immigrant represented by Al Smith, the Irish Catholic Governor of New York, was testing its power in national politics. The Democratic party was the arena of their confrontation.

At the 1924 Democratic Convention in New York City the two factions clashed openly and in full ceremony. In Madison Square Garden the prohibitionist collided with the cockney and the liberal, Protestant glowered at Catholic, the East Side jeered the Nebraska spread, and Smith battled William Gibbs McAdoo to a 100-ballot stalemate. The tensions, indeed the very chaos of that scene belied the notion, sometimes expressed by observers then and since, that during the decade of Republican ascendancy the Democratic party was torpid. And when in the years of the Great Depression the party regained some measure of internal harmony, its objectives redefined, and its center of gravity now clearly shifted to the city, it was able to demonstrate both the strength of its parts and the political effectiveness of their new arrangement.

Ultimately the conflict of the 1920's was one of values: those "Protestant" virtues and comfortable if narrow tastes to which nineteenth-century village America had adhered, set against the standards—scarcely less moralistic perhaps, and at times scarcely less provincial—of the modern American city and the enthusiasms of its communal enclaves: Roman ritual, Jewish scholarship, the disciplines of celibacy, and the pleasures of the saloon. And of course, there was the fact of urban cosmopolitanism, the sophistication and enlightened curiosity that might give their character to one city dweller even while his neighbor held to the secure institutions of the Old Country. The mere existence of a cosmopolitan outlook could awaken fears and hostilities on the part of a receding and beleaguered small-town culture.

A number of specific themes and issues defined the larger conflict. Anti-Catholicism—a phenomenon possessing its own independent existence as well as a connection with other attitudes—has a well-chronicled history older than that of the nation itself. Another question of long standing was that of prohibition. Since the late 1840's it had helped to separate the immigrants of that day, the Irish and the Germans, from many old-stock Americans; but the victory of the prohibitionists was incomplete until the ratification of the Eighteenth Amendment in 1920, and that victory was soon to vanish in new strife over the issue. The movement for immigration restriction originated fairly early in the nineteenth century, and as the population expanded, the arguments for restriction, both social and economic, assumed force and an increasing ability to generate ill feeling. In the 1920's Congress debated with passionate intensity bills curtailing immigration.

Other events contributed specifically to rural-urban confrontation in that decade: the assembly-line automobile, the radio, and the movies. Each provided a physical, cultural invasion of the country by the city; country folk could see and hear the city as it moved out upon them. Add to this World War I, with its aggressions, its raucous patriotism, its concern over hyphenism; and even the census report of 1920 that declared the cities to have outdistanced the country in population. While the census declaration was arbitrary in many ways, it must have had its imaginative effect on the American consciousness. An analogous report in 1890 had announced the end of the frontier, and it had some part in prompting Frederick Jackson Turner to his frontier thesis that helped to shape the American imagination. So too the census of 1920 could have brought the American city to a new awareness of political and social strength, and the American hinterland to a heightened state of fear and militance.[1]

But why in the twenties did the urban-rural antagonisms center within the Democratic party? There was at least one ephemeral reason: only the Democrats needed to suffer the

[1] Census reports must be read and evaluated with care; semantic ambiguities particularly complicate the reports that locate the changing areas of rural and urban America. To census officials in 1920, for example, "rural" referred to farms and towns of fewer than 2,500. A small town of 5,000, or even a small city of 25,000, located in the middle of a farming area and dependent on farming for its economic well-being, might in fact possess a rural character unrevealed in the reports. Nor were dwellers in the large cities necessarily untouched by country ways. Even in New York and Chicago there were men and women residing who had come too recently from the country to be truly urban in outlook. And nationality groups recently arrived on American shores often adhered to some of the mores of the European village. While the ghettos of New York and other big cities presented the ethnic variety and the viewpoint of a new American urbanism, that urbanism itself reproduced many of the institutions of County Cork or the southern Italian plains —above all, the church of the European peasant. And urban provinciality itself sometimes fully rivaled in its narrowness the vision of upstate New York or the Middle West and South.

While the census reports of 1920 were perhaps premature in calling America urban, those of 1930 most assuredly were not. The Census Bureau did not hold to a consistent standard in its definition of rural and urban; but if the discrepancies be leveled and a single reasonable measure imposed, we will find 14,365,512 more urban dwellers recorded in 1930 than in the previous report. See United States Bureau of the Census, *Fifteenth Census of the United States: 1930. Population*, I, 7–8.

divisions of the presidential nominating process. In 1924 and 1928 the choice for the incumbent Republicans was predetermined, and even in 1920 the Republican candidate, once nominated, attracted a diversity within the political and social spectra. More basically, however, the composition of the two parties was such as to assure that the Democratic would be the party of deeper social and ethnic conflict. The Republican cause was that of the middling elements in American civilization, in country and city alike, and appealed to a wide range of incomes and occupations, while for decades the Democracy had attracted the extremes—the most aggressively Jeffersonian or populist of the farmers, particularly in the South, and the most powerful of the urban immigrant machines. And the city immigrant was of necessity the symbolic urbanite; alienated in varying degrees from American society as a whole, he had to take his identity as an American exclusively from his immediate surroundings.

We might fix on two moments in the history of the Democratic party—the age of Jefferson and the time of Jackson. During these periods, the party adopted a distinctly rural or frontier countenance and established certain traditions and assumptions about itself upon which the country faction of a later era could draw. Yet the Democrats were by no means the uniquely rural party. In the early and middle nineteenth century, no national political organization, whether Democratic, Whig, or anti-slavery, could have survived even temporarily without drawing massive rural support. The Civil War and Reconstruction won for the Democrats the agricultural South, but settled the Republican party upon sections of middle and western America. In the early twentieth century, it was the politics of William Jennings Bryan that shaped the rural Democracy.

Bryan's earliest appeal to the countryside was as an economic reformer. In 1896 he adopted a free-silver program that had its passionate adherents among the agrarians, and very few among the city dwellers. Of the fifty most populous counties in the nation, forty-five gave pluralities to McKinley in the November election; of the remaining five that went for Bryan, four were in the traditionally Democratic South. The combined population of the twenty-three McKinley states was 44.8 per cent urban—if an urban community be defined as one having a population of 2,500 or more—while the twenty-two that went for Bryan were 21.4 per cent urban. A comparison with the previous presidential election is telling: the Democratic plurality of 162,000 in the eighty-five principal cities in 1892 was replaced in 1896 by a Republican plurality of 464,000. Outside the most urban areas the 1896 election told another story. Bryan improved on Cleveland's record in the agrarian states and carried 1,551 of the nation's 2,738 counties. With Populist help he also increased the Democratic vote in thirty of the nation's forty-five states.[2]

Thereafter Bryan turned to a more general kind of reform. His program was to embody policies of urban as well as rural progressivism, yet its expression and its energy were of the character of middle-border protest. By 1912 he had proposed a graduated income tax and government ownership of the railroads; he fought against the abuse of the labor injunction; he pioneered in proposing a bank deposit guarantee similar to that

[2] For a view of the 1896 election returns in a long-range context, see Tables I and II. McKinley's success in the cities and Bryan's in the country do not constitute *prima facie* evidence of urban-rural tension in the elections. V. O. Key, Jr., sees a more distinct sectional antagonism in the returns: "A Theory of Critical Elections," *Journal of Politics,* XVII (February 1955), 15–16. On the emphasis given to free silver in the campaign, see Paul W. Glad: *McKinley, Bryan, and the People* (Philadelphia, 1964), pp. 137–8, 164–5, 167, 173–5, 179–84, 206. All national, state, city, and county tallies—hereafter not footnoted—for the years 1916 and before are to be found in Edgar Eugene Robinson: *The Presidential Vote, 1896–1932* (Stanford, 1934); those for 1920 through 1940 are in Richard M. Scammon: *America at the Polls: A Handbook of American Presidential Election Statistics, 1920–1964* (Pittsburgh, 1965). United States Bureau of the Census, *Tenth Census: Population,* I, 9–57.

forced upon Franklin Roosevelt in 1933. Impelled by a Jacksonian faith, he championed sundry democratic reforms: initiative, referendum, and recall; direct primaries; a single-term presidency; woman suffrage; and the movement against the lame-duck Congress. If these programs appear shallow next to those of the New Deal, they were radical compared to those of the preceding generation. William Allen White later observed that Bryan had "stood for as much of the idea of socialism as the American mind will confess to." If Bryan reformism did not compete successfully against Republican progressivism in most of the Central and Western states, it did win for the party in 1900 and 1908 a larger proportionate vote there than the Democrats had been winning before 1896. This support, coupled with that of the South, and set against the success of the Republican progressives and conservatives among at least the non-immigrant urban classes, gave the national Democratic vote a strongly rural complexion.[3]

Of itself, the popular support that Bryan won in these elections may not have had a more than temporary influence upon the party, which was always too heterogeneous to sustain a Bryan stereotype. In 1912, however, he helped secure the Democratic nomination for his fellow progressive, Woodrow Wilson, and thereupon agrarian progressivism became an even stronger force within the Democracy. Upon his victory, Wilson felt obligated—despite some qualms—to choose the Nebraskan as his Secretary of State, and Bryan gave unstinting support in working for a version of Wilson's reform program more far-reaching even than that which Wilson himself had set forth during the campaign. But the growing respect between the two leaders ended abruptly in 1915. Wilson's harsh note to Germany

[3] President Theodore Roosevelt had incorporated into his politics and even, in part, into law a reform program similar to Bryan's, as George Mowry points out in his *Theodore Roosevelt and the Progressive Movement* (Madison, Wisc., 1946), p. 35. White is quoted in Paul W. Glad: *The Trumpet Soundeth: William Jennings Bryan and His Democracy, 1896–1912* (Lincoln, Neb., 1960), p. 158.

on submarine warfare clashed with the neutralist conscience of his Secretary.[4]

Yet in spite of their failure to agree on handling the German problem, these two progressive Democrats pursued common policies—from interference in Latin American affairs to regulation of big business—and thereby gave a measure of coherence to the Democratic party program. Wilson was attentive to agricultural protest, though sometimes at variance with its leaders, and was disposed to share the rural and small-town aversion to the city. Both Wilson and Bryan worked more diligently than any other statesmen of their time for an international organization to settle world problems peaceably. The issue of prohibition was one of the few on which the two were far apart.

In at least one major respect their characters were as similar as their politics. For better or worse, each man brought a strong sense of Christian morality directly into American politics. Both profoundly believed that for every problem there was a "moral" course of action. And each man could stand intractably behind his commitments. Bryan, for instance, refused to abandon free silver, even after 1900 when that program had lost its initial popularity and he could have campaigned more effectively on a policy of anti-imperialism alone.[5] As distinctive in its stubborn courage as in its political folly was Wilson's intransigence on the League of Nations.

Similar in moral rigor and in their legislative programs, the two men also drew overlapping political support. It is true that some urban political leaders, such as Roger Sullivan of Chicago, had played an important role in nominating Wilson in 1912, whereas Bryan had identified certain urban bosses with large corporate interests. But Sullivan had supported Wilson in part to prevent a possible stalemate which would result in Bryan's nomination. In rhetorical thrusts at Wall Street and Tammany,

[4] *New Republic*, II (March 13, 1915), 139–40; Arthur S. Link: *Wilson: The New Freedom* (Princeton, 1956), pp. 206–7, 213, 222.
[5] Glad: *The Trumpet Soundeth*, pp. 59–60.

as well as in his snubbing of Boss Charles Murphy of New York in the 1912 campaign, Wilson showed the same independence of urban machines that had characterized his tenure as governor of New Jersey. In the 1912 convention, Bryan's attachment to Wilson had developed largely because of Murphy's opposition to the Princetonian. And in both 1912 and 1916, Wilson drew even more support from the countryside than had Bryan. In 1916 twenty-three states of the South and Far West voted for Wilson, and the biggest cities did not figure greatly in the electoral victory. Wilson did improve on Bryan's vote in the eastern cities, but he also carried almost all of the wheat states, and thereby outdid Bryan in his home territory. At the same time, patronage dealt out by Postmaster General Burleson maintained rapport between Wilson and the urban machines, which, with the aid of Burleson and presidential aide Joe Tumulty, were actually strengthened at the expense of some urban progressives. But if in some measure Wilson may have harmonized the city and the country wings of the party, most fundamentally he "emerged as the present heir of the great populist-Bryan tradition."[6]

The Wilson coalition of 1916 was based upon agrarian and peace sentiment, as well as upon Wilson's impressive record of reform, and was strongest in its rural component. Had the election been decided in the nation's ten major cities, Charles Evans Hughes would clearly have won. And the nation's industrial states, with the exception of New Hampshire, Ohio, Washington, and California, went entirely to Hughes. The voters in the South and West, who formed the backbone of the rural Wilson

[6] Arthur S. Link: *Wilson: The Road to the White House* (Princeton, 1947), pp. 353–4, 403–4, 433, 465, 495, 527; *Wilson: The New Freedom*, p. 160; and "Woodrow Wilson and the Democratic Party," *Review of Politics*, XVIII (April 1956), 146, 150 ff.; John Blum: *Woodrow Wilson* (Boston, 1956), p. 114, and *Joe Tumulty and the Wilson Era* (Boston, 1951), pp. 152–3; Glad: *The Trumpet Soundeth*, p. 172; Mortimer Smith: *William J. Gaynor, Mayor of New York* (Chicago, 1951), p. 145; Seward Livermore: *Politics Is Adjourned: Woodrow Wilson and the War Congress, 1916–1918* (Middletown, Conn., 1964), p. 240.

coalition of 1916, cast their ballots for the incumbent presidential candidate as the statesman who "kept us out of war"; in their quest for peace they looked also to Bryan, who campaigned for Wilson throughout the West and South, as they looked to him in matters of social reform.

By the 1920's, then, the Democratic party had laid for itself in the hinterland a solid progressive foundation, and progressive in the manner of Bryan. Somewhere in the process, moreover, the country Democracy was acquiring more and more clearly a tone that had always been present in the progressive movement itself—a tone of moralism, the style of the Jeremiad.

The aims of the rural faction became larger than the economic and political; it sought no less than the rescue of traditional American virtue, and that virtue it identified with the countryside, which must now resist the moral corruption of the cities— their political machines, their saloons, their strange religious faiths—even as it must also resist their financial perfidy. Bryan led the way. Of the election of 1916 he exulted to a meeting of prohibitionists—he had enlisted in the cause by about 1909— that the party had "won without the aid of the cities, and . . . received the support of nearly all the prohibition states . . ."; in *The Commoner* he wrote that the election was a victory for "the West and South without the aid or consent of the East. The scepter has passed from New York, and this is sufficient glory for one year."[7] This was to be the moral tone of Bryan's heir apparent of the early twenties, William Gibbs McAdoo, who deferred to the Bible Belt and, like Bryan, became a strong prohibitionist. To be sure, "the impassioned criticism of the social order, which Bryan had brought to the Democratic party . . . was not for McAdoo," as Herbert Agar has noted. The enterprising McAdoo frequently indulged in Populist rhetoric, but he lacked a strong emotional or intellectual commitment to populist

[7] On Bryan's symbolic importance in the 1916 convention, see Arthur S. Link: *Wilson: Campaigns for Progressivism and Peace* (Princeton, 1965), pp. 44–5, 47, and *The New York Times*, June 16, 1916, p. 1, which called Bryan "the outstanding figure of the convention." Bryan is quoted in *The Commoner*, XVI (November 1916), 1.

reform. McAdoo, moreover, was not so conspicuously country-bred as Bryan; he had lived in New York City for many years, and he numbered Bernard Baruch of that city among his important supporters. Nevertheless, his utterances were replete with condemnations of the city as the home of Wall Street and with praise of the country as the hope of America.[8]

The later career of Bryan indicated the continuity of the progressive with the moralist phase of the country faction. He never relinquished his commitment either to progressive reform or to the Democratic party. When in 1920 the Prohibitionists, meeting in Lincoln, Nebraska, tendered their nomination to Bryan, the honor was insufficient to lure him from the Democratic organization. Staying within the party was for Bryan a simple matter of loyalty and faith. In another setback to the prohibition forces, Bryan swallowed hard in 1920 and voted for the wet Democratic candidate James Cox.[9]

And in contrast to the stereotype of the aging Nebraskan, the seedy figure with the palm-leaf fan, furnished by H. L.

[8] According to Arthur Schlesinger, Jr., the "facile and plastic" McAdoo made himself over in the image of Bryan. *The Crisis of the Old Order, 1919–1932* (Boston, 1957), p. 94. William Watts Ball of North Carolina, among others, preferred Bryan to McAdoo, whom he called "mercenary" and "shoddy." Ball to [?] Watson, August 28, 1924, Ball Papers. Not until the 1924 convention did Bryan, who apparently relished the role of an elder statesman, work for McAdoo's nomination. But he supported the efforts of Robert Woolley to take control of the party away from National Chairman George White and the urban faction in 1921. It was evidently the candidacy of Smith, which Bryan had termed "impossible," that forced the older Democrat to give some support to McAdoo's camp. Post to Bryan, February 8, 1921, Bryan to Post, February 28, 1921, and March 1, 1921, Post Papers; Woolley, unpublished memoir, Chap. xxx, Woolley Papers; J. J. Alexander to Thomas B. Love, May 10, 1924, Love Papers; *The New York Times*, October 13, 1923, p. 1; December 31, 1923, p. 7; May 11, 1924, p. 1; July 8, 1924, p. 1; Agar: *Pursuit of Happiness* (Cambridge, Mass., 1938), p. 340; New York *World*, June 23, 1924, pp. 1, 23.

[9] *The Commoner*, XX (May 6, 1920), 1; *New Republic*, XXI (January 28, 1920), 258; Lawrence Levine: *Defender of the Faith: William Jennings Bryan; The Last Decade, 1915–1925* (New York, 1965), pp. 170–4.

Mencken, the more generous and more accurate portrait by Lawrence Levine shows Bryan in his last years working to rekindle reform within the party. In 1919 he stood by his peace principles when he gave strong endorsements to the League, though he did severely criticize the President for failing to compromise on the issue of Article X of the League Covenant. He also remained consistent in his concern for economic progressivism. Before the presidential election of 1920 the Commoner lauded the achievements of Wilson's first term, which he considered a fruition of his own work, but he charged Wilson with the responsibility for the demise of progressive Democracy after 1916. In 1920 he also urged the Nebraska Constitutional Convention "to authorize the state, the counties, and the cities to take over and operate any industry they please. . . . The right of the community is superior to the right of any individual." The next year he came out with a bold new program of twenty-two miscellaneous progressive planks, which included proposals for a department of education in the President's cabinet, government ownership of certain monopolies, and an excess-profits tax. In 1923 Bryan was still enunciating a simple radicalism directed especially, but not wholly, to the needs of the farmer; he also called for an alliance with progressive Republicans to secure legislative goals. Claude Bowers, among others, praised Bryan's lifelong efforts in behalf of reform: "Almost everything we've got today in the way of reforms originated with Bryan. . . . And yet everybody thinks of him now because of his prohibition views and on account of that evolution trial."[1]

At one point in the twenties Bryan remarked: "I don't think there is a busier man than I am. I have got to keep the Demo-

[1] Bowers: Oral History Memoir, Columbia University, 1954; see also William Gibbs McAdoo: *Crowded Years* (Boston, 1931), p. 337. On Bryan's political influence in the twenties, see Levine: *Defender of the Faith*, pp. 186–8 and *passim; The New York Times*, February 17, 1921, p. 3; March 18, 1923, VIII, 1; April 2, 1923, pp. 1, 6; and William E. Dodd: *Woodrow Wilson and His Work* (New York, 1922), p. 431. *Review of Reviews*, CXII (July 1920), 42; *The Commoner*, XX (February 1920), 8–9; Bryan to Henry T. Rainey, January 2, 1924, Rainey Papers.

cratic party straight, and I have got to see that Prohibition is enforced, and I have got to see that religion is defended." William Allen White exaggerated when he said that Bryan dominated the platform committee of the Democratic National Convention of 1924, but even in New York his presence was imposing. The New York *Herald-Tribune* called Bryan's July 2 speech to the convention his "greatest flight of oratory in years." Many of the country delegates at the old Madison Square Garden clung to him as a symbol of righteousness in the face of the jeering Irishmen and Italians with whom Tammany had packed the galleries. But in New York, Bryan saw with grief that his was an embattled America. When he addressed the delegates, applause greeted his remark that this would probably be his last convention. "I may change my mind," he threatened, but his life was in fact nearing a close.[2]

The following summer he appeared at the Scopes trial in Dayton, Tennessee. Bryan's belief in reform had always been sustained by his faith in a beneficent God, and in the era of Republican normalcy he had turned increasingly to the Protestant churches, which he had always viewed as agencies of reform. Even in his gesture at Dayton—the culmination of the events through which, philosophically and practically, he severed himself from the rising urban Democracy—his loyalty to the fundamentalist faith was in part a loyalty to his own special religious-moral brand of social reform, as well as to what Walter Lippmann called his "dogma of majority rule." In a passage from a lecture on the evils of Darwinism that he did not live to deliver, Bryan said of the evolution theory that "by paralyzing the hope of reform, it discourages those who labor for the improvement of man's condition. . . . Evolution chills

[2] White: *Politics: The Citizen's Business* (New York, 1924), p. 69; *Christian Register*, III (July 10, 1924), 104; W. J. Dwyer to Breckinridge Long [1925?], Long Papers; *The New York Times*, July 2, 1924, p. 5; *Official Report of the Proceedings of the Democratic National Convention . . . [of] . . . 1924* (Indianapolis, 1925), p. 327; Paxton Hibben: *The Peerless Leader: William Jennings Bryan* (New York, 1929), p. 379.

the enthusiasm [for social reform] by substituting aeons for years." But this observation did not interest his followers, who had turned to simpler moralist concerns and a mood of pure moral antagonism to the city.[3]

The alliance between the Democratic party and the major immigrant groups had its origin in the early national period, when the Jeffersonians opposed the anti-Jacobin and anti-Irish Alien and Sedition Acts. New Americans found their way into the local organizations of the Democratic-Republicans and then the Democrats, and in their turn attracted later comers. As the Democrats stood by their immigrant supporters against the Protestant nativism of the late 1840's and early 1850's, the party drew even larger numbers; and an appeal for the votes of the economically deprived also strengthened the party among the immigrants. Most of the recruiting was among the Irish, partly because they were by far the most numerous of the immigrants during the first half of the nineteenth century, partly because they were almost solidly Roman Catholic and therefore the most unified in their opposition to nativism, while the Germans—after the Irish the largest group—were divided in religion and more often settled in rural areas away from the influence of Democratic political machines.

The traditions of Ireland and the experiences of three generations of American Irish help to explain the Irish role in the Democratic party. Under English domination, where common-law institutions reinforced the relationship between the ruled and the ruling people, the Irish learned to bargain at the local level for the favors of the central government. In their Church and in their anti-English secret societies the Irish learned loyalty

[3] William Allen White wrote that "the passing of Bryan has changed the whole aspect of the Democratic party. He was the one living force that held his party in check against the new order." New York *Herald-Tribune*, June 25, 1928, p. 3. Lippmann: *Men of Destiny* (New York, 1927), p. 45; *American Review of Reviews*, LXXII (September 1925), 312–13.

and discipline; and in the early-nineteenth-century Catholic Association movement, which in several ways functioned as a political party, they strengthened their feeling for political power. Once in America, the Irish used the Democratic party as a secular extension of their identity. Shunning union with a middle class that had ordained a Protestant America, they introduced to the party their national and Catholic traditions of discipline, hierarchy, and communal solidarity. Pluralism was discouraged by the parochial school system and by the social and religious influences of parish priests who distrusted Protestant reformers. It was opportune that the Irish settled in the American cities, where their cultural traditions would be well adapted to political life.[4]

Before the Civil War, some important urban Democratic machines—notably Tammany Hall—were acquiring an Irish stamp.[5] Even by mid-century, the city was pressing the immigrant communities into compact political units representing a considerable part of the urban populations among which they lived. Cities provided, therefore, a means of effective and self-

[4] Edward M. Levine: *The Irish and Irish Politicians* (Notre Dame, Ind., 1966), pp. 4–10, 30, 35–51, 65–9, 83, 87, 98–101, 116, 125–9; Nathan Glazer and Daniel P. Moynihan: *Beyond the Melting Pot: The Negroes, Puerto Ricans, Italians, and Irish of New York* (Cambridge, Mass., 1964), pp. 221–38.

[5] On the Democracy's longstanding attraction for the Irish, see Oscar Handlin: "The Immigrant in American Politics," in David F. Bowers, ed.: *Foreign Influence in American Life* (Princeton, 1944), pp. 88–90, and Carl Wittke: *The Irish in America* (Baton Rouge, 1956), pp. 105–13; on the Irish in New York State, Florence E. Gibson: *The Attitudes of the New York Irish Toward State and National Affairs, 1848–1892* (New York, 1951), pp. 14, 56, 88–90, 103, 451, and Lee Benson: *The Concept of Jacksonian Democracy: New York as a Test Case* (Princeton, 1961), pp. 171–3, 321–3; on the Boston Irish, J. Joseph Huthmacher: *Massachusetts People and Politics, 1919–1933* (Cambridge, Mass., 1959), p. 14 and *passim*; on the Irish in Chicago, Harold F. Gosnell: *Machine Politics: Chicago Model* (Chicago, 1937), pp. 45, 64–6, 101–2. On federalist antipathy for the Irish, see Wilfred E. Binkley: *American Political Parties: Their Natural History* (3rd rev. edn.; New York, 1958), pp. 79–80.

conscious political expression denied to the rural immigrant settlements.

In the decades that followed the Civil War, the Irish seized not only the Democratic city machines but many of the cities themselves—New York, Brooklyn, Jersey City, Boston, and San Francisco. But after about 1885 the current of migration began to shift: the preponderance would now be from the South and East of Europe rather than the North and West. On whom would the newer Americans bestow their political allegiance?

At first the Irish, instead of cultivating these potential allies, guarded their own command of urban politics as tenaciously as they maintained control within the American Catholic Church. In several cities the Republicans tried to win the votes of new immigrants—with some lasting success in such cases as the New Haven Italians and the Boston Jews. But the Republicans had inherited some of the nativism as well as the propertied identity of the Federalist-Whig tradition, and by the 1890's the nativist American Protective Association and the Republican party were closely linked in several states. In time, moreover, the Irish warmed to the other white ethnic elements; in Chicago by the 1920's Irish Democrats even learned to address meetings in Italian. Between the newer immigrants and the Irish there was enough similarity of interests—in economic status (despite the edge Irish-Americans had over the more recent comers), often in religion, in the very fact of immigrant background and estrangement from old-stock American society—to overcome mutual antagonisms and pull most of the southern and eastern Europeans into the Irish machines. In considerable measure, Democrats captured the new immigrant as well as the old.[6]

[6] Of the Chicago Italians, for example, Giovanni E. Schiavo wrote in 1928 that "brought up in a corrupt political environment, under the influence of Irish politicians, the Italian has not yet evolved a political conscience of his own. He is still following in the footsteps of the Irish. His methods, his ambitions, his ideals, his goals are the same as those of the Irish." *The Italians in Chicago* (Chicago, 1928), p. 104. On the ties of Republican state parties to the APA, see Wittke: *The Irish*

Between 1894 and the 1920's the Democratic party itself could not be called the party of the cities. Some cities with a predominantly native-born population were traditionally Whig and then Republican; some others were ruled by immigrant Republican machines. As Carl Degler has shown, moreover, there was a period in the late nineteenth century and into the twentieth when the Republican party, uninhibited by Jeffersonian precepts against "energetic" government and therefore free to innovate, was able to appeal widely to city voters as the party of industrial growth and economic experiment.[7] From the Homestead Act to the Dingley Tariff, the income tax to the Blair Education Bill, the Republican party stood for a social and economic nationalism that would appeal to a range of classes at the same time that it spoke the shibboleths of free enterprise and laissez faire. Theodore Roosevelt and other progressives of the early twentieth century called for a strong national government and worked to establish an urban-rural harmony of interests. Doubtless some urban immigrants at the time were won by this image; perhaps ethnic conflict repelled a few of them from the Irish and into the Republican organizations. But the Irishmen, possessing their traditional and highly effective Democratic machines, held their loyalty to the Democracy with only some temporary defection in a few special elections such as 1920, and with a few political deviants like the Republican organizations that captured the Irish of Philadelphia and Rochester. They provided the Democrats with a faithful city immigrant-stock constituency larger than any single bloc the Republicans could

in America, p. 124; on Republican anti-Catholicism after the Civil War, Robert D. Cross: *The Emergence of Liberal Catholicism in America* (Cambridge, Mass., 1958), p. 24; on Irish domination of the Catholic Church, Wittke: *The Irish in America*, pp. 91–5, and Oscar Handlin: *Boston's Immigrants* (rev. edn.; Cambridge, Mass., 1959), pp. 165–7. Robert E. Lane: *Political Life* (New Haven, 1958), p. 241; Oscar Handlin: *The American People in the Twentieth Century* (Cambridge, Mass., 1954), p. 216; Gosnell: *Machine Politics*, p. 24.
[7] Carl N. Degler: "The Nineteenth Century," in William H. Nelson, ed.: *Theory and Practice in American Politics* (Chicago, 1964), pp. 25–42.

usually hope to muster, a constituency broadened more and more by the absorption of new ethnic elements. And in the twenties the immigrants, totally lacking in blood connection with the American hinterland, and thrust by the rural nativist movement into a position of counterattack, were at the forefront of national urban politics. Increasingly they were introducing into the Democratic party a character absent from the Republican: a city gesture, a cockney edge. The Irish continued in their leadership of the city machines. Meanwhile, their new immigrant allies were coming to a full involvement in politics, and at some point in the twenties, as Tables I and II show, the Democrats won the cities.

For the immigrants who came here around the turn of the century, American politics had been a strange business. The new arrival from Italy or the east of Europe was indrawn; he reverenced family, church, and, suffusing all else, his own nationality. He was, in the words of Robert Lane, "pitifully conservative." "Political apathy," declares Lane, "is a function of peasant . . . origin with its associated views of government as part of a natural order beyond control." Even for the Irish, the Catholic Church had at first discouraged political participation, viewing itself as a sanctuary from the harshness of life in the urban ghetto. The segregation of its flock heightened the innate conservatism of the communicants, but the Catholic hierarchy soon found itself unwilling and unable to support the nominal separation of church and state. Church-related issues and pressures on the clergy were as intensive for the Catholic as for the Protestant churches; and the policy of sheltering immigrants from political life was gradually abandoned.[8]

After living in America for a time, the immigrants began to see that his economic and social status could be raised by shaping his activities to political means and ends. The urban machines

[8] Lane: *Political Life*, pp. 244, 251; Handlin: "The Immigrant and American Politics," pp. 90–2. On the attitude of the Catholic Church, see Cross: *The Emergence of Liberal Catholicism*, p. 25, as well as Lane, *passim*.

TABLE I

Urban Presidential Vote: Per Cent Democratic, 1876–1940*

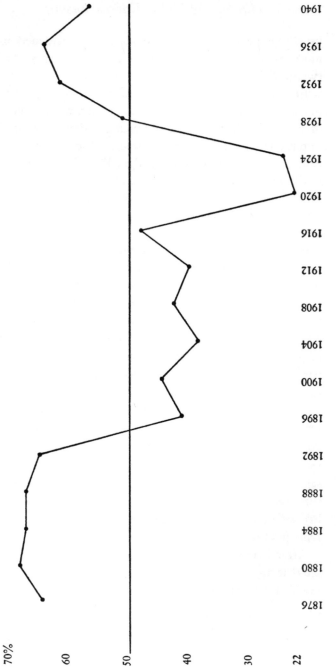

* Based on the ten largest cities as identified in the nearest decennial census.

TABLE II

Urban Congressional Representation: Per Cent Democratic, 1876–1940*

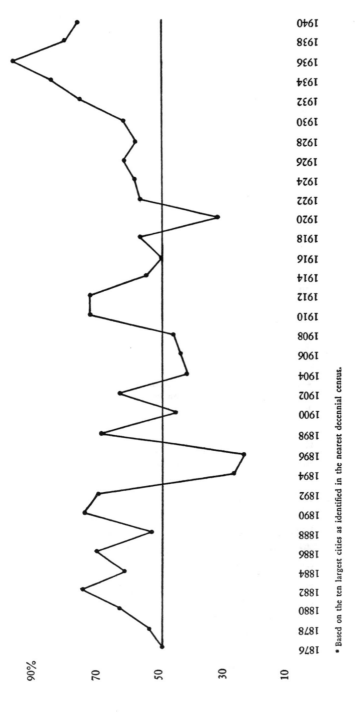

* Based on the ten largest cities as identified in the nearest decennial census.

TABLE III

Participation of Ethnic and Old Stock in Presidential Elections,
1896–1940*

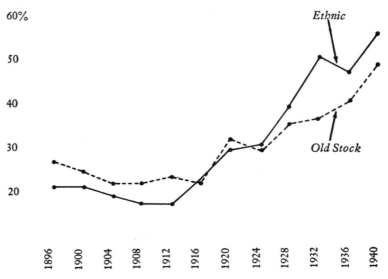

* Based on those cities identified as ethnic and old stock by Carl Degler: "American Political Parties and the Rise of the City: An Interpretation," *Journal of American History*, LI (June 1964), 55–6.

themselves drew the immigrant toward political participation, since they controlled many city jobs, offered police and fire protection, and performed other important functions. If the Italian or Jew was to be offered some patronage or perhaps even a minor slot or two for his kind on the city ticket, then he would have to appear regularly at the polls. Immigrant nationalism, directing itself to issues promoted by the foreign language or nationality press, sharpened political sensitivities, and these were strengthened further as second-generation Americans gained in education and in understanding of political matters. Unions, by requiring naturalization, also brought the new American into politics. Immigrant participation—which is charted in Table III—rose markedly during the foreign-policy debate of 1916 and continued its increase during the 1920's. In 1924 the immigrants of at least one big city, Chicago, were voting as heavily as native whites. The years of neutrality, of the great war, and of that war's unsettling aftermath had awakened the immigrant-stock citizen to the importance of the government as his agent in international relations; and in the twenties, national events touched him directly as immigrant, or as Catholic, or as representative of the ways and aspirations of the city. The movement for immigration restriction sustained his interest in events in Washington, as did the fight to repeal prohibition. The "new immigrant" communities of the postwar era, moreover, were just a bit further up the social and economic scale—certainly a little more firmly rooted—than they had been in their earliest years; and along with improvement in status and opportunity came a quickened energy, an increase in knowledge of political affairs, and a heightened sense of the distance the immigrant had yet to span in the attainment of equality. Apathy once had measured the paucity of his expectations; heightened political participation now represented his new hopes and ambitions. The Great Depression brought the immigrant even more heavily into politics. In later generations, as the immigrant became better assimilated and more economically successful, his political concern, except in relation to European wars, would wane.[9]

Despite the enormous influx of eastern Europeans, the Irish influence remained stronger than that of the newer groups far into the twentieth century, at least in New York, Boston, Chicago, and San Francisco. As late as the administrations of Franklin Roosevelt and Harry Truman, immigrant-stock executive appointees were overwhelmingly Catholic Irish—"a vivid testimonial," according to Samuel Lubell, "of the extent to which the Irish have dominated the Democratic party."[1] Yet until the 1920's the Irish produced no leader who might claim national eminence. A few Irish Democrats, such as Joe Tumulty, had served their party with distinction. But the first national

[9] Lane: *Political Life*, pp. 244–51; Harold F. Gosnell: *Getting Out the Vote* (Chicago, 1927), p. 87.
[1] *The Future of American Politics* (rev. edn.; New York, 1956), p. 83.

figure of the Irish Democracy, though his ancestry was in fact mixed, was Governor Alfred E. Smith of New York. Smith became the spokesman of urban Democracy because he was a machine man—the less so as his career progressed, but his feel for machine politics never left him. As the machine had fixed most of the immigrants to the Democratic party, Smith, as a product of Boss Charles Murphy's Tammany Hall, was their logical representative. The other ethnic and racial minorities easily identified with Al Smith, who radiated warmth and genial impulsiveness. Hitherto, immigrants of different nationalities had often quarreled more strenuously among themselves than against the nativists; but Smith's affability, his stand on prohibition, and the urban-rural tensions of the day molded the city immigrant Democracy into a force of unprecedented cohesion.

The career of Al Smith in the New York Assembly represents in microcosm the politics of the ghetto in its combination of pragmatic reform and pragmatic service to the machine. Smith entered the Assembly in 1904, and in 1911 became Democratic majority leader and chairman of the Ways and Means Committee. He introduced several reform measures designed to eradicate various social injustices and business malpractices— measures representative of the kind of bread-and-butter progressivism that the immigrant condition generates. Among his important accomplishments were the reorganization of the lower criminal courts in New York and a law restraining the issue of fraudulent stock. His factory inspection tours after the tragic Triangle Shirtwaist Factory fire of 1911 led to some important labor legislation, such as that limiting the work of women and children; and in 1914 he supported a far-reaching conservation program. But Smith was often forced to subordinate his own progressive instincts to the will of Charles Murphy, who supported reform only when it seemed likely to pass anyway or was dictated by political expediency. As governor of New York, Charles Evans Hughes introduced a spate of reform measures to the legislature. To embarrass the governor, Tammany joined with the Old Guard Republicans to defeat much of Hughes's program, and Smith was instrumental in carrying out Murphy's orders to demolish the governor's proposals. Smith forced the Assembly Democrats to vote against strengthening the public service commissions—which were a threat to patronage—and against state regulation of the telephone and telegraph. As one student of Smith's Assembly career puts it: "He had achieved notoriety for using his extensive legislative talents against the popular reforms Governor Hughes had sought to institute." Under pressure from Murphy, Smith also pushed through the "West Side grab," an overly generous franchise for a right of way to the grateful New York Central Railroad in New York City. He also wrote the notorious Levy election law that strengthened Tammany's hold on the city. It is only necessary to read the reports of the Citizens' Union of New York during some of his Assembly years to see unquestioned evidence of Smith's frequent readiness to subordinate principles of good government to political aggrandizement.[2]

When Charles Murphy died in 1924, Al Smith eulogized that he had "made of his life a lesson and an example to the youth of the country." Unhappily, it was an example vastly inferior to that of Smith himself. Murphy won a measure of respectability by keeping his hands off the courts and out of the public till, and his religious background apparently cut off prostitution as a source of income; but he was resourceful at profiting from city franchises and private contracts. J. Joseph Huthmacher, in an effort to show the urban lineage of progressivism, refers to him as "that rather obscure progressive figure." And Murphy does deserve credit, whatever his motives, for committing his well-disciplined following to a variety of substantial reforms. But he has been lauded for supporting some reforms, such as workmen's compensation, that had passed almost unanimously, and for others, like the direct primary, that he earlier opposed.

[2] Revealing on the contradictions of Smith's career in the Assembly is a 1964 St. John's University doctoral dissertation by Louis D. Silveri: "The Political Education of Alfred E. Smith: The Assembly Years, 1904–1915"; the quotation is from p. 156. Citizens' Union: *Report of the Commission on Legislation, 1909* (New York, 1910), pp. 17–19.

Murphy acquiesced in that primary which he and Smith had fought so bitterly, but acquiesced only after a Democratic debacle at the polls followed the ruthless impeachment of Governor Sulzer. If Murphy gave his blessing to some reforms, he stood in the way of many more. It would be a misreading of his character, and of Smith's background, to ignore the comments on Murphy made by certain contemporaries. Uninterested in reform, he was "arrogant and selfish," according to the New York *Evening Post;* he was more interested in "money and power," insisted the writer of a Tammany exposé. The New York Times said Murphy "was the exemplar and beneficiary of a system which . . . condemns New York City to suffer from . . . the lowest moral standards in public office." "Mr. Murphy and his machine," noted the *New Republic,* "were successful only by making a mockery of the processes of political democracy"; in the city government of 1924, according to *The Nation,* "there is endless graft. . . . The system [Murphy] headed was the same corrupt one which has for generations degraded New York. . . ." The liberal journals were surely closer to the mark than the loyal governor on the occasion of Murphy's death.[3]

As the more constructive activities of Smith's legislative career indicate, he did not merely stagnate under the aegis of Murphy's organization. And in 1915 he emerged a statesman through his widely acclaimed understanding of governmental affairs at the New York State Constitutional Convention. In 1918 he became governor of New York in a rise that testified to the growing

[3] Miss Nancy Weiss, in a forthcoming book on Murphy, presents a balanced portrait of that political figure, whom she credits with bringing Tammany a measure of respectability that helped to make possible the presidential candidacy of Governor Smith. New York *Tribune,* June 17, 1903, p. 1; Huthmacher: "Charles Evans Hughes and Charles Francis Murphy: The Metamorphosis of Progressivism," *New York History,* XLVI (June 1965), 25–40; New York *Evening Post,* January 5, 1919, p. 2; Morris Werner: *Tammany Hall* (New York, 1928), p. 322; *The New York Times,* April 26, 1924, p. 24; *New Republic,* XXXVII (April 19, 1924), 323; XXXVIII (May 7, 1924), 269; LVIII (May 5, 1929), 320; *The Nation,* CXVIII (May 21, 1924), 574; CXXXI (August 27, 1930), 214

power of the immigrant urban supporters as well as to his popularity among an even wider public; his political career up to that time was one of genuine, if only partial, growth in stature from his early position as loyal Tammany henchman. His outlook as governor—even after he became independent of Tammany—would remain conservative in several basic ways. Yet there is no question but that the endeavors in which he excelled, such as administrative reform and labor legislation, entitle him to the highest rank among New York governors and the reputation of a farsighted progressive. In his inaugural address in 1919 he asked that cities be given the right to regulate their own utilities, and he urged state intervention to relieve the postwar housing shortage; during the next year he vetoed a number of laws passed by a legislature in the grip of the Red Scare; and he gave Belle Moskowitz a free hand in choosing members of a Reconstruction Commission to reorganize the state's administrative structure. Before his term was out, the *New Republic* called him "one of the ablest governors New York has ever had."[4]

Before the twenties, the career of Alfred E. Smith struck a nice balance between his instinct for pragmatic reform and his adherence to the machine. Indeed, a harmony existed between certain kinds of reform and the urban machine: a harmony of spirit, technique, and often of economic objective. And although by 1928 Governor Smith had drifted from both of these positions, he remained the fit representative of the plebeian city electorate in its clash with the rural and nativist. The emotional South, where Bryan had moved in the early twenties, and the belligerent ruralism of parts of the West were to be found in the same political party with another emotional quantity, the urban Irish. But the immediate ground for political conflict was prepared in the latter days of the Wilson era, when a progressive Democratic coalition disintegrated, and the elements that had composed it began to regroup into mutually antagonistic factions.

[4] *The New York Times*, January 2, 1919, p. 4; *The Nation*, CVIII (January 11, 1919), 38; *New Republic*, XXIV (November 3, 1920), 226.

CHAPTER II

The Wilson Coalition

In 1912 the Progressive movement, advanced in earlier days by the flamboyant energy and skill of Theodore Roosevelt and the workmanlike experimentation of Robert La Follette, was delivered into the sober keeping of President Woodrow Wilson. By 1916, progressives could look with satisfaction on the manner in which the Chief Executive and his party were forwarding the cause of reform. In that year, President Wilson—winner of only a plurality of the popular vote in 1912—was able to forge a coalition of voters strong enough to win him a second term; and the condition of the Democratic party, like that of the Progressive movement whose life the party had helped to sustain, seemed comparatively sound and its future promising.

The winning coalition assembled elements harmonious enough for 1916, though by no means permanently compatible. Since more voters than usual crossed party lines to give the minority party a victory, the contest belonged to what political scientists have labeled "deviating" elections. Wilson's reform legislation attracted a spectrum of progressive voters ranging from middle-class Americans, who would be content with a few restraints upon the activity of finance and industry, to socialists bent on the eventual destruction of American capitalism. The President captured not only the loyal Democratic followers of William Jennings Bryan, but also some of Theodore Roosevelt's Progressive adherents who saw Wilson enact, one by one, the important elements in the Bull Moose platform of 1912. Among Wilson's supporters, in fact, were a number of businessmen who had believed in the viability of the New Nationalism preached by the Roosevelt progressives; for Wilson had in effect begun to accept the distinction between good and bad trusts, and he had dulled the cutting edge of the new regulatory agencies, the Federal Trade Commission and the Tariff Commission, with his conservative appointees. However they might deplore the Adamson Act and Child Labor Act, businessmen could appreciate the continuing economic prosperity (as could all elements in the coalition), the conservative tariff plank in the 1916 platform, and the stability that Wilson had brought to the currency system. Particularly appreciated in the banking world was the Kern Act of 1916, which eased restrictions on interlocking directorates. Probably the Republican party continued to attract a majority of men from the business world, but Wilsonianism made significant inroads.[1]

Farmers occupied a vital place in the Wilson coalition. They warmed to the antimonopoly measures and agricultural education programs of Wilson's government, its regulation of railroad rates and promotion of good roads, its generous loans to agriculture coupled with the advancement of credit against ware-

[1] For a view of the election that emphasizes long-range trends, see the important work of political scientists: Angus Campbell *et al.*: *The American Voter* (New York, 1960), p. 533. The Republican rift of 1910 had not yet healed in 1916; indeed, the issues of the war had renewed the feuding among Republican leaders. Arthur S. Link: *Wilson: Confusions and Crises, 1915–1916* (Princeton, 1964), pp. 319–21. John Garraty: *Right-Hand Man: The Life of George W. Perkins* (New York, 1960), p. 356; *New Republic*, VIII (September 2, 1916), 103–4; *The Commoner*, XVI (October 1916), 1–2; 14–15; George H. Mayer: *The Republican Party, 1854–1964* (New York, 1964), p. 342; Robert H. Wiebe: *Businessmen and Reform* (Cambridge, Mass., 1962), pp. 152–4.

house stocks. These reforms came into law not through Wilson's own initiative—indeed, he had at first blocked the rural credits bill, and apparently he signed the Federal Farm Loan Act of 1916 mainly for reasons of political expediency—yet they were products of his administration.[2]

By 1915 and 1916, labor as well as agriculture found that it could look to Wilson. To be sure, the labor legislation of Wilson's early days in office had been disappointing; but the approach of a presidential election, the threat of strikes that might endanger the administration's preparedness program, and the reports of Frank P. Walsh's United States Commission on Industrial Relations and its successor, the Committee on Industrial Relations, together impelled the administration toward a stronger labor policy. The new labor program included the controversial Adamson law, making the eight-hour day mandatory on interstate carriers, a measure for which Wilson's support was essential; the Keating-Owen Child Labor Act, which epitomized the best impulses of the Progressive Era; the Kern-McGillicuddy law, which provided workmen's compensation for federal employees; and the La Follette Seamen's Act, which Wilson supported after coming to know the desperate labor conditions in the merchant marine. Labor might also take satisfaction from the appointment to the bench of Louis D. Brandeis over the staunch opposition of Senate conservatives—a nomination that was of the greatest significance in the face of labor's gloomy experiences before the Supreme Court. Equally gratifying was the dedicated service of the President's Secretary of Labor William B. Wilson, formerly an official of the United Mine Workers.[3]

[2] *Wallace's Farmer*, XIV (June 24, 1916), 1190; William Allen White to Franklin D. Roosevelt, April 6, 1916, White Papers; Arthur S. Link: *Wilson: The New Freedom* (Princeton, 1956), pp. 262–3.
[3] Marc Karson: *American Labor Unions and Politics, 1900–1918* (Carbondale, Ill., 1958), pp. 77, 80, 82–4, 88–9; Richard J. Fenno, Jr.: *The President's Cabinet* (New York, 1959), pp. 73–4; John S. Smith: "Organized Labor and Government in the Wilson Era," unpublished doctoral dissertation, Catholic University, 1962; *American Federa-*

At least as important as progressivism in winning converts to Wilson was peace. With the bellicose Teddy Roosevelt once more backing the Republican party, to which he could impart a measure of his own chauvinism, the Democrats identified their party with the cause of peace and credited their President with keeping us out of war—both in Mexico and in Europe. Wilson had tempered his preparedness program when in April 1916 he appointed as Secretary of War the pacifist-inclined Newton D. Baker. And in the passage of the 1916 Jones Act for governing the Philippines, Wilson also pleased the anti-imperialists. The peace program attracted not only native-born isolationists, pacifists, and agrarian socialists, but also immigrant groups whose ancestral homelands would profit by continued American nonintervention in the European conflict. Among them were the Irish, some Germans and Austrians, and Scandinavians who desired to emulate the neutral stance of their native countries. Admittedly, Wilson must have alienated many immigrants with his charges of hyphenism and his inaction on behalf of Catholics in Mexico, and others were piqued by what they interpreted as Wilson's partiality toward the British. The German press in particular denounced Wilson, and Hughes became known as the German-American candidate. Yet many Germans thought Wilson would not fight if re-elected and that Hughes eventually would. Hughes, moreover, lost votes by his approval of Theodore Roosevelt's speeches. As Carl Wittke observed: "The slogan, 'He kept us out of war,' probably was as irresistible to many German-Americans as it was to millions of other voters, particularly in the Middle and Far West."[4]

---

tionist, XXIII (July 1916), 541, and (November 1916), 1068; see also AFL Executive Council Minutes, July 24, 1916, and July 29, 1916, AFL Papers.

[4] Wilson also attracted immigrants through his veto, in 1915, of a bill that would require a literacy test for entrance into the United States. Among the Irish, strong Democratic traditions and Wilson's labor record strengthened resistance to Hughes. For some statistics on Irish and German voting in 1916, see the relevant tables in Chapter VIII. Wittke: *German-Americans and the World War* (Columbus, 1936), pp. 98, 100–1,

To the union of progressives and isolationists was added the South, long loyal to the Democratic party and strongly influential in the Wilson Administration. The alliance that carried Wilson into his second term was preponderantly rural in composition, an alliance of South and West; he failed to carry the industrial states of Massachusetts, Rhode Island, Connecticut, New York, New Jersey, Pennsylvania, Michigan, and Illinois. Urban progressivism and labor gave the alliance vitality and a distinctive character, but the electoral strength, with few exceptions, came entirely from states as rural as the Presbyterian manse occupied by Wilson's father.[5]

Yet only four years after its making, the Wilson coalition lay in ruins. Warren Harding and normalcy[6] won the election of 1920 by an almost two-to-one margin, collecting 60.3 per cent of the total vote against 34.1 per cent for the Democratic candidate, James M. Cox. The party had lost the power to unite a diversity of classes and interests; and even when some of these would return to their Democratic allegiance, they would do so

---

111, 282; Link: *Wilson, Confusions and Crises*, pp. 278–9; Louis L. Gerson: *The Hyphenate in Recent American Politics and Diplomacy* (Lawrence, Kan., 1964), p. 68; Mayer: *The Republican Party*, p. 346; *The New York Times*, November 12, 1916, p. 6; *The Public*, XIX (November 17, 1916), 1092; William M. Leary, Jr., "Woodrow Wilson, Irish Americans and the Election of 1916," *Journal of American History*, LIV (June 1967), 57–72.
[5] Senator Gilbert Hitchcock of Nevada rated peace first and progressivism second as reasons for what he described as "a transfer of political power from the East to the West . . . and from the crowded industrial centers to the small cities and farms." Chicago *News*, November 11, 1916, p. 2. In 1916 the presidential vote in the ten largest cities taken together was Republican. The Democrats had virtually conceded the East in 1916, and the labor vote contributed significantly to their victory only in Washington, and in states never yet carried by the Democrats in a two-party contest—New Hampshire, Ohio, and California. John Blum: *Woodrow Wilson* (Boston, 1956), pp. 81, 125; *The New York Times*, November 12, 1916, pp. 1, 6, 7; Arthur S. Link: *Woodrow Wilson and the Progressive Era, 1910–1917* (New York, 1954), pp. 249 ff.; Karson: *American Labor Unions*, pp. 88–9.
[6] Warren Harding did not coin the word "normalcy." For at least two nineteenth-century usages, see *The Oxford English Dictionary* (Oxford, 1933), VII, 208.

not as participants in an articulate progressive movement sustained by a national organization and leadership, but as self-consciously antagonistic factions.

To some extent, it is true, the appearance of precipitous decline was unreal, for the defeat of 1920 came at the end of a period in which the Democrats had enjoyed a success disproportionate to their basic political resources. It is in the congressional elections of the Wilsonian era that is seen most clearly the transience of Democratic victory. In 1910 a serious rift among Republican leaders threw the House to the Democrats, and in 1912 the further cleavage of the opposition into separate candidates, Progressive and regular, stabilized the Democratic lead. But once the Republican split began to close, the party was quickly restored to its normal congressional strength. In 1914—with some Progressive candidates still in the field—the Republicans increased their representation by sixty-six seats, in 1916 by an additional sixteen. The year 1918 was by no means an unusually successful year for the Republicans, though it was a turning point in the sense that they won control of both houses of Congress. In the face of a more united opposition party, the Democratic presidential victory of 1916 was itself a near miracle. It testified to the success of Wilson and his program and the powerful effect of the European war upon the electorate; it signified an approval of particular measures and personalities, rather than an assertion of a durable and persistent Democratic power. It is therefore reasonable to surmise that the victories of the Wilson coalition may have constituted in part an interruption rather than a basic shift in party alignments, touching upon particular issues rather than fundamental party loyalties.

Nevertheless, the four years from 1916 to 1920 were portentous for the Democratic party, for its relative political power was to become even smaller than it had been during the period of Republican ascendancy that preceded the Wilsonian era. One group after another deserted the Democracy until it was left with only a meager corps of supporters.

The debacle of 1920 was foreshadowed in the congressional election of 1918 when control of the House of Representatives slipped to the Republicans. In eight states of the interior—Indiana, Ohio, Illinois, Kentucky, Missouri, Kansas, Nebraska, and Colorado—the Republican party carried twenty-three districts that in 1916 had gone Democratic. The ebbing of Democratic strength in these states made a serious and permanent breach in the Wilson coalition. But of itself the election spelled no massive repudiation of Wilson or the Democratic party; in fact, the Democrats won a substantial majority of the popular congressional vote. In the Northeast, South, and Far West, they did surprisingly well, gaining one more seat than they lost. The vote is noteworthy, however, because it represents the first serious breach in the Wilsonian alliance.[7]

What caused the defection in the agricultural interior? Some of it may have been no more than the return of traditionally Republican voters to an allegiance they had only temporarily left either for Republican or Wilsonian progressivism, or for a Wilson peace that had not been forthcoming; some of it may have been isolationism—whatever isolationism could have been active even in the spirited days of Belleau Wood and the Argonne. But mid-American isolationism flourished in the cities as well as the country, while the rural areas alone abandoned the Democratic party in 1918. A different explanation for the behavior of the Central States can be measured statistically. The

[7] These figures were obtained by a comparison of the first *Congressional Directory* of the Sixty-fifth Congress (1st Sess., April 1917) with the first of the Sixty-sixth Congress (1st Sess., July 1919); no April issue was published in 1919. At its initiation, the Sixty-fifth Congress had 215 Republicans, 215 Democrats, and 5 Independents. The net Republican gain of 22 from the Democrats gives the count of the new House: 237 Republicans, 193 Democrats, 4 Independents, and 1 contested seat in Wisconsin. In the Senate the Democrats also performed badly in the American mid-continent: winning a lone seat in Massachusetts, they lost in Colorado, Illinois, Kansas, and Missouri, as well as in Delaware and New Hampshire. On the popular vote, see C. G. Hoag: "Analysis of the Official Returns of the Congressional Elections of 1918," *The Public*, XXI (May 25, 1919), 545.

Democrats could conceivably have retained control of the House of Representatives, had they not committed a series of errors in agricultural policy. Their biggest mistake was to favor the cotton growers of the South over the wheat farmers of the interior.[8]

Much of the resentment in the wheat states in 1918 was directed against the Lever Act of August 1917, which allowed the Food Administration to fix the cost of wheat as low as $2.00 a bushel. The price of $2.20 fixed by the government should have been high enough to stimulate production and low enough to discourage inflation. But the farmers were not satisfied. The price of $2.20 was a precipitous drop from the $3.40 reached in the spring of 1917; and even the average market price that had prevailed in the five preceding months was almost $2.60. The Allies had purchased heavily in wheat futures and, by demanding delivery that spring, temporarily pushed prices upward. Worse still for the wheat farmers, the crop of 1917, like that of 1916, was small owing to drought and freezing. They also protested against a new system of wheat grading put into effect

[8] The wheat issue in the campaign is explored by Livermore in *Politics Is Adjourned*, pp. 170–6, 192–5. This chapter gives quantitative support to his argument but differs with his assumption that the election of 1918 was in every sense a "political upset" (p. 2). Of course, the Democrats did lose their tenuous control of the House and Senate—admittedly spelling trouble for Wilson's League—but the nature of the returns did not indicate any sudden nationwide dissatisfaction with the Democratic party. Even the net Republican gain over 1916 of twenty-two seats from the Democrats was not especially significant, since the average off-year loss by the party in power in this century has been forty-two seats. It is when the election results of 1918 are measured against Wilson's famous appeal for a vote of confidence that the Republican showing appears to be a crucial triumph in the revival of Republican strength. See also Josephus Daniels' manuscript diary, December 10, 1918, and Senator Thomas P. Gore: "The Wheat Farmer's Dilemma," *Forum*, LX (September 1918), 257–66. Ray A. Billington: "The Origins of Middle Western Isolationism," *Political Science Quarterly*, LX (March 1945), 44–64; William G. Carleton: "Isolationism and the Middle West," *Mississippi Valley Historical Review*, XXXIII (December 1946), 380–2; Selig Adler: *The Isolationist Impulse: Its Twentieth-Century Reaction* (New York, 1957).

in 1917 under the Grain Standards Act, a system that would benefit millers and grain buyers more than the farmers themselves. Even in 1918, though acreage had been vastly increased, the yield—still hampered by droughts—reached only the prewar average. On June 7, 1918, Wilson vetoed a bill to raise the ceiling on wheat to $2.40 a bushel. Just a few months before, he had encouraged farmers to sow wheat on land normally devoted to other crops; and those farmers who followed the President regarded his veto as an economic betrayal. It was put to them that it was a patriotic duty to submit to low prices in a time of inflation, but, so it seemed, the principle was inconsistent in its application.[9]

For while the administration was hampering the wheat farmer, southern Democrats were keeping raw cotton off the list of price-controlled items. This unequal treatment of the two sections antagonized the wheat areas; and, as wartime cotton prices spiraled upward—increasing substantially more than the controlled wheat prices—old sectional jealousies revived. During the campaign the Republicans seized upon the failure of the Democrats to heed the farm protest. And in the final results, the Republicans gained in the wheat areas in strikingly close proportion, district by district, to the extent of wheat acreage.

In ten states that led in the production of wheat, the Democrats were victorious in not one of the congressional districts the Republicans had carried in 1916, while the Republicans won twenty-one that had gone Democratic in the previous election. The Republicans gained in Indiana (4), Kansas (4), Missouri (3), Washington (1), Nebraska (3), Ohio (5), and Illinois (1). Some of these districts contained a substantial number of

---

[9] For the administration's injunction to farmers, see the New York *Herald-Tribune*, February 19, 1918, p. 4. Secretary of Agriculture Houston wrote to Herbert Hoover of the Food Administration, complaining that the minimum price had turned out to be the maximum price as well, and the Assistant Secretary at about the same time admitted that "wheat is perhaps but little if any more profitable than at prices prevailing two or three years ago." Agriculture File 234-403, National Archives. See also File 234-142. United States Department of Agriculture, *Monthly Crop Report*, IV (May 1918), 53; George Akerson to John G. Brown, October 19, 1928, Hoover Papers.

TABLE IV

Wheat Acreage in the Ten Leading Wheat States and Republican House Gains in 1918

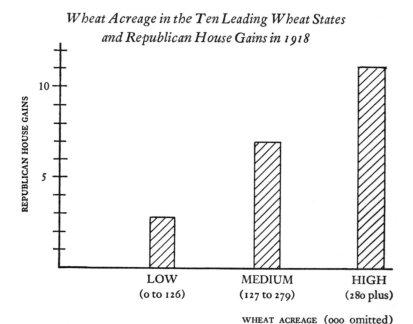

WHEAT ACREAGE (ooo omitted)

German-Americans, who might be expected to oppose the Democrats; but in most of the areas, including those in Missouri, the German vote could not have been the determining factor. There are ninety-six congressional districts in these seven states. Table IV, which represents Republican House gains from the region, is based upon an arrangement of these districts into three groups of high, medium, and low wheat acreage, each group containing thirty-two districts. The Republicans won eleven seats in districts of highest acreage; seven in the middle districts; and three in the areas of lowest wheat acreage. Only in Ohio were any of these seats formerly occupied by one-term Democratic congressmen, whose tenure might have been contingent on short-lived conditions.[1]

[1] Wheat areas in other parts of the country also replaced their Democratic congressmen with Republicans; these include the seventh district in California, the first in Maryland, the third in Colorado, the twentieth in Pennsylvania, the second in Michigan, and the eighth in Kentucky. Years later, in a letter to Josephus Daniels, Vance McCormick, Democratic National Chairman in 1916, confirmed the importance of the farm is-

Although the error most costly to the Democrats in 1918 was the rigid wheat ceiling, the administration also antagonized rural interests in other ways. Its wartime purchase, at slightly less than the market price, of virtually the entire wool supply introduced further uncertainty into an already precarious market and, together with anticipated cutbacks in government orders after the Armistice, contributed to a serious wool depression lasting from October 1918 to March 1919. The government's policy favored operators of large farms over the small wool growers located far from Washington, and it penalized them further by needlessly holding up crop payments. In several congressional districts with high wool production, Democratic seats were lost. The government was generous in its loans to the southern cattlemen of Texas and Oklahoma even as it withheld assistance from middle-western herd owners—and the Republicans pointed to the sectional discrimination. Finally, the Railroad Administration raised the cost of shipping grain beyond the point for which a slight rise in the price ceiling could compensate, while a shortage in cars lengthened time in transit, and a rule that the burden of proving negligence should fall to the shipper made it more difficult to prosecute claims for lost goods.[2]

---

sue. March 24, 1941, McCormick Papers. Shifts were determined by a comparison between the last *Congressional Directory* of the Sixty-fifth Congress (1st Sess., April 1919) and the first of the Sixty-sixth Congress (1st Sess., July 1919). County figures on wheat acreage are found in the United States Bureau of the Census, *Fourteenth Census: Agriculture,* V, V₁, V₁₁, VI₁₁₁. Maps of the congressional districts, indicating what counties they include, are found in most issues of the *Congressional Directory.* Frank M. Surface: *The Grain Trade During the World War* (New York, 1928), pp. 24, 28, 59–60, 68, 76, 121.

[2] Wool districts lost include the twenty-third in Pennsylvania, the first in New Mexico, and the fifth in Washington (also one of the low-acreage wheat districts represented in Table IV). Agriculture File WIB-17D–A2, Box 34 and Boxes 19–33, National Archives; Katharine Snodgrass: "Price Fluctuations in the Woolen Industry," *Annals of the American Academy,* LXXXIX (May 1920), 55–60, esp. 57–8. Corroborative evidence that the cattle loan policy of the administration, whether or not by design, was in practice partial to the South may be found in the Federal Farm Loan Board, *Second Annual Report,* November 30, 1918, p. 19.

Together, the Wilson Administration's agricultural policies heightened western jealousies toward the South's dominant position in the Democratic party. And that southern ascendancy was startlingly apparent. President Wilson, born in Virginia and raised in Georgia, often identified himself with his native section. His first cabinet consisted of five representatives from the South and only four from the rest of the nation. Racial segregation was applied with increased rigor to workers in some federal agencies. In Congress, where many important committees were chaired by men from south of the Mason-Dixon line, the extent of southern control was greater even than in the executive. From the North came complaints over favoritism to the South in distribution of patronage, as well as over the crucial matter of agricultural price-fixing. As John W. Burke, the Treasurer of the United States, wrote to Joe Tumulty: "During the campaign in the last election the argument we had to meet everywhere was 'the South is in the saddle; it has the legislative [*sic*] and the executive.' "[3]

The Republican gain of 1918 was the outcome of a campaign waged in a spirit of sectionalism over particular and ephemeral issues. Of course, some more basic grievances against Wilson had accumulated during the war—high taxes and government-imposed economic planning had been particularly irritating. But the normal disillusionment that ensues at the end of a war had not had time to develop. Most interest groups had as much

---

District 6, Missouri, number of National Farm Loan Associations: 112; number of loans, 1,577; total amount loaned, $3,855,230. District 10, Texas, number of National Farm Loan Associations: 288; number of loans, 5,250; total amount loaned, $13,568,461. McAdoo to W. P. G. Harding, October 25, 1918, McAdoo Papers.

[3] John W. Burke to Joe Tumulty, November 17, 1919, Wilson Papers; Senator Thomas Walsh to W. M. Johnston, November 12, 1918, T. J. Walsh Papers; *Current Opinion*, LXV (December 1918), 350–2; Chicago *Daily Tribune*, October 22, 1918, p. 1; October 31, 1918, p. 1; *Literary Digest*, LIX (November 16, 1918), 14–15; *The New York Times*, November 7, 1918, p. 20; Arthur S. Link: *Wilson: The Road to the White House* (Princeton, 1947), pp. 2 ff.; J. Leonard Bates: *The Origins of Teapot Dome* (Urbana, Ill., 1963), pp. 152, 156.

reason to be satisfied in 1918 as in 1916. During the war, the federal government had increased its activities in behalf of labor, strengthening the good relations of the prewar era; the Republicans, wrote Senator Borah of Idaho in October 1918, have through their inaction "handed the labor vote of this country practically en masse to the president."[4] The war may have set the stage for the quickening reaction against Wilson in 1919 and 1920; after all, our part in the conflict could be taken as a betrayal of the peace slogan of 1916. But it was the uncertainty of peace, the failure to withdraw once victory had been won, that apparently brought home to the voter of 1920 the message of that betrayal; hence the elections of 1918 preceded the period of most intense isolationist reaction.

Since in considerable measure the Democrats lost upon sectional issues, the election probably cannot be viewed as a clear repudiation of Wilson's plea for a vote of confidence—which *The New York Times* thought had won votes for his party—and in no sense was it a national repudiation of Wilson. Outside of the wheat districts, the 1918 House returns show not Democratic weakness but persisting strength, which was probably nourished by wartime prosperity. They indicate a continuing trust in Wilson and demonstrate a nation's gratitude for the recent defeat of Germany.[5] Finally, they signify that while by 1918 a wedge had already been driven into the Wilson coalition, it is the period between 1918 and 1920 that must be examined most carefully to explain the Democratic defeat of 1920. It was in these divisive times after the war that grievances against the Wilson Administration most rapidly accumulated, and the

[4] Borah to Shad Hodges, October 10, 1918, Borah Papers.
[5] Vice President Marshall remarked that "the war is a Democratic asset." Homer Cummings, Democratic National Chairman, asked rhetorically if the voters wanted General Pershing to stop his brilliant advances, and James W. Gerard, former ambassador to Germany and a good Democrat, announced that the Kaiser would be encouraged if the electorate repudiated Wilson. *The New York Times*, October 28, 1918, p. 1; November 1, 1918, p. 14; November 4, 1918, p. 6.

cohesive force of Wilsonianism—cohesive both for the Democracy and for the nation as a whole—dissolved.

The tensions of 1919, to which the Wilson Administration fell victim, were to a great extent the product of America's involvement in the great conflict. Institutions and customs that once maintained the social equilibrium had been altered or destroyed, in part by the governmental controls of wartime, in part by the emotional and social disturbances of war itself. Workers, having become accustomed to a measure of war prosperity and to collective bargaining enforced by the War Labor Board, anxiously sought to preserve their gains as the government prepared to withdraw from the economy; but labor faced employers even more resolute in wishing to restore the days of open contract, and applying in their struggle against collective bargaining the rhetoric of the "American Plan." Farmers cried for various forms of aid from a Congress deaf to their pleas, and as price supports came near to ending, pleaded with a cabinet equally unmindful of their plight. In northern cities Negroes attempted to hold on to their wartime jobs as soldiers returned home looking for work. Negroes themselves came back from the trenches, bringing with them an aggressive edge their fathers had never possessed. Forced up by the war, the cost of living played on the anxieties of the population. Following the success of the Russian Revolution and its spread to Central Europe, an aggressive Attorney General, A. Mitchell Palmer, aroused by frightened citizens, clashed with liberals of all shades in his ill-defined attempt to suppress revolutionary plots. Debate on the League of Nations separated idealist from realist, and realist from isolationist. Vainly, the progressives worked to resist the course of reaction.

The atmosphere of conflict was thickened by a state of mind for which the war itself had in large part prepared the condition. Social unrest characterizes any postwar period. Wars impose upon a people a discipline beyond their normal capacities; in turn, their hopes for the postwar era expand indefinitely, only to be followed by disillusionment and frustration. Our participation in World War I, moreover, was too brief to expend the reserve of fighting spirit manufactured by the Committee on Public Information. That wartime propaganda agency had planned a symphony in creed and emotion that was to reach its crescendo by the middle of 1919. Though the war ended sooner than had been expected, the emotion lingered on, no longer fixed and steadied by the pursuit of victory, and some of it turned to a distorted patriotism, to suspicion, to antiradicalism. In its dual temper of anger and of tiredness, the time was unfavorable to the maintenance of progressivism.

An economic dislocation brought on by the return of peace contributed to the unsettled political conditions of 1919 and 1920. But the extent and nature of the dislocation must be identified carefully, for on the surface conditions appeared quite good. Demobilization of the armed forces created some brief hardship early in 1919, but no lasting unemployment problem; nor did the mass revocation of military orders induce an immediate deflation. For according to Paul Samuelson: "*Economically*, the first World War lasted until 1920." The economy was kept active: money was spent on demobilization itself, consumer savings and dismissal pay for veterans were soon in circulation as pantry shelves were restocked and as servicemen returned, business contracts were settled, the military deficit had to be financed, and the Treasury desired to postpone any contraction until after the floating of a last major war loan and further loans to European countries. These monetary policies sparked a revival in automobile production, housebuilding, and numerous related industries which eased the readjustment for the nine million who had been engaged in defense work and the four million soldiers returned to peacetime life.

Industrial production declined a maximum of ten per cent by the middle of 1919, but in the last six months of the year it reached a new high point. Such figures do not record the vast shifting of jobs and resulting hardships that must have occurred in 1919. Yet a need for credit in that year that might have stimulated the economy for the duration was not met, and when government spending and industrial expansion both halted in 1920, unemployment rose sharply. As the hard times closed in upon them, workingmen and farmers condemned an administration whose earlier sympathy for the common man seemed to have vanished.[6]

As a prelude to the privations of unemployment, a steady rise in the cost of living, particularly in food prices, had angered and perplexed consumers. Despite the wartime controls on prices of certain items, the cost of living almost doubled between 1914 and 1920, and in New York City it rose twenty-eight per cent between 1919 and 1920 alone. The people, according to a correspondent of Mark Sullivan, are "more interested in the price of beefsteak and a pair of shoes" than in Wilson's League of Nations. The Wilson Administration had proposed that an industrial board in the Commerce Department be allowed to set maximum prices, but George Peek, lacking authority to keep steel prices down, resigned as its head in May 1919; and Congress had denied further funds to Herbert Hoover's Food Administration, forcing it out of existence in June. By the late spring of 1920 the index of living costs began to fall but the high prices of the preceding years, though worldwide in origin, had done political damage to the administration—but so too would a system of price and wage controls. Added irritants were the scarcities that persisted after the war as labor unions struck and the economy pursued its uneven course. The inadequate supply of coal, for example, caused widespread anxiety that reached its worst proportions just before election day. Viewing the high cost of living as the nation's greatest postwar problem, the Federal Reserve Board acted against the inflation of 1919 and early 1920 by raising the rediscount rate, curtailing credit, and dis-

[6] Samuelson and Everett E. Hagen: *After the War* (Washington, D.C.: National Labor Relations Board; 1943), p. 21; George H. Soule: *Prosperity Decade* (New York, 1947), pp. 83–4.

couraging expansion. A major depression began in 1920, soon enough to contribute to the defeat of the administration in the fall.[7]

Labor presented the Wilson Administration with a particularly vexing and embarrassing problem, for it appeared responsible in considerable part for the nation's social unrest and economic trouble. In several of the strikes organized to retain and extend wartime gains, the Justice Department seemed quick to side with management. In September, Wilson asked laborers not to strike for higher wages, since strikes would raise even further the high cost of living, and he denounced the Boston police strike as a "crime against civilization." When the bituminous coal miners went out on strike in November, Attorney General Palmer obtained two federal court injunctions against the strikers that aroused labor's ire. Following the example of some businessmen, he styled the strikers radicals and their conduct a rehearsal for Communist revolution. Palmer typified a middle class once friendly to labor but now convinced it had become dangerous. Wilson estranged the Railway Brotherhoods by refusing to support the Plumb Plan, which would have given to the workers a role in controlling the country's railroads. And to assuage the hard feelings between capital and labor he called the National Industrial Conference to meet in October. But the AFL withdrew on the grounds that representatives of employers refused—in the face of the steel strike then in effect—to affirm the principle of unrestricted collective bargaining that had widely established itself during the war. In the eyes of fair-minded observers, the conference appeared to reveal only the stubbornness of management.[8]

[7] For cost of living figures, see *The New York Times*, May 3, 1920, p. 1; Samuelson: *After the War*, pp. 13, 31; and the consumer price indexes of the United States Department of Labor (revised in 1962). John A. Peters to Mark Sullivan, 1920 [?], Sullivan Papers; Frederic L. Paxson: *Postwar Years: Normalcy, 1918–1923* (Berkeley, 1948), p. 45; Houston; *Eight Years with Wilson's Cabinet, 1913–1920* (New York, 1926), II, 105 ff.

[8] Editorial reaction of the country's newspapers to the strikes of 1919 is contained in the *Literary Digest*, LXIII (October 25, 1919),

The President and his Secretary of Labor William B. Wilson were apparently preoccupied with the public interest and public mood; but in the end, despite even the generous arbitration of Secretary Wilson in the coal strike and the President's efforts on behalf of the steel workers, labor's dissatisfaction with the economic and political status quo increased as rapidly as the public's dissatisfaction with labor. In early 1920 the Esch-Cummins Act came dangerously close to requiring compulsory government arbitration of labor disputes—a thing that in an era of conservative federal administration would hold little promise for the workers—and the antistrike provision of the act also offended labor. Samuel Gompers blamed this act and the "unrest in the country" on Congress, but the image of the Wilson Administration as a progressive friend of labor was destroyed.[9]

Farmers found themselves in their familiar dilemma of squaring the higher cost of living with declining market prices for their crops. Although the 1918 congressional elections had marked the departure of many farmers from the Democratic party, the Department of Agriculture made little effort to forestall further desertions. For a time the postwar agricultural market prospered as foreign demand sustained the expanded wartime production, but foreign buying declined once credit was withdrawn under the War Finance Corporation, and almost all crops suffered sharply falling prices shortly before the 1920 election. And even though farm mortgages had more than doubled since 1914, Secretary of Agriculture David Houston— a southerner viewed with considerable suspicion by western farmers—along with his successor Edwin T. Meredith, awaited indifferently the end of price supports. To heighten the troubles

---

11, and (November 22, 1919), 11–14. Franklin K. Lane to Woodrow Wilson, October 19, 1919, Serial VI, File 5085, Wilson Papers; Gompers to Lee Seamster, March 29, 1920, Gompers Papers; William B. Wilson to James Duncan, April 22, 1920, William B. Wilson Papers.

9 David Brody: *Labor in Crisis: The Steel Strike of 1919* (Philadelphia, 1965), pp. 102–11. Gompers is quoted in the *American Federationist,* XXVII (July 1920), 656–7.

of the Wilson Administration among the farmers, the new Esch-Cummins law, passed in January 1920, permitted the railroads to raise their rates by thirty-five to forty per cent, and the Federal Reserve Board gave no effective help to agriculture. Farm prices fell by one third in the year before the election, while the prices of farm supplies remained steady.[1]

Closely joined to the unsteadiness of the postwar economy was an injurious psychological mood. "There is a strange poison in the air," observed Wilson's son-in-law, William Gibbs Mc-Adoo, in 1920.[2] There was indeed. The poison had gathered during the war, and even with the coming of peace and the elimination of the immediate center of infection it was working its way throughout the social body and mind.

The duty of spreading a patriotic war spirit had fallen to the highly efficient Committee on Public Information. The unit owed much of its effectiveness to its chairman George Creel, a Denver progressive who shrewdly worked upon chauvinistic feelings already present in American society and brought to a new intensity a national mood that blended aggression and sincere idealism, patriotic dedication and xenophobia. The success of the Creel Committee, as measured by sales of war bonds and subscriptions to Liberty Loans, went beyond expectations. Liberals in government failed to foresee, however, that wartime propaganda and repression might have harmful aftereffects in a time of peace, that the psychological gratifications of war would be hard to surrender.

In Bolshevism, symbol alike of anarchy and of treacherous retreat from wartime alliance, the aroused American temper found in postwar days a new object to stand surrogate for the defeated Hun. Stories of Bolshevik cruelty replaced those of

---

[1] United States Department of Labor, *Statistical Abstract, 1920* (Washington, D.C., 1921), p. 464; Arthur S. Link: "The Federal Reserve Policy and the Agricultural Depression of 1920–1921," *Agricultural History*, XX (July 1946), 166–75; Benedict Crowell and Robert Forrest Wilson: *Demobilization: Our Industrial and Military Demobilization After the Armistice, 1918–1920* (New Haven, 1921), pp. 126–44.

[2] McAdoo to Jouett Shouse, September 17, 1920, McAdoo Papers.

German atrocities, and it was rumored that Germans had instigated the Russian upheaval. Indeed, Bolshevism was the enemy in Siberia, where in February 1919, American troops suffered considerable casualties. And when the international ambitions of the Bolsheviks became publicized, organizations such as the American Vigilantes International sprang up to combat them, and the newly formed American Legion went on the alert. At the same time Lenin's revolution stirred the Socialists of America to new hope and expression. The massive labor agitation of 1919 added to the fear of insurrection from the left.

During the war the Creel Committee had asked citizens to report those who spread pessimistic stories about the fighting or cried for peace. In response the American Protective League arose; made up of business and professional men, it acquired a semiofficial status during the war as an arm of the Bureau of Investigation. The League publication *The Spyglass* directed its postwar attention to the Communist menace. The first of many antisocialist riots instigated by veterans occurred in New York just a few weeks after the war had ended. Soldiers seeking employment in large cities frequently turned violently upon Socialist agitators. The formation of the Comintern the following March further heightened anxiety. Soon various representatives of public sentiment were calling on the Justice Department directly to act against all radicals as well as to keep wartime political prisoners in jail. And at the head of the department was a man with both an aggressive temper and presidential ambitions.

Although Attorney General Palmer at first displayed a judicious attitude, in keeping with his earlier career as a moderate, political opportunism and a lifelong distrust of foreigners and their ways eventually warped his sober judgment. The explosion of a bomb in front of his house spurred him to fanaticism. Red propaganda, he reportedly claimed, gave him "the creeps," and he maintained that the Reds were not going to "get him." But his notorious actions occurred only after alarmist reports from J. Edgar Hoover, newly appointed head of the antiradical division in the Bureau of Investigation, convinced him that the country faced a revolution.[3]

Ignoring fundamental canons of human and civil rights, Palmer, late in 1919 and after, caused the unlawful imprisonment of hundreds of aliens suspected of revolutionary sentiment. Even while opposing immigration restriction, he attempted summarily to deport as many foreign-born radicals as he could. Anthony Caminetti, Commissioner of Immigration in the Department of Labor, temporarily prevailed on his superiors to condone many deportations. The policy itself was not new, but its massive implementation was. The activity of the Justice Department would have its brief effect upon the composition of the Democratic party, since it deepened the estrangement from the party of immigrant voters and of some libertarians and labor unionists who saw the deportations as a potentially dangerous weapon in the hands of employers; but in intensifying the social and political reaction, the Red Scare may have done even greater damage to the Democracy. For Wilsonian reform had been the mainstay of Democratic presidential politics since 1912; and in the new political climate of America, much of the popular reform impulse withered and died.[4]

[3] In April 1919, Palmer told Governor Cox of Ohio that current charges of pro-Germanism in the Cincinnati schools "consisted chiefly of gossip" and "hearsay." As late as June 1919, Palmer argued that more repression would play into the hands of the radicals; in July he told Wilson he thought the sedition sentence of Eugene Debs "too long"; in October he opposed restrictions on immigration; and even in November he thought some of the Senate bills "too drastic." Palmer to Cox, April 30, 1919; see also Palmer to John Lord O'Brien, April 27, 1919, and file 100–374, Justice Files, National Archives; Palmer to Wilson, July 30, 1919, Wilson Papers; *The Nation*, CVIII (June 14, 1919), 927; Palmer to John S. Starkweather, November 17, 1919, and Palmer to Senator Lawrence C. Phipps, November 19, 1919; Stanley Coben: *A. Mitchell Palmer: Politician* (New York, 1963), pp. 155–6, 185–6, 198–9, 203, 205, 207, 212; Donald Johnson: *The Challenge to American Freedoms: World War I and the Rise of the American Civil Liberties Union* (Lexington, Ky., 1963), pp. 119–75.
[4] Stanley Coben has contributed a new interpretation of the Red Scare. He sees it as a complicated social-psychological movement in response to a national disequilibrium induced by radicalism, major strikes, federal controls, the high cost of living, and an unsteady economy. Coben

The "deportations delirium" itself ended abruptly early in the election year of 1920. Palmer's predictions of social unrest failed to materialize, labor agitation decreased, and he encountered the opposition of aroused liberals. Even George Creel, no insignificant spokesman for full-blooded Americanism, worked with the American Civil Liberties Union to free imprisoned radicals. Finally, Palmer met his match in Acting Secretary of Labor Louis Post, whom the Attorney General called "a Bolshevik himself." The authority to deport radicals lay only with the Secretary of Labor, and Post—convinced by an IWW brief concerning encroachment on the rights of radicals—refused to act on about eighty per cent of the approximately 2,700 cases sent to him by the Justice Department. To remove the obstacle, an angry House Judiciary Committee started impeachment hearings against Post; but despite his seventy-one years, the Acting Secretary stymied the committee with a storehouse of irrefutable and damning facts about the deportation cases. Curious citizens who came to scoff at Post remained to applaud when he reprimanded the committee members for abusing the Bill of Rights.[5]

---

finds the term "revitalization movement," as it is formulated by one anthropologist, to be applicable to the Red Scare; the phrase describes a mass attempt to verify accustomed ways of thinking and to destroy foreign influences. "A Study in Nativism: The American Red Scare of 1919-20," *Political Science Quarterly*, LXXI (March 1964), 52-75; Anthony F. C. Wallace: "Revitalization Movements," *American Anthropologist*, LVIII (April 1956), 264-81.

[5] According to the Detroit *News* of April 23, 1920, the President, perhaps through fear of angering organized labor, sided with Post against Palmer—a corroboration of Wilson's alleged caution to the Attorney General not to let the country "see Red." William Preston, Jr.: *Aliens and Dissenters: Federal Suppression of Radicals, 1903-1933* (Cambridge, Mass., 1963), pp. 224-5; Frederic C. Howe: *The Confessions of a Reformer* (New York, 1925), p. 327; Howe to W. B. Wilson, October 9, 1919, William B. Wilson Papers, Pennsylvania Historical Society; *The New York Times*, May 9, 1920, p. 12; Labor Department File 167-255A, National Archives; United States Department of Labor, *Annual Report of the Commission on Immigration, 1920* (Washington, D.C., 1921), pp. 32-4; *Annual Report . . . , 1921* (Washington, D.C., 1922), pp. 14-15; Post: *The Deportations Delirium of Nineteen-Twenty* (Chicago, 1923).

In its larger significance, the Post-Palmer skirmish was symptomatic of emerging political disorder within the Democratic party. The conflict was one of many in an administration that had lost its power to discipline itself or its party, and to unite and stimulate Congress to act on pressing national problems. This near abandonment of party discipline, especially on the part of Wilson, who alone was in a position effectively to govern the Democratic administration, goes far in explaining the disaster that struck the party in 1920.

During the first months of peace, Wilson's schedule made it impossible for him to provide the domestic leadership so sorely needed by his party and his country. He spent the month after the congressional elections of 1918 preparing for the Paris peace conference. On December 2 he left for Paris, and, except for a ten-day trip home in the late winter to sign bills and attend to unavoidable domestic duties, his work kept him abroad until July 8, a period of about seven months. On the winter journey home, he met his cabinet, talked to a fairly complacent conference of governors and mayors about unemployment, and had dinner with members of the Senate Foreign Relations Committee; but a ten-day whirlwind of activity could not replace constant presidential concern and leadership. While President Wilson was abroad, his Secretary of State wrote: "The Democrats in Congress, without his personal leadership, simply went to pieces."[6]

In the weeks to come, the fight over the League of Nations consumed much of Wilson's time, and he continued to give little attention to domestic and party affairs. "There is no real note of leadership coming out of the White House," complained *The Nation* in August. Although weakened by a severe attack of influenza, on September 3, 1919, Wilson began a tour to generate support for his League. On September 25, he had a physical breakdown in Pueblo, Colorado, and shortly afterward suffered a paralyzing cerebral hemorrhage. Since that affliction often leaves some of the bodily and mental functions unim-

[6] Lansing Private Memoranda, December 14, 1919.

paired, and a few of Wilson's visitors during the last year and a half of his presidency found him apparently hale, their testimony has occasionally been taken as evidence that his illness did not seriously damage his capacities. But the opposite was the case. The cerebral thrombosis—its symptoms resemble those of a ruptured blood vessel or stroke—prevented him from performing effectively the complex activity of a President; he was rarely able to work more than an hour or two a day or to sustain more than a few minutes of dictation. In the middle of 1920, Dr. Cary T. Grayson, Wilson's physician, spoke of the President's gradual mental deterioration. Had illness not struck him down, Wilson might have continued as the strong party leader he had described in his *Congressional Government;* as it was, his party floundered for lack of direction, all the more so because earlier he had accustomed it to the vigorous leadership of a prime minister. "Thanks to Mr. Wilson's domination of his party," observed *The Nation,* "[few Democratic leaders] retain any special capacity for independent thought or constructive statesmanship."[7]

The President's absence forced an unaccustomed degree of independence on even the least active cabinet members, whom he had regarded primarily as administrators rather than as members of an important political body. Secretary of the Treasury McAdoo, the most competent executive, had already resigned. Secretary of the Interior Franklin K. Lane, on leaving the cabinet in 1920, complained that government officials would not make decisions and shrank from responsibility. But inexperienced though they were at independent leadership, the more ambitious secretaries jumped at the opportunity to direct government policy. The most flagrant exercise of autonomous power was by Attorney General Palmer, who issued his famous

[7] *The Nation,* CVII (November 9, 1918), 545; CIX (August 2, 1919), 133. On Wilson's illness, see John Garraty: *Woodrow Wilson* (New York, 1956), p. 182; Arthur Walworth: *Woodrow Wilson,* I: *World Prophet* (New York, 1958), p. 400; and the bibliographical note in John Blum: *Joe Tumulty and the Wilson Era* (Boston, 1951), p. 312 (see also, pp. 214, 216).

injunction against the United Mine Workers less than two months after Wilson's collapse. Palmer's actions in the Red Scare severely divided Wilson's advisers: Tumulty, Lansing, and Burleson supported him in opposition to William B. Wilson, Lane, and Daniels. Secretary of State Robert Lansing acquired Wilson's enmity by calling cabinet meetings without the President's consent; according to Josephus Daniels and others, Lansing wanted Vice President Thomas Marshall to take over the government.

The new executive leadership frequently took on a conservative character. Fundamental decisions on economic policy lay chiefly with Carter Glass and David F. Houston, successors to McAdoo in the Treasury; and both Houston and Glass wanted the ailing postwar economy to mend itself. Lincoln Colcord of *The Nation* diagnosed the situation in an article entitled "The Administration Adrift":

> So with the President out of commission, it has been Carter Glass and Mr. Burleson, and Mr. Houston, all Bourbon southerners, who have dominated the Administration and formulated its policies during this critical time. . . . There seems to be little doubt that the leaders of the Bourbon Democracy have utilized the full power and prestige of the Presidency to work their own ends.[8]

Wilson's loss of political flexibility and leadership is revealed in his handling of executive appointments and patronage, which had been used so skillfully by subordinates during his first term.

[8] Between the end of the war and the election of 1920 six of the nine cabinet officers had to be replaced. Wilson's conception of party leadership is discussed in Link: *Wilson: The New Freedom*, pp. 145–7. David Houston, among others, recalls encroachments by Congress on executive domain after Wilson's illness. *Eight Years with Wilson's Cabinet*, II, pp. 71–90; Houston to Woodrow Wilson, April 15, 1920, Houston Papers, Library of Congress. On Wilson's declining role as party leader, see George Creel: *The War, the World, and Wilson* (New York, 1920), p. 134. Richard F. Fenno, Jr.: *The President's Cabinet* (New York, 1959), pp. 119–20. Colcord is quoted in *The Nation*, CIX (November 15, 1919), 635–6; Lane in *The New York Times*, March 1, 1920, p. 1.

Several cabinet members privately resented many of Wilson's new appointments, which were motivated by a strange mixture of nonpartisanship and spite. On February 19, 1919, McAdoo, now out of the government, wrote to Carter Glass about the "universal complaints" being directed against Wilson's willingness to appoint "irregular party men" who were often prominent Republicans. On December 13, McAdoo was again corresponding with Glass on the problem, insisting now that Wilson's cavalier handling of patronage had "enormously weakened the Democratic Party." The appointment of a former Bull Mooser, Bainbridge Colby, as Secretary of State early in 1920, further irritated loyal Democrats. No less politically injudicious was the attitude of Postmaster General Burleson, who dispensed more patronage than the rest of the cabinet added together. When Wilson, heeding a recommendation of the Civil Service Reform League, exercised his wartime power by ordering postmasters to take competitive examinations, Burleson, a faithful subordinate with a gift for antagonizing, executed the order with impartiality unbecoming a party man. Formerly a stabilizing influence in the Administration, the Post Office chief became in later days a source of party turmoil. In 1919, Robert Woolley of the Interstate Commerce Commission told Colonel House that Burleson "must resign—or be forced to—if there is to be a shred of the Democratic Party left to go into the campaign of 1920."[9]

[9] Complaints about the distribution of patronage are a characteristic of American politics in any era; it was Wilson's absence from active political duty that gave patronage its special importance. Some of the recriminations that plagued Wilson's second term are collected in Raymond Hanks: "The Democratic Party in 1920: The Rupture of the Wilsonian Synthesis," unpublished doctoral dissertation, University of Chicago, 1960. McAdoo's letters to Glass are in the McAdoo Papers; Woolley's letter to House, dated June 17, 1919, is in the Ray Stannard Baker Papers. On Burleson's willingness to go outside the party for good postmasters, see the Thomas B. Love Papers, "1920 Campaign," Folder 1. *The Nation*, discussing conflicts in the cabinet, denounced Burleson as the "least fit" member of that body, CX (January 3, 1920), 844. See also Fenno, *The President's Cabinet*, pp. 222–3.

Another indication of the President's declining role as leader was his failure to offer a progressive postwar domestic program. "Can anyone," asked Walter Lippmann late in 1919, "name a single reform initiated or carried through since the Armistice?" Wilson did send three messages to Congress, but they scarcely mention proposed reforms. No program of reconstruction was broached for fear it would cause anti-administration sentiment. Conservationists in particular were discouraged; but for a liberal filibuster, a "giveaway" water-power act would have passed early in 1919. Even such significant and progressive legislation as was passed had for the most part been initiated in prewar days, whereas other measures, such as the Transportation Act of 1920, which labor vigorously opposed, were steps backward from the radical nationalization of wartime. In referring to the railroad act, the *New Republic* condemned "the unfortunate legislation of 1920. . . . It was the fitting product of a mediocre, spineless and leaderless Congress"; the General Leasing Act of 1920 failed to prevent the outrageous scandals of Teapot Dome. A decade later the same journal observed: "Wilson through the force of his own personality carried his party into a position of progressivism which was not native to it, and from which it promptly backslid as soon as his individual authority was removed. By 1920, there was little evidence left in the party of the spirit which in 1913 was busy inaugurating the Federal Reserve Board and so many other measures of reform." In its last years the Wilson Administration had little to offer progressive Americans, and its repressive measures repelled the liberals.[1]

The one issue that might have rallied liberal support was the League of Nations, and yet in fact the League added to Democratic disharmony, as well as to the strength of the Republican

---

[1] The Merchant Marine Act of 1920 was one of the most notable achievements of the session, but, like the Water Power and General Leasing Acts, it too was an inheritance from the prewar era. *New Republic*, XX (November 12, 1919), 315; XXVI (March 23, 1921), 92–9; LVIII (May 8, 1929), 320; Bates: *Origins of Teapot Dome*, pp. 165, 179–80, 200, 211; Philip Taft: *The AF of L in the Time of Gompers* (New York, 1957), p. 469.

attack. It was indeed on foreign policy more than on any other question in the postwar era that the Progressive movement fragmented, dividing into what have been labeled its internationalist, realist, and isolationist parts. For a time the League was able to ride the crest of an internationalism expounded by Wilson in his cherished wish to "make the world safe for democracy"; it was promoted to a degree by the same spirit of wartime idealism that also unleashed the more chauvinistic impulses of the day. Evidence of the League's initial strength was ubiquitous. Newspapers supported it overwhelmingly, and even thirty-two state legislatures endorsed some kind of international organization. But the League—still little more than a pleasant notion in most people's minds—was pushed into the background by the immediacy of domestic problems, and a shift in the sentiment of the people was soon to come.[2]

The President's conduct at Versailles did its part to trigger the reaction against the League. Republicans were the first to be estranged. Already, in his appeal in 1918 for a Democratic Congress to further his policies, Wilson had invited a partisan response from the Republican party; and by failing to take influential Republicans with him to Paris, or to keep the Senate leaders informed of the treaty-making progress, he further widened the breach. And it is ironic that his failure to provide a few favors to Republicans in a matter where political diplomacy would have done some good came at a moment when administrative patronage was being distributed with a bipartisanship destructive of party unity. Wilson's highhanded indifference to the advice and feelings of the Republicans—his apparent assumption, at Versailles and thereafter, that it was the duty of the Senate Republicans, as it was the duty of the Democrats, to provide a rubber stamp for a Wilson treaty—lost him a good deal of the support that he might otherwise have commanded. Of course, if

[2] William Allen White later wrote of a "height of aspiration" lasting from the Armistice to early 1919. But "perhaps there was no reality to that day," he said, "but only an emotional fiz [*sic*]. . . ." White to W. D. Guthrie, July 10, 1923, White Papers.

Wilson had triumphed in peace as he had in war, the Republican cause would have been less hopeful. But he did not. The Republicans, by fastening their argument upon Article X of the League Covenant—a controversial statement guaranteeing the integrity of national boundaries—and by representing the provision as a binding commitment that would involve American soldiers in an unending series of wars and police actions, brought many of their listeners to a new idea of the League as an instrument not for peace but for bloody international adventure. And Wilson stiffened the opposition when he assailed the anti-League senators as "bungalow minds" whose heads were "knots tied to keep their bodies from unravelling."[3]

A more surprising effect of Wilson's performance at Versailles was the desertion of many ardent liberals who could have been expected to rekindle the idealism of 1917 and 1918. Unprepared for the conflict between ideals and self-interest, they abandoned the Treaty of Versailles after becoming convinced that at the conference, and in his earlier defense pacts with England and France, the President had betrayed his own principles. And by tying the League to the treaty, he invited greater opposition than he would otherwise have encountered. For example, the *New Republic* observed in 1920 that the Fourteen Points really belonged to the liberals of the world, not to Wilson, who had negotiated them so badly. Those liberals who had been suspicious of Wilson from the first had their fears con-

[3] It is possible, of course, that the President could on no account have secured Republican cooperation. However tactful he might have been, a handful of powerful isolationist Republican senators would have threatened the Chairman of the Senate Foreign Relations Committee with a party bolt in 1920. And despite Henry Cabot Lodge's own milder sentiments, Lodge might have backed the isolationists, if only to prevent a revolt within his party similar to the Bull Moose rebellion of recent and searing memory.

On May 10, 1919, Colonel House wrote in his diary that Wilson "has built up a fire there [in the Republican Congress] which is now beginning to scorch him and it will become worse and worse as his term wanes. It was all so useless and it has hampered him in the exercise of his public work."

firmed; for those who trusted him, the disillusionment was deep. The protests of some of Wilson's own advisers increased the ranks of men who wanted no part of a League tied to a punitive and "reactionary" peace treaty—one that perpetuated existing injustices and so could only lead to another war. Mounting evidence of Allied perfidy in bringing on the war also disillusioned the liberals. *The Nation* imaginatively charged that the international banking interests, operating through Elihu Root, were pushing the League. Domestic events strengthened their belief that the President had relinquished his role as a reform leader. As they saw it, the shambles at Versailles was matched by the repression of the Palmer raids.[4]

For those who continued to support a League, Harding's own rather disingenuous use of the issue was one reason for the failure to recognize that the organization stood in peril. At one point Harding—who in the Senate had voted for the League with reservations—proposed scrapping it, but later he left the door ajar to "an association of nations"; he thereby muddied the issue and helped to prevent the election from becoming the referendum on the League that Wilson had asked for in his message at the Jackson Day dinner. The confusion among proponents of world power as to Harding's real intention was illustrated when on October 14, 1920, a Committee of Thirty-One, made up preponderantly of Republican internationalists such as Herbert Hoover, Charles Evans Hughes, and former President Taft, sincerely pledged themselves and their party to a League; in fact, it was because of the Committee's position that the *New Republic* claimed to anticipate a Republican League in the event of Democratic failure.[5]

The Republicans were hostile, the liberals cool or confused, and the old-stock Americans were increasingly alarmed over foreign entanglement. The Democrats could ill afford to draw into the League debate still another and steadily expanding

[4] *New Republic*, XXIV (September 9, 1920), 18; *The Nation*, CIX (July 5, 1919), 3.
[5] XXIV (September 16, 1920), 35.

force in American politics: the organized immigrant, perhaps more intractably hostile to Versailles than was any native American faction apart from the irreconcilables. The most staunchly Democratic of all the immigrant groups, the Irish, saw the League as an instrument of oppression in the hands of the British. Yet in his January plea that the election of 1920 be a "solemn referendum" on the League, Wilson laid the party open to the animosity of the national minorities.[6] Political bosses, such as Charles Murphy of New York, Thomas Taggart of Indiana, and George Brennan of Illinois, pleaded against the idea. They saw that to make the League a central issue in the campaign would shatter Democratic foreign blocs in Boston, New York, Chicago, and other large cities heavily populated by immigrants or Americans of immigrant extraction for whom the Treaty of Versailles represented a slighting, a betrayal, or an oppression of the old countries. For once the chauvinism of the immigrant was joined to the chauvinism of the native isolationist.

The Democratic party was left with almost no one to defend the League but an ailing President hampered by the constitutional requirement that he share with the Senate his jurisdiction over foreign policy. Long before the presidential campaign of 1920 and Harding's additional blows against the League, the continuing and fruitless debates in and out of the Senate—along with Wilson's infuriating proprietary attitude toward the League—were wearying voters whose wartime idealism paled with each passing day. A growing weariness first arose among Republicans, immigrants, and disillusioned liberals, and among Communists who thought of the League as a rival to their own international movement; and gradually the skepticism came to permeate the mind of the whole nation. The press, antagonized by Wilson's censorship policies as well as his handling of the news from the Versailles Conference, was in a mood to promote

[6] At the Jefferson Day dinner Wilson's "solemn referendum" message was read, while Bryan, in what was one more open split among Democrats, spoke for conditional ratification. Homer Cummings wrote: "The President *must* compromise [on the League] or he will wreck his party." Personal memorandum, January 28, 1920.

the change in sentiment. Many Democrats, anxious to have a winning issue in the 1920 election, had at first resisted compromising on the League. It was the fate of the Democratic party to become a political scapegoat in the League struggle wherein the issues were unclear and distorted. One correspondent wrote to Franklin Roosevelt: "I fear . . . that the Wilson League of Nations is about the most effective millstone that any party, bent on suicide, has tied about its neck to date."[7]

The presidential campaign would be an ordeal for any Democratic candidate who should attempt to face up to the burdens of the League and of intraparty disorder; yet three leading Democrats actively sought their party's nomination. Among James Cox, William Gibbs McAdoo, and A. Mitchell Palmer, the Attorney General was by far the weakest candidate. Palmer timed his campaign badly, incurring ridicule when his grave predictions about a May Day Communist insurrection proved baseless. Another obvious handicap was that in his home state, traditionally Republican Pennsylvania, he had performed badly in earlier races. Worse still, his performance during the Red Scare and his treatment of the unions during the coal strike alienated both liberals and labor leaders, who made him a symbol of the reaction and betrayal that appeared to characterize the Wilson Administration during its second term. In the early Michigan primary, where he campaigned actively, the Attorney General ran some distance behind Herbert Hoover, Governor Edward Edwards of New Jersey, McAdoo, and William Jennings Bryan, all of whom had tried to stay off the ballot. His name did crop up at the convention, where he inspired extraordinary enthusiasm among some delegates and was favored by some urban bosses; but he had little following as a second-choice possibility and was inconceivable as a consensus candidate.[8]

[7] Barbara Leahy to Roosevelt, June 9, 1920, Roosevelt Papers.
[8] On Palmer's bid to win the presidential nomination, see Coben: *A. Mitchell Palmer*, pp. 246–67. Wilson himself, ten days before the convention, reportedly told Carter Glass that Palmer would be a "weak" candidate. Robert K. Murray: *Red Scare* (Minneapolis, 1955), p. 260.

The name of William Gibbs McAdoo recalled, far more than Palmer's, the liberal achievements of Wilson's first term. Although McAdoo's progressivism was never predictable, people correctly identified him with the reforms of those early years as well as with the pro-labor Railroad Administration he later came to head. McAdoo was the most distinctly Wilsonian candidate—many of his supporters had held administration posts; and throughout the war McAdoo had worked closely with such loyal Wilsonians as Josephus Daniels and Carter Glass. Yet in an attempt to dissociate himself from an already faltering administration and to present himself as an unencumbered presidential candidate, McAdoo had quit his government posts at the end of 1918, catching the spirit of the times when he said he was leaving to make some money. According to Newton Baker, Wilson resented the loss of his able cabinet member on the eve of his European trip. Like other administration men, McAdoo lost touch with Wilson during the League dispute, when the Chief Executive was withdrawing more and more into his own moral and psychological realm. And McAdoo's standing with Wilson was not improved when in April of 1919, in conversation with the President, he announced that his own reservations about the League coincided with those of Elihu Root. McAdoo's correspondence and planning throughout 1919 and 1920 indicate that he was waiting for some paternal word and that in truth he was staking his hopes for 1920 upon the President's recommendation; but Wilson never endorsed him.[9]

[9] Colonel House wrote in his diary: "McAdoo remarked that he and the other Cabinet Members were nothing but clerks. This is not true of McAdoo, and that is why the President gets along less well with him." House manuscript diary, September 24, 1918. According to Josephus Daniels, Wilson declared to Burleson that McAdoo was not fit for the presidency. *The Wilson Era: Years of War and After, 1917–1923* (Chapel Hill, N.C., 1946), p. 553. McAdoo apparently "nettled" Wilson in cabinet meetings with his "emphatic manner and language." Fenno: *The President's Cabinet*, p. 122. McAdoo suggested to Tumulty that Democrats as well as Republicans should offer amendments to the Covenant. McAdoo to Tumulty, March 27, 1919. On Wilson's resenting the loss of McAdoo in 1918, see also Charles S. Hamlin's manuscript diary, February 5, 1924.

If McAdoo had persisted in his efforts to win the nomination, he would probably have been successful.[1] He turned aside because he thought the Democratic party had by 1920 temporarily lost its standing with the electorate, and because Wilson, who apparently favored his own renomination, would not give McAdoo the support that the former Secretary of the Treasury thought he would need in the campaign. In failing to endorse any of the candidates, the President signaled his own burdensome availability;[2] and probably more than coincidence accounts for the circumstance that McAdoo's decision to withdraw came just after the publication in the New York *World* of an article by Louis Siebold, based on an interview with Wilson and portraying the President as a healthy man and a logical candidate.[3] Inordinately ambitious and too canny to risk his political future on an imperfectly staged campaign, McAdoo was forced to hold back until 1924; meanwhile, he sent a bronze medal bearing a likeness of himself, together with a list of his accomplishments, to all his convention supporters.

[1] Although unpopular with urban bosses with whom he had not fully cooperated on patronage matters, McAdoo's popularity with many voters was certain. He ran first, Cox fifth, in the *Literary Digest* poll prior to the convention, LXV (June 12, 1920), 20; see also Mark Sullivan in *Collier's*, LXV (June 19, 1920), 9, 18. Josephus Daniels noted in his diary on January 29, 1920, that "McAdoo seems our strongest man." E. David Cronon, ed.: *The Cabinet Diaries of Josephus Daniels, 1913–1921* (Lincoln, Neb., 1963), p. 488. For reference to a "McAdoo Menace" letter prepared by leading Republicans, see David H. Stratton: "Splattered with Oil: William G. McAdoo and the 1924 Presidential Nomination," *Southwestern Social Science Quarterly*, XLIV (June 1963), 62.

[2] Nothing in Wilson's own Anglophile constitutional theory precluded his running for a third term; continuity of leadership was, in fact, central to that theory. Whatever his inclinations, his illness had severed his party support. Kurt Wimer: "Woodrow Wilson and a Third Term," *Pennsylvania History*, XXIX (April 1962), 193–211; Wesley Bagby: "Woodrow Wilson, a Third Term, and the Solemn Referendum," *American Historical Review*, LX (April 1955), 567–75; and Cronon, ed.: *Cabinet Diaries*, p. 497.

[3] Burleson told House that McAdoo wanted a positive expression from Wilson before the convention that the President was not a candidate—and got none. House Diary, June 3, 1921; *The New York Times*, June 19, 1920, p. 21. The Siebold interview is in the New York *World*, June 18, 1920, pp. 1–2.

James Cox, serving an unusual third term as governor of Ohio, found his way into politics as a newspaper publisher. His recommendation in April 1919 that the teaching of German be prohibited in all of Ohio's elementary schools (the measure was adopted, but only one other state, Nebraska, saw fit to impose a similar restriction) and his keen interest in movie censorship marred his earlier constructive record, as other policies had damaged that of Cox's fellow progressive, Wilson. More important in the eyes of the electorate was the matter of Cox's divorce in 1911 and remarriage in 1917—there were children by each wife. Before the Democratic convention, Mark Sullivan was calling the divorce an insurmountable obstacle to Cox's nomination.[4]

In contrast to the other major candidates, Cox was not identified with the Wilson Administration, and he was not a prohibitionist; he had run as an avowed "wet" in the 1918 gubernatorial election. These two negative virtues intrigued city bosses, particularly Charles Murphy of New York, whose hostility to Wilson dated back to the President's days as governor of New Jersey. In May of 1920, Murphy and his counterparts from other large cities attended a "stop McAdoo" meeting in French Lick Springs, Indiana, which outlined strategy that later secured the nomination of Cox. Edmond H. Moore, Cox's manager, arranged with Palmer's forces to oppose McAdoo jointly. In further pursuance of the policy sketched at French Lick Springs, Moore persuaded many of the Palmer and McAdoo delegates to name Cox as their second choices; the wisdom of this tactic revealed itself during the balloting at the convention, for Palmer and McAdoo, who might have pooled their strength in the interest of some other veteran of the Wilson Administrations, came close to possessing between them the two-thirds vote needed for nomination. When Palmer withdrew, his votes were divided

---

[4] Bagby: *The Road to Normalcy*, p. 154; Wittke: *German-Americans*, p. 181. Palmer wrote Cox in April 1919 that there was no need for restrictive legislation against radicals. April 30, 1919, Justice File 167-200, National Archives. Mark Sullivan to Henry Watterson, April 14, 1920, Watterson Papers.

among several candidates, though they might logically have gone to the other Wilsonian. Pennsylvania, perhaps, was showing its gratitude to Ohio, which had opposed a resolution to drop from each successive ballot the nominee with the lowest strength.[5]

With aid from the Murphy-Taggart-Brennan alliance of machine bosses, Cox finally won the nomination on the forty-fourth ballot. Even at the outset the mood of the delegates had been sober, since they believed with virtual unanimity that no Democrat could win in November; the length of the balloting brought the convention to a still further dispiriting anticlimax.

Ironically, it was Cox's running mate who had the brighter future. Franklin Roosevelt was chosen for the magic of his surname and for the geographical and political balance he would bring to the ticket. Although he had served as Assistant Secretary of the Navy, he had become *persona non grata* with Wilson, owing in part to his tactless remark in 1919 that "any man with common sense could save ten per cent of our government expenses." He continued in the 1920 campaign to denounce government waste and inefficiency. Roosevelt was a much less dominating figure in 1920 than he was to become in the thirties. In personality he thought it expedient to cast himself in the role of the Bull Moose Roosevelt; he cultivated the exclamation "Bully!" along with the politics of the Square Deal. And the papers quoted him as saying: "The Volstead Act—ridiculous!" Yet in 400 formal speeches delivered between August and November, Roosevelt projected his own young, attractive, and friendly personality before the public. Although his argument for the League of Nations was marred by excessive sarcasm, a Republican wired Senator Burt New that "Roosevelt is making friends."[6]

[5] *The New York Times*, May 9, 1920, pp. 1–2; James M. Cox: *Journey Through My Years* (New York, 1946), p. 226.
[6] In a post-election meeting with Cox, Roosevelt predicted, prophetically enough, that the Democrats would not elect a President until a fairly serious depression had occurred. Arthur Schlesinger, Jr.: *The Crisis of the Old Order, 1919–1933* (Boston, 1957), p. 366. The slight against Wilson

The convention adopted a perfunctory and defensive platform that happened to be the longest in the party's history up
to 1920. The first and most significant plank was an endorsement
of the League of Nations linked with an evasive statement about
a willingness to accept "interpretive" amendments; and both
Cox and Roosevelt, who later conferred with the President on
the League, gave the issue chief emphasis during the campaign.
The Wilson men who controlled the platform committee also
paid homage to the struggle for arbitration in industrial disputes
and for abolition of child labor. But even at that, the Democratic
platform was hardly more forward looking than the Republican,
which through the efforts of William Allen White and other
progressives contained a call for the recognition of the Soviet
government, American participation in the World Court, and
acknowledgment of labor's right to bargain collectively. In
rejecting an extreme dry plank, a gesture that again was quite
in keeping with Wilsonianism, the Democratic platform offended Bryan and the prohibitionists. Foreshadowing the in-
ternecine strife that was to plague the party in the twenties,
Bryan called the wet plank "a plagarisn [*sic*] from the Brewer's
Blue Book." In *The Commoner* he wrote that "The nomination of Governor Cox signalizes the surrender of the Democratic Party into the hands of the reactionaries." Bryan finally
cast a reluctant vote for Cox.[7]

---

was contained in an address at the Harvard Union, February 26, 1919;
quoted in Frank Freidel: *Franklin D. Roosevelt: The Ordeal* (Boston,
1954), p. 35. See also Cronon, ed.: *Cabinet Diaries*, pp. 490, 497–8. Grady J.
Gravlee: "A Rhetorical Study of Franklin D. Roosevelt's 1920 Campaign,"
unpublished doctoral dissertation, Louisiana State University, 1963.
[7] "If . . . Bryan," wrote George White, "made a speech in behalf of the
Governor during the campaign, I did not hear of it and I am sure he
positively declined to endorse Governor Cox's candidacy." White to W. B.
Fields, February 5, 1921, George White Papers. Alfred Lief, however,
remembered one speech that Bryan gave on behalf of Cox. *Democracy's
Norris* (New York, 1939), p. 222. J. Harvey McCarthy to Bryan, Novem-
ber 8, 1920, in George White Papers; William Jennings Bryan to Pat
Harrison, 1920, Bryan Papers; *The Commoner*, XX (July 1920), 13;
Lawrence Levine: *Defender of the Faith: William Jennings Bryan; The
Last Decade, 1915–1925* (New York, 1965), pp. 172–4.

Bound to the disastrous issue of the League, and pitted against a popular political mood that forecast almost certain defeat, Cox and Roosevelt faced another more immediate and practical problem: a party organization that had been nearly dormant since the 1918 congressional elections. Here, as within the administration itself, the Democracy revealed its growing incapacity to order itself or to define its purposes; and again much of the trouble might be traced to the President who was neglecting the affairs of his own party. McAdoo had earlier detected the weakened condition of the party machinery. Worrying, perhaps, over his own possible candidacy, he wrote to Daniel Roper on January 28, 1919, that he was "quite concerned over the organization of the National Committee. We have been drifting for a long time. There is neither direction nor energy ... in our organization, and unless these are infused into it and promptly, we shall go into the 1920 campaign with a terrible handicap." Even in the midst of that campaign Joe Tumulty telegraphed Cox in exasperation:

> The campaign so far as the National Organization is concerned, is an utter and tragic failure. There is no executive or campaign committee; no plan of campaign; no contact be-between the National Organization and the various state organizations. . . . No bureau of the National Committee is functioning. They have not merely ceased to function, they have never functioned at all. A condition of demoralization and chaos, which is as difficult to understand as to describe, exists.

Claude Bowers, hard at work on his *Party Battles of the Jackson Period*, in 1921 summed up the situation by comparing the Democratic party organization of his own day with that of Jackson's time. "The Wilson period," wrote the lifelong Democrat Bowers to McAdoo, "had not behind it the fighting, sleepless organization, nor has it the brilliant propogandists [*sic*] like Kendall and Blair. . . . The organization men of those days worked ceaselessly, day by day, year by year. . . ." Bowers complained of "the miserably weak publicity that has been sent out —occasionally—between races or drinks—from our National Committee."[8]

Cox did little to improve the efficiency of the national organization. In order to resolve intraparty bickering, he appointed the neutral and ineffectual George White of Ohio to the post of Democratic National Chairman. Of White, one Ohioan wrote: "His indolence in the campaign of 1920 was commented on by [Senator] Pat Harrison and everyone around headquarters. . . ." White was notably tardy in the formation of a finance committee, with the result that the party even had difficulty in maintaining its offices in Chicago, and in Montana the presidential campaign train nearly stopped for lack of funds. In 1920 the Republicans raised a campaign fund more than three times as great as that of the Democrats, whereas in 1916 Wilson's campaign had been almost as well financed as Hughes's. In contrast to the Democrats, the Republicans surpassed even their memorable performances of Mark Hanna's day. Will Hays was magnificent in his efforts to revivify his party. He had conferences with almost all Republican congressmen, and gathered from each of them lengthy press releases to send to friendly papers. He hired expert salaried fund raisers. To obtain full cooperation from state organizations, he set up a system of partially matching grants for the national campaign. In addition, Hays cultivated the various ethnic voters, scrupulously noting in his records the disposition of Thrace and Macedonia and the landlocked condition of Magyar territory; and he excelled at mitigating factionalism within his own party. Finally, Hays was not overly scrupulous about the propaganda he spread, which identified anarchism and Bolshevism with the Democrats. With good cause, a post-election correspondent of Roosevelt complained of "the poison scattered by Mr. Hays."[9]

[8] Bowers to McAdoo, January 18, 1921, and McAdoo to Roper, McAdoo Papers; Tumulty to Cox, September 23, 1920, Tumulty Papers; Blum's *Tumulty*, p. 167.
[9] On White's performance see Homer Cummings' personal memorandum, October 5, 1920; Daniel C. Roper: *Fifty Years of Public Life* (Durham,

Cox himself waged a tireless campaign, yet it was as ineffective as it was energetic. He charged the Republicans with accepting improper campaign contributions, but when challenged was unable to prove his accusation. His changing stands suggested to the minds of some columnists the confusions of Warren Harding; the Syracuse *Herald* said that the candidates were "as alike as two peas." After a meeting with the President, Cox decided to support the Wilson League and attacked its hyphenated opponents; but later in the campaign—too late to regain immigrant support—he made known his desire for clarifying amendments and proposed a reservation to the crucial Article X. In further incongruity to the dour Wilson, he wore a loud checkered overcoat and sporting hat as he pleaded for the League. He made three "wet" speeches in the campaign and then he appeared to run dry. He also shifted his stand on exclusion of Orientals. Moderate on the issue at first, he later adhered to the party's platform, which called the white racist sentiments of the West Coast "a true expression of the judgment of our people." The *New Republic* dismissed Cox: "If [he] has done anything or said anything . . . to earn the confidence of liberals, beyond repeating the tamest platitudes of Victorian progressives, we have not run across any report of it."[1]

N.C., 1941), p. 210; Bagby: *The Road to Normalcy*, pp. 129–30. According to Blum, Moore hampered the party organization even more than did White. See Blum's *Tumulty*, p. 249. On Hays see his "The Republican Position," *Forum*, LX (August 1918), 129–36, and W. D. Jamieson to McAdoo, September 21, 1919, McAdoo Papers; Robert G. Tucker to Hays, October 4, 1920, Hays Papers; W. H. Thompson to Roosevelt, November 13, 1920, Roosevelt Papers; Mayer: *The Republican Party*, p. 369.

[1] Ed Moore had been antagonized by Cox's overtures to Wilson. Moore wrote to George White in 1923: "You know what I said to you about Cox when, after we nominated him, he ran out on us and went to Canossa to make his peace with Wilson." August 13, 1923, White Papers. New York *World*, September 12, 1920, p. 12; Arthur Mullen: *Western Democrat* (New York, 1940), p. 185; Garraty: *Henry Cabot Lodge* (New York, 1953), p. 399; Cronon, ed.: *Cabinet Diaries*, p. 562; Andrew Sinclair: *The Available Man: The Life Behind the Masks of Warren Gamaliel Harding* (New York, 1965), p. 166; *New Republic*, XXIV (September 22, 1920), 83; (October 13, 1920), 153–4.

Over the fortunes of Cox hung the long and dark shadow of Woodrow Wilson. The real Republican quarry was always the incumbent President, not the Ohio governor. On the general issue of a League the people may have been undecided or indifferent, but toward the Wilson League considerable numbers were by 1920 unquestionably hostile, as they had become estranged from the austere and unbending President himself. It was Wilson who must bear final blame, if blame can be ascribed to a man in his physical and mental condition, for injudicious appointments that divided the cabinet and to that extent weakened the party. It was Wilson, the progressive friend of the farmer and the laborer, who had presided over an administration that managed in its last years to alienate from the Democracy substantial segments of labor and agriculture. In its toleration of men like Palmer and Burleson, moreover, the Wilson Administration helped to sustain the illiberal mood that served as a principal agent of its own rule. Secretary of the Interior Franklin K. Lane remarked just before the election: "Wilson is as unpopular as he once was popular . . . [he] bears down his party to defeat." And defeat came.[2]

For Cox's poor showing in November, cautious analysts offered "the backwash of war" as a general explanation. But the election involved one noticeable variable: the large numbers of

[2] According to Thomas Bailey, "The crippled Wilson, not the dynamic Cox, was running in 1920." *Woodrow Wilson and the Great Betrayal* (New York, 1945), p. 342. The Des Moines *Register* noted that Cox plaintively shouted to an audience: "Wilson's not running this year, Cox is running." October 8, 1920, p. 1. H. L. Mencken observed in the Baltimore *Sun* that "the heaviest burden that the Democratic party has to carry in this campaign is the burden of Dr. Wilson's unpopularity. He is disliked for a hundred and one different reasons. . . . It is months since I last encountered a genuine Wilson man." September 13, 1920, in Malcolm Moos, ed.: *A Carnival of Buncombe* (Baltimore, 1956), p. 21. In 1919, before the President's illness, an effort of indeterminate momentum to impeach Wilson on twenty-three counts had originated in St. Louis; see the pamphlet signed by John C. Meyers in the Dodd Papers, September 1921 to April 1922, S–Z. Franklin K. Lane to Benjamin I. Wheeler, October 28, 1920, *The Letters of Franklin K. Lane*, eds. Anne W. Lane and Louise H. Wall (Boston, 1922), p. 359.

women who cast their first votes in 1920. And some commentators suggested that the Republicans owed their great pluralities to the newly adopted Nineteenth Amendment. It was true enough that southern states and southern Democrats in Congress had notoriously opposed passage of woman suffrage. The view that in 1920 women were especially predisposed to Republicanism arose in part from a frequently cited statistical study by Stuart A. Rice and Malcolm M. Willey, which was based on election returns in Illinois. In that state records of voting by sex were kept in 1920—records that reveal greater Republican support among women than among men. But in concluding that women were in 1920 the more strongly Republican of the sexes, Rice and Willey failed to take into account the special circumstances created by the state's large immigrant-stock population, which was rather evenly distributed among the counties. Even in 1920, Chicago's immigrants gave more support to the Democratic party in proportion to their numbers than did the rest of the city's population. Yet America's women of immigrant stock showed greater hesitancy to make use of their new privilege than did their more emancipated native American sisters,[3] and as a result their sentiment, which might have somewhat weakened the Republican lead among Illinois women, went to a large extent unregistered, while the sentiment of their husbands and brothers, which diluted the Republican lead among the state's male voters, was counted. But it is certain that in Illinois, and probably in much of the nation, the female vote if not the female sentiment was more heavily Republican than the

[3] That immigrant-stock women lagged behind women of native extraction in the exercise of the vote may be demonstrated with particular clarity in Boston. In the twenty-six wards of that city, registration was obtained by sex; and it can be seen that immigrant districts were typically districts of lowest female registration. The only native American areas that had a correspondingly low registration of women voters were the Negro and lower-class native wards, where social restrictions on women also existed. In the Negro sections, perhaps, the Democrats rather than the Republicans were the gainers. Bureau of Elections, Boston, *Boston City Document Number Ten* (Boston, 1921).

male, and was therefore of some benefit to the victorious party.[4]

Though the overwhelming Democratic defeat was the expression of a whole national mood, a number of important groups did register at the polls their special hopes and frustrations. Perhaps the most interesting feature of the 1920 election was the voting behavior of the immigrants clustered in the eastern cities. Table V, which is based on five assembly districts with the highest immigrant or native-born populations in each of three cities, reveals the striking rate at which voters of foreign stock fell away from the Democratic party. In New York, for example, the vote for Cox among immigrants dropped off 29.4 per cent from Wilson's total, compared to the nationwide shift of 15.2 per cent. The Socialists of New York benefited more than the Republicans from the shift.[5]

The Democratic losses of 1920, unlike those of 1918, were not merely sectional: the weakened party received less than its normal minority vote in every part of the nation. The passage of the Esch-Cummins Act, as well as the negative labor record of the second Wilson Administration, cooled labor toward the Democrats; in the Northeast, labor leaders and particularly

[4] Rice and Willey: "A Sex Cleavage in the Presidential Election of 1920," *The Journal of the American Statistical Association*, XIX (December 1928), 519–20. Foreign white stock comprised 60 per cent of Chicago's population and 40 per cent of the downstate total. United States Bureau of the Census, *Abstract of the Fourteenth Census of the United States*, 1920, pp. 18, 50, 372, 378. Two Illinois counties (Union and Greene) where the female vote for Cox eclipsed that for Harding were among the handful of counties with an insignificant population of foreign white stock. Charles E. Merriam and Harold F. Gosnell: *Nonvoting: Causes and Methods of Control* (Chicago, 1924), pp. 28–32; Harold F. Gosnell: *Getting Out the Vote* (Chicago, 1927), pp. 83–4; Andrew Sinclair: *The Better Half: The Emancipation of the American Woman* (New York, 1965), *passim;* Doris Stevens: *Jailed for Freedom* (New York, 1920), pp. 327–8; United States Bureau of the Census, *Fourteenth Census, Population,* III, 457–8.
[5] Chapter VIII contains a more comprehensive commentary on ethnic voting in 1920. *The New York Times*, November 9, 1916, p. 4; November 4, 1920, p. 4; Chicago *Daily Tribune*, November 9, 1916, p. 4; November 4, 1920, p. 3; Boston *Municipal Register, 1917,* p. 293; *1921,* p. 271; United States Bureau of the Census, *Fourteenth Census, Population, passim.*

TABLE V

The Presidential Vote in New York, Boston, and Chicago— Immigrant and Native

	Immigrant Districts		Native-Born		Citywide	
	1916	1920	1916	1920	1916	1920
New York City	D49.3	D19.9	D42.4	D23.7	D52.9	D27.3
	R45.2	R50.0	R57.6	R69.8	R47.1	R60.0
	s 5.5	s28.6		s 4.5		
Chicago*	D60.4	D36.2	D37.7	D22.0	D47.5	D26.3
	R39.6	R63.8	R62.3	R78.0	R52.5	R73.7
Boston*	D71.7	D45.8	D51.2	D33.0	D60.1	D40.3
	R28.3	R54.2	R48.8	R67.0	R39.9	R59.7

* Two-party vote.

railroad men had been disappointed in the selection of Cox over their candidate, McAdoo; and southern support for prohibition must have further injured the Democratic cause among urban workingmen. Though Samuel Gompers' interest in the League had led him to endorse Cox, the AFL in 1920 was more anti-Republican than pro-Democratic. Daniel Tobin of the Teamsters Union was one of the few important labor leaders to back Cox enthusiastically; and some labor groups were so angered at Palmer and Burleson that they refused to endorse the Democratic candidate at all. Business groups remembered that the redistributive tax policies of war had been forced on the country by southern congressmen, who had also promoted government control of the railroads and utilities. The wheat districts in the central states, as in 1918, opposed the party they had in considerable extent supported in 1916, and falling prices for corn and wool also made their mark on the farm vote. In the face of agricultural deflation, Cox himself suggested that more land be reclaimed for agricultural use. The Democracy suffered most in the Far West, where the Wilson popularity of 1916 dissolved in antipathy toward Versailles and its favored treatment of Japan. Key Pittman, Cox's campaign manager in the Far West, thought the fight there was hopeless and let it go almost by default. Even in the South Democrats did badly, losing Tennessee and many prohibition areas for the first time since the Civil War.[6]

The Wilson coalition has been called unstable because it appeared in the middle of a long period of Republican ascendancy. And it is true enough, as the authors of *The American Voter* have shown, that voter preference, as a latent disposition, survives occasional apostasies—and ever since 1894 the Republicans had been the majority party. But a resumption of normal voting patterns only partly explains the sharp reaction against Wilson. To account for this unusual two-to-one loss, the particular mental climate of postwar America deserves special emphasis. The Wilson coalition, even apart from its inherent instability, was a victim to the reversal in political feeling that often develops in postwar times, and that is reflected in the defeat of Clemenceau and of Australia's Hughes, the eclipse of Lloyd George after his khaki victory of 1918—all men of Wilson's time—and, of course, Churchill's downfall in 1945 and the Republican victory in the American elections of 1946.

[6] In the one third of the wheat districts that had the highest acreage, the vote cast for the Democratic presidential candidate was 21 per cent less of the total than it had been in 1916, whereas the loss was 13 per cent in each of the remaining districts. United States Department of Agriculture, *Yearbook of Agriculture, 1928* (Washington, D.C., 1929), pp. 686, 714, 959. *American Federationist*, XXVII (July 1920), 656–7; (August 1920), 737–8; Arvil E. Harris: "Organized Labor in Party Politics, 1906–1932," unpublished doctoral dissertation, State University of Iowa, 1937, p. 310. John Higham in *Strangers in the Land* (New Brunswick, N.J., 1955), p. 265, says that "in California anti-Japanese hysteria, quiescent during the war, broke out again in the latter part of 1919 and rose to unprecedented heights during the election of 1920"; see also Roger Daniels: *The Politics of Prejudice: The Anti-Japanese Movement in California and the Struggle for Japanese Exclusion* (Berkeley, 1962), pp. 79–105. Will Hays considered all the western states to be the battleground of the 1920 campaign. *The New York Times*, June 15, 1920, pp. 1–2. Pittman's view is recorded in Fred Israel: *Nevada's Key Pittman* (Lincoln, Neb., 1963), p. 45; see also Cronon, ed.: *Cabinet Diaries* [October 7, 1920], p. 561–2.

The collapse of Wilsonianism represented the collapse of a philosophy—the "fusion of the peace cause with the idea of progressive democracy," as Arthur Link has called it—in interaction with the decay of a political structure. The philosophy fell victim to the war. Our entry into the conflict not only mocked the idealism of peace but more significantly forced a replacement of economic progressivism by a program of mobilization, and then after 1918 worked its harm upon progressivism in the issues and the very atmosphere it left behind: disillusion, the Red Scare, the League. With no political philosophy to give it direction, the structure of leadership had to disintegrate also. In the necessarily harsh decision-making of war it lost its progressive bearings and its political acumen—witness the clumsy handling of the agricultural problem in 1918. Later it almost ceased to exist when Wilson, abandoned to the League question and broken in health, became incapable of imposing order upon Congress, his party, and his own cabinet. Even in the techniques of patronage the administration grew inept.

The result was the disaster of 1920. Possibly that defeat had little directly to do with the character of the Democratic party in the years that followed. Some of the elements that turned against the Democratic party, like the wheat farmers, were merely moving back to Republican convictions they had never basically abandoned; the immigrants, on the other hand, would soon resume their loyalty to the national Democratic party. The importance of the election as a prelude to the twenties is its demonstration that the party no longer possessed, as it briefly had in Wilsonianism, a principle of cohesion. In 1920 it could not hold the groups and interests it had brought together in 1916, and for more than a decade it would be unable to unify to any significant political end the factions that it loosely incorporated.

CHAPTER III

The Divisive Themes

In Norfolk, Virginia, Spartanburg, South Carolina, and Snowdoun, Alabama, Ku Klux Klansmen in 1924 marched in spectacular parades. As was customary, the marchers usually draped themselves in white sheets symbolic of Christian purity and bore aloft hundreds of American flags; but the parades culminated in unique and lurid naturalization ceremonies, with all the trappings of Christian baptism, for thousands of sometimes reluctant aliens. The incidents dramatized a tension between native American and foreigner that ought to be as closely identified with the decade of the twenties as hedonism or Babbittry. Ethnic conflict pitting old stock against a new had existed throughout much of America's past.[1] But the coming of the "new immi-

---

[1] According to Walter Dean Burnham, "Profound antagonisms in culture and political style between the cosmopolitan, immigrant, wet, largely non-Protestant components of American urban populations and the parochial, dry, Anglo-Saxon Protestant inhabitants of rural areas can be traced back at least to the 1840s." And Lee Benson observed of New York State in the 1830's: "Immigrant Irish Catholics and native puritanical Protestants viewed each other as negative reference groups whose values, beliefs, attitudes, and ways of life clashed fiercely." Burnham: "The Changing Shape

grant"—less kin to older Americans than had been the earlier immigrants from the north of Europe, and far more alien in manner and tradition—raised that conflict to an almost unprecedented intensity. For while John Higham has demonstrated that much more than the new immigration contributed to a heightening of nativist feeling, it cannot be doubted that the recent arrivals gave rise to the fear that unassimilable elements were being injected into the tissue of American culture. Jews from Russia and the Balkans sometimes brought with them dangerous political ideas, as well as an exotic religion. Roman Catholic immigrants from southern Europe swelled the congregations of that suspect faith. And the World War had strengthened the notion that degenerating influences came from outside America and from alien sources within.[2]

In justification of their attitudes, nativist Americans advanced theories about the innate inferiority of the recent immigrant. Professor William MacDougall, a Harvard social psychologist, gave some of the theories of Anglo-Saxon supremacy academic backing; Madison Grant put them into more popular form in *The Passing of the Great Race;* and the historical writer Kenneth

---

of the American Political Universe," *American Political Science Review,* LIX (March 1965), 26; Benson: *The Concept of Jacksonian Democracy: New York as a Test Case* (Princeton, 1961), p. 322. *The Searchlight,* V (July 12, 1924), 1, 7.

[2] The president of the Clarksville, Tennessee, Kiwanis Club, spoke for his own organization—and for much of the nation at large: "In the last thirty years the tide of immigration has undergone a decided and alarming change. Prior to that time the overwhelming majority of entrants were of a racial stock akin to our own and therefore easily assimilable. . . . In latter years the inflow has been of a distinctly different and inferior character, Italians, southern Slovenes, Magyars, and natives of the Mid-Littoral, the latter admittedly the very antithesis of the Anglo-Saxon. These people have not the same ideals and aspirations of the Northern peoples. Among them the most revolting diseases are far more prevalent. Their ethical standards are entirely at variance with our own. They are unable to appreciate our conceptions of political liberty. Their ideas of right and wrong are so diametrically opposed to our own that no reconciliation between them is possible." F. J. Runyon to Senator Kenneth McKellar of Tennessee, March 19, 1924, McKellar Papers. Higham: *Strangers in the Land* (New Brunswick, N.J., 1955).

Roberts marketed them in the *Saturday Evening Post*. Most extensively of all, the Ku Klux Klan spread the idea that the newest arrivals would weaken the character of American society. Protesting the "Mississippi of foreign elements" that made our cities into "Sodoms and Gomorrahs," Hiram Evans of the Klan spurred the fight for restrictive legislation designed to restore the balance of peoples that had held in nineteenth-century America. The restriction movement was, however, far more broadly based than the Klan. "What a spectre is presented to the country," wrote a correspondent of Senator Kenneth McKellar, the Tennessee Democrat: "A foreign bloc, representing the Jewish, Italian, Russian, and Polish provinces of New York, Massachusetts, and other sections . . . defying the American Congress on the Immigration bill. . . . What would 'Old Hickory' . . . have said and done?" Replying that he was in "entire accord" with his constituent's indignation, McKellar, like most other senators from the South and West, pledged himself "heartily in favor of the strictest kind of immigration laws." A handful of urban congressmen opposed such legislation.[3]

For the computing of immigration quotas that would maintain within the nation already existent proportions of ethnic stock, Governor Smith of New York favored using the census of 1920 as the base line; while Hiram Evans preferred that of 1890, when the new immigrants had as yet only begun to swell their numbers.[4] Before the end of 1924, and partly in response to

[3] See, for example, MacDougall's books, *Ethics and Some Modern World Problems* (New York, 1924), pp. 21, 49–50, 73 ff., and *Is America Safe for Democracy?* (New York, 1921). On his influence upon nativist thinking, see *Christian Register*, CIV (July 10, 1924), 657. Demand for Grant's book (New York, 1916) carried it through several printings in the 1920's, and Grant himself contributed political leadership in the South and West for racist goals. Some of Roberts' essays are collected in *Why Europe Leaves Home* (New York, 1922); see also Gino Speranza: *Race or Nation* (Indianapolis, 1925), and Lothrop Stoddard's *Rising Tide of Color* (New York, 1920). Hiram Evans: "The Ku Klux Klan," *The Landmark*, VI (April 1924), 240; Legrand W. Jones to McKellar, March 19, 1924, McKellar to Jones, March 26, 1924, and McKellar to F. J. Runyon, March 22, 1924, McKellar Papers.
[4] *The New York Times*, August 23, 1928, pp. 2, 3.

postwar immigration that threatened to acquire unprecedented proportions, Congress passed new and lower quotas based on national origins as listed in the 1890 census, and so solved the problem to Evans' satisfaction. But while the 1924 law, which was to take effect fully by the end of the decade, may have calmed a few hysterical nativists, the belief continued to be widespread that a large alien population resided within America and that it must be carefully watched and controlled.

The city was the embodiment of all that was "foreign" to American life. To the more apprehensive rural followers of Bryan and McAdoo, New York City, the birthplace of Al Smith and the scene of the convulsive Democratic Convention of 1924, seemed a fusion of Babel and the Cities of the Plain. What place could there be in American culture for a metropolis where in 1920 fully three quarters of the white stock were themselves foreign born or the children of foreign-born parents?[5] And in the thinking of nativists, immigration was of a piece with the other ills of the great city. New York was the home of Wall Street, a name anathema to men who had once heeded Populist leaders. The city, moreover, housed a number of cultural attractions that rural manhood deemed snobbish and effete. The legitimate theater, until recently an affront to the American conscience, made its home in New York along with opera sung in a foreign language. Then there was the ease with which liquor could be bought in Manhattan during the days of prohibition; for this the ruralists blamed Tammany Hall, itself a further symbol of the corrupt city. Diversions encouraged by Tammany, and sanctioned in laws signed by Governor Al Smith, included Sunday baseball and professional boxing. Books and magazines, some of them less than wholesome, were pub-

[5] It may be that the Protestants among the older city immigrants developed a nativism as strong as that of the ruralists, but the dialogue on the issue was between the city and country. Walter Laidlaw, ed.: *Statistical Sources for Demographic Studies of Greater New York, 1920* (New York, 1922), p. xxix; for more comprehensive data on the foreign-born population, see Laidlaw's *Population of the City of New York, 1890–1930* (New York, 1932), pp. 245–315.

lished in the city. New York stood also for the forces of rationalism and modernism—Harry Emerson Fosdick spoke from the pulpit of the Riverside Church—against which the rural fundamentalist pitted his faith. In the country the agrarian myth survived. Orators might still invoke the words of the young Thomas Jefferson: "Those who labour in the earth are the chosen people of God . . . , whose breasts he has made His peculiar deposit for substantial and genuine virtue. . . . The mobs of the great cities add just so much to the support of pure government, as sores do to the strength of the human body."[6]

The cities, moreover, were formidable in their growth, overtaking the countryside at a moment when it was actually suffering an absolute loss in population.[7] And the twenties were a time of considerable rural poverty and urban prosperity, a time that might tempt the city mind to a condescending superiority and the country mind to jealousy. With the rise in agrarian poverty and the loss of ambitious farm youths to the urban factories went a decline in rural morale.

More than ever before the city and country stood at odds during the 1920's, and by 1924 the tension had clearly entered politics. Urban immigrants had voted with some group solidarity in the elections of 1916 and 1920; and by the early twenties the

[6] In the papers of a prominent southern Methodist clergyman, there appears an unsigned etymological note: "The name 'Manhattan' had its origin from the drunken bout which the Indians called 'Man-na-hatta-nink'—the Delaware Indian name for a place of general drunkenness." July 1928, Warren A. Candler Papers. During the 1928 presidential campaign a broadside of Governor Smith dictating to a Negro woman bore the caption: "We don't care a cuss about what he does in New York, but we don't propose to sit silent and let him jam New York ideas down our throats. The picture is a New York idea. . . ." Special Collections, Columbia University Library. New York *World*, May 10, 1924, p. 1; Thomas Jefferson: *Notes on Virginia*, William H. Peden, ed. (Chapel Hill, N.C., 1955), pp. 164–5. See also Morton and Lucia White: *The Intellectual Versus the City: From Thomas Jefferson to Frank Lloyd Wright* (Cambridge, Mass., 1962), pp. 12–20.

[7] In 1910 there were 44 metropolitan areas with a population of more than 100,000; in 1920 the figure climbed to 56; and by 1930 it had shot up to 99. Warren S. Thompson: *Population: The Growth of Metropolitan Districts in the United States: 1900–1940* (Washington, D.C., 1947), pp. 6–7.

Ku Klux Klan and other xenophobic groups were making their strongest bid. Since the conception of a melting pot seemed fallacious, some native Americans feared a distant future in which the control of political affairs might pass completely from their hands into those of solidly ranked immigrant voters, as had already occurred in Boston and other large cities. Eventually, the Roman Catholic Church might even become the state church of America; prominent Catholic priests had hinted ominously of such things. The high birthrate among the Catholic new-comers made more credible the fear that the Church might come to dominate American politics, first seizing one of the parties, and finally the nation. Those with greater knowledge of the situation saw a milder but more immediate ill. Mark Sullivan, himself no nativist, spoke for some intelligent native Americans when he protested that "the mere existence of a considerable number of foreigners who act together in politics is a present vivid obstacle to political action in the free and spontaneous interest of the nation as a whole. . . ."[8] To a considerable extent, then, urban-rural conflict was at its deepest level a reflection of the cleavage between the native-stock American and the immigrant—a cleavage constantly more distinct than the division between city and country, or between an urban East and a rural West and South.

That the forces of urbanism eventually brought new vigor to the Democratic party seems to be beyond question; they helped create for it, by the thirties, a powerful new identity, and they contributed their legions of voters to its electoral army. But it is a possibility, incapable of definite proof but worthy of suggestion, that even the factional strife of the twenties was doing its part in revitalizing the Democracy. Struggles between rural and urban Democrats over the divisive issues of the Ku Klux Klan, Roman Catholicism, and prohibition increased the self-consciousness and aggressiveness of both factions even as it

[8] John A. Ryan and Moorhouse F. X. Millar: *The State and the Church* (New York, 1922), pp. 33–5; *World's Work*, XLVII (February 1924), 441.

weakened the whole party; and in the increased militance of its camps lay a source of future strength for the entire party. Even the losers, the drys and the Klansmen, created in men like Hugo Black of Alabama powerful leaders who would long outlast the decade. The strength of faction was still more impressive in city areas, where the Democratic contingent among urban congressmen was on the increase and where Senator David I. Walsh of Massachusetts came into increasing prominence as a spokesman for a rapidly industrializing section. And once the personalities who symbolized conflict within the party—William Jennings Bryan, William Gibbs McAdoo, and Alfred E. Smith—had passed from national politics the social issues they represented lost much of their political meaning and the stage was set for a rapprochement between city and country Democrats.[9]

The organized expression of ethnic hatred in America was the Ku Klux Klan, which was revived in Atlanta, Georgia, in 1915 while the racist movie *Birth of a Nation* was showing at a local theater. Colonel William J. Simmons had organized the new Klan, but the leadership fell in 1920 to Edward Y. Clarke and Mrs. Elizabeth Tyler, whose Southern Publicity Association had hitherto been engaged in promoting the Red Cross. About 1922 Hiram Evans, a Dallas dentist, took over from Clarke and helped to bring the Klan into national politics. In the early twenties, the frustrations of a serious depression, a fresh wave of immigration, the dramatized relationship of a few Italians and Sicilians to crime syndicates, and the incentive that a

[9] Black's reliance on Klan support is discussed in Daniel M. Berman: "Hugo Black, Southerner. II. The Negro," *American University Law Review*, X (1961), 35–42. Black renounced the Klan in the thirties. Like other politicians, he had been forced to choose between accepting the organization's support or risking political failure. Many reports also exist of Harry Truman's alleged reliance on Klan support; see, for instance, Norman F. Weaver: "The Knights of the Ku Klux Klan in Wisconsin, Indiana, Ohio, and Michigan," unpublished doctoral dissertation, University of Wisconsin, 1954, p. 82. Walsh's career and his popularity in immigrant areas are described in J. Joseph Huthmacher: *Massachusetts People and Politics, 1919–1933* (Cambridge, Mass., 1959), *passim.*

large initiation fee offered to Klan organizers all combined to swell the Klan's following.

The Klan of the twenties resembled its predecessor of Reconstruction in its attitudes toward the Negro. The industrial demands of World War I had enabled many Negroes to secure jobs that earlier would have been out of their reach, and to move into new areas where their presence was unwelcome. Their more favorable economic and social status antagonized unemployed white veterans, and on such embittered feelings the Klan thrived.[1] Hiram Evans proposed sterilization of undesirable elements within the Negro race; but he also considered African resettlement, and in 1922 met with Marcus Garvey, the Negro nationalist, to discuss the policy. The new Klan, however, was not a direct ideological descendant of the earlier movement, which had contented itself with simple white supremacy; the twentieth-century organization, partly commercial in its nature, drew its members from a broader spectrum and could more definitely trace its ancestry and its attitudes to nativist groups. The immigrant, particularly the Catholic, took his place alongside the Negro as a target of the nativists, victim of a hostility that proceeded only in part from economic frustrations similar to those that helped turn the white man against the colored.[2] Klan strength coincided with areas in which nativism had ap-

[1] But coincidentally with the rise of the Klan, the conscience of the South was tightening against at least the worst form of Negrophobia. During the years of the Klan's most rapid growth, the number of lynchings in the South fell off markedly. Lynching figures are taken from Jessie P. Guzman *et al.*, eds.: *The Negro Yearbook, 1952* (New York, 1952), p. 278; identical government figures are available for the years since 1919 in *Crime of Lynching*, United States Senate: Committee on the Judiciary, *Hearings* (Washington, D.C., 1948), p. 30.

1910	67	1915	51	1920	53	1925	17
1911	60	1916	50	1921	59	1926	23
1912	61	1917	36	1922	51	1927	16
1913	51	1918	60	1923	29	1928	10
1914	51	1919	76	1924	16	1929	7

[2] On the Klan's anti-Catholicism, see John Mecklin: *The Ku Klux Klan: A Study of the American Mind* (New York, 1924), pp. 28, 38.

peared in the past, notably the Middle West and South. In the Middle West, where the anti-Catholic American Protective Association had shown its colors in the 1890's, Klansmen were endorsed by former members of the APA. In the South a narrow denominationalism contributed to a bitter and vigorous anti-Romanism directed against the recent immigrants. The appearance of new centers of nativist and, later, Klan sentiment could be explained by population shifts. Oregon and Washington, for example, were originally settled by immigrants from the Mississippi Valley who belonged to the old American stock from which earlier nativism had drawn its support. California had its peculiar problem of Oriental immigration.

The conduct and reputation of the Ku Klux Klan that followed World War II have somewhat distorted our view of the earlier organization. "The Klan," H. L. Mencken affirmed, albeit scornfully, "was just what it pretended to be—an order devoted to the ideals most Americans held sacred."[3] Whatever abnormality existed was among certain leaders and in the culture that produced it; most Klansmen were probably more devoted to group fraternalism than to nativism and violence. The organization probably appealed most to the lower middle classes rather than to the poorest, who could ill afford the ten dollar initiation fee and the high costs of regalia. Though perhaps among the native born in more influential or fast-growing cities, the Klan played a crucial role within that segment of the rural Protestant community whose religious and moral spokesman was William Jennings Bryan and whose political concern in the twenties was prohibition. Bryan himself deplored the Klan and never was a member. But to win the support of Bryan's rural America, the order offered itself as an arm of the Protestant churches and patriotic organizations, for which it already possessed an affinity; and upon religion and patriotism the Klan built its mystique.

The Klan's famous symbol was the burning cross. The chap-

[3] William Manchester: *H. L. Mencken: Disturber of the Peace* (New York, 1950), p. 146.

lain, or Kludd, was an important official; he opened each Klavern meeting with a prayer, perhaps reminding an assembled gathering, as did one Klan "prayer book," that "the living Christ is a Klansman's only criterion of character." Before an altar, a central piece of Klan equipment, the Kludd delivered the Kloxology. Religious songs became Klan songs: "There's a Church in the Valley by the Wildwood" became "There's a Cross that Is Burning in the Wildwood"; "Onward Christian Soldiers" was metamorphosed into "Onward Valiant Klansmen." Christian burial ceremonies were occasionally graced by flowers spelling "KKK" spread over the grave. And deeply ingrained in Klan consciousness was an aggressive patriotism. A Grand Dragon noted that "one of our great duties in disseminating the principles of Klancraft is to forever and ever preach the gospel of patriotism, never allowing a national or state event in which our flag is being commemorated to pass by without making special effort [to create] . . . love and respect in the hearts of all men for our starry banner." At an initiation ceremony, a Klokard (clerk or lecturer) erected a flag-draped altar, and stood a second American flag to its left. A Klan Khoral Klub sometimes would sing "The Star Spangled Banner." The most effective of all Klan songs were familiar tunes that combined religious with patriotic appeal. And in its devotion to the United States and to Old Glory, the Klan is especially to be distinguished from the southern organization of post-Confederate days.[4]

The politics of Klansmanship in its heroic days and after were frequently intertwined with the politics of the major parties. The influence of the Klan was swelled by politicians who joined as they would any fraternal organization that might deliver votes, and by others who would use it in the service of their personal ambition. And in adhering to the Klan, such men made it all the stronger, all the more desirable to political hopefuls. Its power, like that of other clubs, was therefore self-generating;

[4] *The Knights of the Ku Klux Klan of the Realm of Oklahoma vs. the State of Kansas, ex. rel.,* p. 183; Emerson Loucks: *The Ku Klux Klan in Pennsylvania* (New York, 1936), pp. 121-2.

it was capable of drawing members especially at the local level where its intimate, grass-roots character made support of it a necessity to neighborhood politicians, especially where the organization trimmed its program to local needs. Significantly enough, the Klan promoted opposition to reapportionment of the rurally dominated state legislatures, especially in swiftly urbanizing states like Illinois and Indiana. In Texas, Arkansas, Wisconsin, West Virginia, and other states, elections were sometimes held within the Klaverns prior to regular party primaries; and directions were often given to support various bills in the state legislatures. The Indiana "Military Machine" was designed to bring out every available Klan vote on election day.[5] Though it was strongest in local politics, the order was frequently credited with aiding in the election of senators and governors, who would sometimes respond to the pressures of the organization. Late in 1923 the *New Republic* pointed out that the Klan virtually dominated the politics of Oklahoma, Arkansas, Indiana, and Texas, and enjoyed a degree of political influence in Ohio, Oregon, Maine, Connecticut, New Jersey, and elsewhere. The year 1924 was to represent the high point of the Klan's political influence.[6]

As a rule, the Klan attached itself to the dominant political party. Consequently, its deepest infiltration of the Democratic party was in the South. From Oklahoma and Texas to Virginia, Klan power in the South's party of tradition was formidable. Throughout the rest of the country, however, the Klan allied itself primarily with the Republicans and made overtures to the Democracy in most cases only when it desired to widen its already considerable influence. Democratic politicians sometimes welcomed the Klan's support, as they would any bloc of potential voters, and the Klan sometimes even controlled the

5 Charles C. Alexander: "Secrecy Bids for Power: The Ku Klux Klan in Texas Politics in the 1920's," *Mid-America*, XLVI (January 1964), 9–10; *The New York Times*, August 1, 1922, p. 21; W. D. Harry to William Allen White, September 23, 1924, White Papers; Weaver: "The Knights of the Ku Klux Klan," p. 195.
6 *New Republic*, XXXVI (November 21, 1923), 321.

Democratic factions. In Missouri the Klan was used as an outright Democratic weapon to intimidate Negroes who had recently moved northward out of the black belt. But outside the South the Klan usually assumed a Republican coloration; and at times it encountered organized Democratic opposition.[7]

In Indiana, for instance, one Democrat boasted that while in 1924 "the Klan simply swallowed the G.O.P.," his party was meeting the issue squarely. Although the Klan was reported to be in control of "a very large majority of the Democratic organizations," the state Democratic party, under the influence of the Indiana boss Tom Taggart, denounced the Klan—but Governor Vic Donahey then did not endorse the platform. Similar disavowals of Klan support were adopted at Democratic state conventions in Connecticut, New Mexico, Ohio, and Kansas—states where the Klan was supporting the Republicans. All of the Klan "victories" reported by *The New York Times* in its 1924 election analysis were Republican successes; this circumstance was testimony that in the two or three years prior to 1924 Klan membership rolls had been growing much faster outside than inside the South.[8]

Before the 1924 presidential election the Klan constituted a potentially powerful bloc; conservative estimates of its active strength in 1924 range in the neighborhood of only two million, but a greater number of members had been enrolled at one time or another. Since the order was made up almost wholly of male citizens, the ranks who might vote the Klan's way must have been further swelled by dutiful wives. Even

[7] In Texas, Oklahoma, and Georgia the Klan occasionally supported Republicans; and in Oregon, Ohio, and Iowa it sometimes backed Democrats. David Chalmers: *Hooded Americanism* (New York, 1965), p. 81.
[8] William H. Rickens to Senator Samuel M. Ralston, May 19, 1924. In Ralston's telegram to Taggart announcing withdrawal as a presidential candidate at the 1924 convention, the Senator complained that he was being tied to the Klan. June 1, 1924, Ralston Papers. Meredith Nicholson to Robert Bridges, 1924, Nicholson Papers; Edgar I. Fuller, *The Visible of the Invisible Empire* (Denver, 1925), p. 125; *Literary Digest*, LXXXI (May 24, 1924), 14; *The New York Times*, November 6, 1924, pp. 1, 3; Chalmers: *Hooded Americanism*, pp. 145, 267.

where the Klan did not function, many people favored its principles, and in areas where it was strong, those who hesitated to join might sympathize with its point of view and perhaps follow its lead. While members of the Klan belonged to opposing political parties, a candidate designated by the Klan could often be assured of both Democratic and Republican votes. In 1922 the chairman of the congressional committee that had investigated the order was defeated in part by Klan opposition, as were two Jewish congressmen in Indiana and Texas. Hiram Evans of Dallas, who worked assiduously to bring the Klan into politics, claimed that the "Klan vote" was always higher than its membership.[9] The power of the Klan was to be reckoned with at national political conventions, and in no small part because it was of unknown potency.

The Klan's political activities reflected the ambitions of its leaders. Evans and Edward Y. Clarke tried sundry schemes to acquire political power. In 1920 Clarke revealed to Georgia Republicans a plan to "discredit" the Democratic party by linking it to the Roman Catholic Church; later in the year he had a "very satisfactory" conference with Will Hays, saying that Hays had "grasped the possibilities in our plan." In 1923 a document stolen from the Klan's Atlanta headquarters revealed plans for a takeover of the national government. According to an ex-official of the Klan, Evans was brought to the White House in the same year by the sculptor Gutzon Borglum, who introduced the Klan leader to President Harding; letters in the Borglum papers from Evans and to Coolidge prove that such a meeting was indeed arranged. A few weeks after Evans' alleged meeting with the Chief Executive, the order transferred its headquarters from Atlanta, Georgia, to Washington, D.C. As the 1924 election approached, the Klan wooed the Democrats as well. In the spring of 1923 Evans approached Williams Gibbs McAdoo at French Lick Springs, Indiana; purportedly he persuaded McAdoo to be the Klan candidate for President, though

9 Stanley Frost: "The Masked Politics of the Klan," *World's Work*, LV (February 1928), 404.

more accurately Evans had simply chosen to support him. During the coming months the Klan worked against McAdoo's opponents, Smith of New York and Senator Oscar Underwood of Alabama; and Evans spoke glibly of electing McAdoo to put "a Klansman in the White House."[1]

The politics of the Klan naturally centered around religious as well as ethnic issues. Senator Tom Heflin of Alabama eulogized the Klan: "God had raised up this great patriotic organization to unmask popery." Colonel Simmons, in an effort to maintain his waning influence over the Klan he had founded, turned more and more to the berating of Catholics.[2] And Clarke in 1920 set out to use anti-Catholicism as a drawing card to brothers in other fraternal organizations, particularly the Masons with their well-known tradition of anti-Romanism. Senator Tom Watson of Georgia, who before the war had suggested the

[1] Benjamin H. Avin: "The Ku Klux Klan, 1915–1925: A Study in Religious Intolerance," unpublished doctoral dissertation, Georgetown University, 1952, pp. 270–1, 296–7; Borglum to Harding and Evans to Borglum, both early 1923, Borglum Papers. Clarke was said to have boasted that he would be "the most powerful man in the world through the Klan." Francis R. Welch to Calvin Coolidge, Justice Department File 198589–591, National Archives. Fuller: *The Visible of the Invisible Empire*, pp. 51, 62; Marion Monteval: *The Klan Inside Out* (Claremore, Okla., 1924), pp. 139, 140–1; Rice: *The Ku Klux Klan in American Politics*, pp. 98–9. The Grand Titan of Waco, Texas, quoted Evans as saying: "Mr. McAdoo is our man." Grand Titan to M. E. Foster, April 14, 1924, Underwood Papers. In a 1938 senatorial campaign a Klan membership card was used to discredit McAdoo, but it was undoubtedly a forgery. See Chapter IV on McAdoo's relationship with the Klan.

[2] John Mecklin, a sociologist, wrote that "a canvass of the motives for joining the Klan indicates that anti-Catholicism takes precedence over all others." Mecklin: *The Ku Klux Klan*, p. 38. See also Charles P. Sweeney: "The Great Bigotry Merger," *The Nation*, CXV (July 5, 1922), 9, and Breckinridge Long manuscript diary, March 6, 1924. Although the Catholic threat was more immediate, since it was carried in the person of Al Smith, the Jews also came in for an occasional attack. The extravagant Bishop Alma White warned of a Roman Catholic–Hebrew alliance; White even interpreted the sinking of the *Titanic* as representing the wrath of God toward immigrants and Catholics. *Heroes of the Fiery Cross* (Zarephath, N.J., 1928), pp. 27 ff. Henry D. Lindsey to Arthur M. Hyde, October 18, 1922, Hyde Papers.

formation of a new Klan, campaigned in that year on the issue of popery. In a recrudescence of Know-Nothingism, the Klan helped to circulate stories about the American political aspirations of the Pope. Once again it was rumored that the Holy Father wanted to set up a new empire in the Mississippi Valley, although Governor Sidney J. Catts of Florida insisted that the Vatican had the Sunshine State in mind. In the nation's capital some Protestants worried that two cannons at Georgetown University were pointed toward the White House and that various Catholic institutions, as seen on a map published in *The Fundamentalist*, appeared to surround the important government buildings—"the great fortress-like strongholds of the papal government on strategical and commanding heights." In the filagree of the dollar bill was seen a rosary, cross, and head of the Virgin Mary placed there by a wily Jesuit; and Senator Heflin objected violently when cardinal-red drapes were hung in Coolidge's reception rooms. The conception of a Catholic conspiracy was everywhere: a correspondent of Franklin Roosevelt suggested that as a reasonable precaution all nuns be fingerprinted; a Klan paper complained that Catholic women had been sent by the hierarchy to infest the women's clubs of Texas "to prepare for the final takeover"; land overlooking West Point, it was pointed out, had been purchased by the Catholics in preparation for civil war.[3]

When Al Smith became a serious presidential candidate, the New Yorker—who summed up in his person and background

---

[3] Other tales that survive expose the ignorance of the Klansmen. Men who could take seriously a Kligraff or a Kludd would find little difficulty in believing, as did Reverend Doctor C. Lewis Fowler, editor of the *American Standard*, that Harding died from hypnotic telepathic thought waves generated in the minds of Jesuit adepts. Sweeney: "The Great Bigotry Merger," p. 10; W. O. Whitney to Franklin Roosevelt, October 15, 1928, Roosevelt Papers; *The Fundamentalist*, April 13, 1928, p. 2; *The Protestant*, March 24, 1928, p. 4; *American Standard*, August 1, 1924, p. 1; Joe Tumulty to Elbert R. Zaring, January 5, 1924, copy in Senator James D. Phelan Papers; Morton Harrison: "Gentlemen from Indiana," *Atlantic Monthly*, CXLI (May 1928), 679–80. Heflin is quoted in Alma White's *The Ku Klux Klan in Prophecy* (Zarephath, N.J., 1925), p. 17.

much that the Klan feared—became the focus of attack. Governor Smith outraged the Klan in 1923 and again two years later when he signed bills that practically outlawed the organization in New York State. The *Literary Digest* believed that Smith had thereby signed his political death warrant so far as his aspirations for the presidency were concerned.[4] Smith had committed additional crimes against Klan mentality when he signed a bill in 1922 making New York the first state to repeal its prohibition-enforcement law, a predetermined step in nationwide wet strategy.

At the Democratic National Convention in 1924 the Klan exerted strength sufficient to prevent the delegates from censuring their organization by name. In New York as elsewhere, boasted Hiram Evans, the "delegates were afraid of what we might do." At that convention the Klan also fulfilled its purpose regarding the presidential candidacy of Governor Smith: to help prevent the nomination of the New Yorker in that year and to instill enough anti-Catholicism in the mind of the average voter to diminish Smith's chances of ever winning the presidency.[5]

Why the Klan lost its vitality after 1924 and suffered a sharp decline in its membership remains something of a mystery, but it can be seen that around 1925 a number of forces were converging against the order. The confidence shaken by the war and the ensuing depression had returned with the prosperity of the middle and later twenties; it was thin soil for the sustenance of extremism. Disclosures of rampant local terrorism and widespread corruption injured the Klan. In 1924 America was shocked to hear that in Indiana Grand Dragon David Stephenson had sexually assaulted an ex-schoolteacher, driving her to poison and death. Other eminent Klansmen, including Simmons and Evans, became involved in financial scandals, and the Klan

[4] LXXVII (June 9, 1923), 12.
[5] Rice: *The Ku Klux Klan in American Politics*, p. 84. The Klan's political fortunes in 1924 are drawn in *The New York Times*, November 6, 1924, pp. 1, 3.

was blamed for acts of individual extremists. The Klan, it began to appear, had little to offer the American who sought a fortified ground of respectability from which to challenge the morals and respectability of others. In addition, the rhetorical defeat of Bryan at the Scopes trial and his ensuing death in 1925 weakened the rural fundamentalist crusade against the city and the foreigner. The congressional quota system of 1924, sharply limiting immigration from southern and eastern Europe, accomplished an important part of the Klan program and removed a portion of its *raison d'être*. Finally, despite its authoritarian structure, the Klan membership was extremely heterogeneous: particularly after its leaders entered politics, arguments flared between progressives and conservatives, Democrats and Republicans. As leaders quarreled over issues and candidates, the discipline of the order ran afoul of existing political alignments.[6]

The Klan's passing freed the Democratic party of a contentious issue, but it did not signal the passing of intolerance. The mental stereotypes that gave rise to the Klan had far antedated its birth; at its decline, words like "Pope," "Catholic," and "foreigner"—their sinister implications sharpened through the work of the Klan—kept their explosive power to draw forth fear or hatred. One Klansman who withdrew from the order stated that "there was nothing wrong with the Klan principles. But the members—they weren't big enough for the order."[7] The Klan's demise was primarily an organizational failure and not a result of external attacks; and the same feelings that made the Klan flourish in 1924 continued to exist during the 1928 presidential campaign.[8]

[6] Toxologists noted that tooth marks on Stephenson's victim were alone sufficient to have induced death; it was a strange way to preserve the purity of American womanhood that was frequently stated as a Klan goal. *New Republic*, LII (November 16, 1927), 330–2; Monteval: *The Klan Inside Out*, pp. 66 ff.; Carl Degler: "A Century of the Klan," *Journal of Southern History*, XXXI (November 1965), 435–43.

[7] Quoted in Loucks: *The Ku Klux Klan in Pennsylvania*, p. 163.

[8] For interesting defenses of the Klan, see Charles S. Joiner to John W. Davis, November 17, 1924, Davis Papers, and W. D. Wilson to Franklin

The fortunes of the Klan were closely related to the course of religious fundamentalism, which also declined after 1925. The administrative personnel of the two movements were often shared. Some individuals appear to have acquired in the Klan their initial training for work in the fundamentalist movement, particularly in the evangelical churches; others made the transition from fundamentalism to nativism. During the years 1922 to 1928, twenty-six of the thirty-nine anti-Catholic lecturers regularly employed by the Klan were Protestant ministers of the fundamentalist type, and in these same years sixteen Protestant ministers served as Klan officials, not to speak of the thousands of Protestant clergymen who joined the Klan. The National Catholic Bureau of Information compiled a list of sixty-seven ministers preaching pro-Klan sermons or entertaining Klansmen in their homes. The most prominent Klansmen served in the fundamentalist crusade. Colonel Simmons himself had once held a probationary Methodist pulpit, although it had been withdrawn on moral grounds, and Edward Clarke with Mrs. Tyler joined the fundamentalists in the mid-twenties—and the Anti-Saloon League still later in the decade—after leaving the Klan. In many parts of the country, church buildings served as meeting places for the Klan; everywhere ministers were offered free membership, and Klan donations to churches were commonplace. H. L. Mencken, Charles Merz, Virginius Dabney, and others reported on the denominational ties of the Klan or the aid it gave to passing anti-evolution laws.[9]

Roosevelt, December 12, 1924, Roosevelt Papers. For examples of non-Protestant groups that patterned themselves on the Klan, see Weaver: "The Knights of the Ku Klux Klan," pp. 246 ff., and *The New York Times*, September 7, 1923, p. 17; September 16, 1923, I, pt. 2, p. 5; March 22, 1924, p. 12; November 2, 1924, p. 1; November 5, 1924, p. 20.
[9] Michael Williams: *Shadow of the Pope* (New York, 1932), p. 317; Virginius Dabney: *Liberalism in the South* (Chapel Hill, N.C., 1932), p. 282; and *Below the Potomac* (New York, 1942), pp. 248–9; Robert M. Miller: "A Note on the Relationship Between the Protestant Churches and the Revival of the Ku Klux Klan," *Journal of Southern History*, XXII (August 1956), 355–68; J. Fletcher Moore to Bishop Warren A. Candler, July 20, 1928, Candler Papers; Charles C. Alexander: *The Ku Klux*

In many areas of belief and attitude, as well as in personnel, fundamentalism and the Klan occupied common ground. The strongest bond was undoubtedly prohibition, but anti-Catholicism also characterized both movements. Fundamentalist periodicals appearing during the election years bear ample evidence of the fact; while many of these journals scrupulously avoided any commentary on politics, a significant number urged the defeat of Smith on religious grounds.[1] Patriotism, too, was as much a part of the fundamentalist crusade as of the Klan movement. America was, so it seemed, the native home of Christianity; and in the ceremonies of many nativist churches the flag was used to excess.

The nativist and fundamentalist groups together were in partial alliance with the prohibitionist movement—the latter a program of the Protestant churches, particularly though not exclusively the evangelist sects. The chief prohibitionist organization, the Anti-Saloon League, sometimes held meetings in churches—as did the Klan—and disseminated its propaganda through church organizations; and it operated at election time in somewhat the same manner as the Klan. The Klan, moreover, made Protestant prohibition the main tenet of its social program, and constituted itself a police agency for the enforcement of the measure: when drinkers flagrantly defied the law in Klan territory, they risked retaliation from the vigilant night riders. Finally, the drys and the fundamentalists drew upon a similar

---

Klan in the Southwest (Lexington, Ky., 1965), p. 87; Norman F. Furniss: *The Fundamentalist Controversy, 1918–1931* (New Haven, 1954), pp. 62–6; Charles Merz: "The Methodist Lobby," *New Republic,* XLVIII (October 13, 1926), 213–15; H. L. Mencken: *Prejudices: Third Series* (New York, 1922), p. 34.

[1] John Roach Straton, a leading figure in the clerical campaign of 1928 against Smith, had long been editor of *The Fundamentalist,* perhaps the movement's principal periodical. See also the publications of the Rail Splitter Press, of which the editor, William Lloyd Clark, was rabidly anti-Catholic; and *Bob Schuler's Magazine, The Allied Protestant American, Gopher, The United Protestant Advocate, The Protestant Herald,* and *The Protestant Standard. The Baptist Fundamentalist of Texas; Christian Standard,* LXIII (October 27, 1928), 13; *The Protestant; Bible Beliefs.*

rhetoric, constant in its references to battle and wars: a rhetoric that revealed the aggressive instinct that sustained their causes.[2]

It is evident above all that the Klan, the Anti-Saloon League, and the fundamentalist churches held in common a suspicion of the foreigner and his ways—so much so that one may speak of a nativist "mind" often inclusive of fundamentalism and prohibitionism. Advocates of a dry America had reason to fear an immigration from lands where wine and beer flowed like water. "Most of the bootleggers . . . appear to be foreigners," Henry Pratt Fairchild assured his readers in 1926. The New York University sociologist continued: "It can not be purely by chance that a map of 'wetness' in the United States is almost a replica of a map showing the distribution of the foreign born." "I made a list of nearly 500 . . . men recently arrested for violating Prohib. [*sic*]," wrote Billy Sunday. "It reads like a page of directories from Italy, Greece—sprinkling of Irish." And citizens of an older American lineage who feared the corrupting encroachments of the metropolis and its immigrant peoples could hope that prohibition might constitute a barrier against the urban manner.[3]

Yet each of the three reform groups, the Klan, the Anti-Saloon League, and the fundamentalists, could work along separate lines and draw support from overlapping but distinct segments of the population. It was therefore possible to be an

[2] In "Prohibition as a Political Issue," *Journal of Politics*, XXIII (August 1961), 507–25, Charles D. Farris demonstrates the existence of a fundamentalist-dry correlation. *Christian Century*, XLV (January 26, 1928), 103–4; XLV (March 15, 1928), 348–9; see also H. L. Mencken's comment of May 28, 1928, in Malcolm Moos, ed.: *A Carnival of Buncombe* (Baltimore, 1956), p. 156; *The New York Times*, October 7, 1928, p. 1; Norman H. Dohn: "The History of the Anti-Saloon League," unpublished doctoral dissertation, The Ohio State University, 1959, p. 164. "This battle is not a rosewater conflict," observed the Anti-Saloon League *Yearbook* of 1911: "It is war—continuing relentless war." (Westerville, Ohio), p. 4. Furniss: *The Fundamentalist Controversy*, pp. 36, 42.

[3] Fairchild: *The Melting-Pot Mistake* (Boston, 1926), p. 215; William G. McLoughlin, Jr.: *Billy Sunday Was His Real Name* (Chicago, 1955), p. 275.

ardent prohibitionist but to look on the Klan with disgust. Bryan was an idol of the Klansmen. When he died the order fired tall crosses in Dayton and Toledo, Ohio, announcing in one case that "In memory of William Jennings Bryan, the greatest Klansman of our time, this cross is burned; he stood at Armageddon and battled for the Lord." But Bryan was not a Klansman; and before the 1924 election he backed up the Democratic candidate's condemnation of the Klan by name. As a matter of fact, he also aided the Klan when at the 1924 Democratic Convention he pleaded with the delegates to refrain from censuring it by name; yet in the same speech he showed at least a degree of disapproval of the order.[4]

By the third decade of the century, then, a complex of political, social, and moral attitudes had established itself, compounded of nativism, fundamentalism, prohibitionism, and a conviction that the American character resided in the farm and hinterland town. But of the four, it was the cause of prohibition that most broadly realized itself in political action and a legislative program; it drew to its standard Americans of evangelical and of nativist persuasion alike, and possessed a power of symbolism over the minds of diverse social groups, both of advocates and opponents. It was also a strongly coercive reform, aimed at bringing under some kind of control the urban and immigrant population; in fact, the very name of the Anti-Saloon League illustrated the drift of the movement. Founded in 1893, at the start of a great depression, the League singled out not alcohol but an institution—and an institution chiefly urban; the League identified the drinker with a culture, and depended on reverse cultural loyalties for its own sustenance. The "anti" in its title bespoke its basic intolerance of cultural differences. To understand the special nature of the prohibition movement, one must

---

[4] Bryan's objection to prohibition was a broad one; to him liquor was a sign of moral laxity, materialism, and skepticism—which, aided by modern science, were turning the city dwellers into pagans. *The New York Times,* August 30, 1924, p. 1; *Official Report of the Democratic National Convention* ... [of] ... *1924* (Indianapolis, 1925), pp. 303–9.

see that "Prohibition is part of our religion," as the leading dry Wayne Williams put it. The Anti-Saloon League was staffed principally by clergymen; its main source of revenue was contributions solicited through the Protestant churches; and its history was such that one scholar refers to it as "the grown-up child of the Methodist Church." "For thirty-two years," boasted the League's house organ, the *American Issue*, "the League has been controlled and supported by the Church. . . . The Church must meet the challenge of the . . . wets." "The saloon," declared Billy Sunday, "is an infidel. It has no faith in God . . . no religion. It could close every church in the land." Al Smith, on the other hand, condemned the efforts of the Anti-Saloon League "to make God-fearing men and women believe that the Eighteenth Amendment and the Volstead Act are dogmas of religion."[5]

Prohibition was a thoroughly and angrily political question: the *New Republic* called it "the one issue which arouses real excitement . . . the grand old perennial." The Anti-Saloon League provided energy and leadership for the prohibitionist forces; the wets found political expression in the Association Against the Prohibition Amendment. Like the Klan, both organizations helped to weaken still further the existing party system. Founded in 1920 and drawing much of its financial support from the brewers, the AAPA set out to tear away from the prohibitionist organization its veil of Christian sanctity. This task, though difficult, was not impossible, for some of the most

[5] Purley Baker of the Anti-Saloon League despaired that "it has been at the point where the urban population outnumbers the rural people that wrecked Republics have gone down. . . . The peril of this Republic likewise is now clearly seen to be in her cities." Quoted in Andrew Sinclair: *Prohibition: The Era of Excess* (Boston, 1962), p. 9. Richard Hofstadter describes the churches as competing with the saloons in "the business of consolation." Introduction to Sinclair: *Prohibition*, p. vii. Sunday is quoted on p. 63 of Sinclair; Smith in *The New York Times*, October 30, 1928, p. 3. The Anti-Saloon League paid Sunday $1200 for speaking against liquor, and he also received money from the Klan. *Time*, VI (August 10, 1925), 5; XII (November 12, 1928), 8. Gusfield: *Symbolic Crusade* (Urbana, Ill., 1963), pp. 6–11; James H. Timberlake: *Prohibition and the Progressive Movement, 1900–1920* (Cambridge, Mass., 1963), pp. 168–9.

prominent clergymen serving in the dry groups appeared unfit to wear the cloth. W. C. Shupp, Superintendent of the Missouri Anti-Saloon League, secured alcohol withdrawal permits for a drug firm in which he and his son held interests; William H. Anderson, the stormy petrel of the dry lobbyists, was convicted of forgery in embezzling League funds; and Bishop James Cannon, Jr., gambled his money on the stock market. The growing national audience of metropolitan newspapers was introduced to the peccadilloes of these and other League officials, and while they were perhaps not unusual in so large an organization, by the end of the decade the Anti-Saloon League could scarcely declare itself "born of God" or proclaim itself "the Protestant Church in Action Against the Saloon." Furthermore, the more fundamentalist churches had been discredited in the Scopes trial and the decline of the status of "old-time" religion. And when the Anti-Saloon League entered the presidential campaign against Smith in 1928, it invited a close identification in the public mind with anti-Catholicism; as Andrew Sinclair puts it: "The foulness of the religious campaign against Smith seemed part and parcel of the virulence of the dry campaign against him"; and while many Americans were quite willing to cast their vote against Rome, there must have been at least a considerable number of Protestants who were repelled by the conduct of Smith's more violent opponents. So despite the formidable support upon which the League might call, the advocates of repeal of prohibition were never at a loss for ammunition.[6]

But during the twenties the League remained an effective political pressure group, holding sway over diverse groups of people. In none of the congresses elected during the decade were

[6] Anderson said the wets were "a lot of unwashed, wild-eyed foreigners in New York City who have no comprehension of the spirit of America." Carter Glass to Wayne Wheeler, November 1, 1930, Glass Papers; Sinclair: *Prohibition*, p. 304; Anderson: *The Church in Action Against the Saloon* (Westerville, Ohio, 1910), *passim; New Republic*, XLVIII (October 27, 1926), 25. On corruption in the League see Peter H. Odegard: *Pressure Politics* (New York, 1928), pp. 219–43.

the wets heavily represented. In 1922 the AAPA approved 249 candidates, thereby furnishing the Anti-Saloon League and its expert lobbyists with an official list of candidates to oppose: under fire from the League, some office seekers repudiated their AAPA endorsement. Similar tactics backfired in 1924 when late in the campaign the Association listed 262 House candidates as "unsatisfactory"; of these 219 were elected, and only two of the thirteen new senators were acceptable to the organization. In 1926 the results were even worse for the wets, and the Congress elected in 1928 was the dryest of all, with only seventy-five wets in the House and fifteen in the Senate. Not until 1930, when the AAPA worked very closely with the candidates, did considerable wet strength materialize; in the elections of that year 166 wet candidates for the House and twenty-two for the Senate were successful.[7]

The major political battleground for prohibition during the twenties was the Democratic party. There the opposing forces were personified in the party leaders Bryan and Smith: the one totally committed to the crusade that looked forward to a "millennial Kansas afloat on a nirvana of pure water"; the other a child of the saloon, offspring and faithful representative of a social milieu in which that institution held an honored place. The division was apparent in the Democratic Convention of 1920, where Wayne Wheeler, a Republican, and James Cannon, Jr., a Democrat, worked to prevent the party from adopting Bryan's strongly worded prohibition plank—a plank that would set aside the more sensible dry policy of evaluating individual candidates rather than the party to which they belonged. In 1924 Bryan once more added to the prevailing disharmony by

[7] Wayne Wheeler's biographer speaks of the wets's "usual and asinine mistakes in the [1922] campaign." Of Wheeler, he wrote: "[He] had a code of honor which prevented him hitting below the belt, unless it was absolutely necessary for the sake of the prohibition movement." Justin Steuart: *Wayne Wheeler, Dry Boss* (New York, 1928), pp. 194–6, 233. Dayton Heckman: "Prohibition Passes: The Story of the Association Against the Prohibition Amendment," unpublished doctoral dissertation, Ohio State University, 1939, *passim.*

again introducing the prohibition issue. After Bryan's death Bishop Cannon became the leader of the Democratic drys, and Cannon blended his prohibitionist beliefs with anti-Catholicism. At the convention of 1928, the prohibitionists, now bereft of their leaders Bryan and McAdoo, lost the party to the wet forces; even in collaboration with the anti-Catholic and Klan elements, the drys were unable to persuade the necessary one third of the delegates to veto the selection of Al Smith. During the presidential campaign the urban leaders of the party willingly made it a propaganda agency for the AAPA. Important Democrats such as John J. Raskob and Jouett Shouse were closely identified with the group, and in 1930 the Senate lobby committee included the half-million-dollar 1928 campaign expenditure of the AAPA with the "committees and organizations receiving and expending money in behalf of the Democratic party."[8]

Hoover's defeat of Smith was of course claimed as a triumph by the drys, but on the presidential level the victory was of one party over another, while the drys had been accustomed to dominating both parties. In 1929 the Jones law, stiffening penalties against first violators of the Volstead Act, encountered the lowest wet vote recorded so far in both houses of Congress, yet the vote itself registered a slight but discernible change that was related to the new urban strength of the Democratic party. Although the wet tabulation in the House was thirty-eight votes shorter than had been the anti-prohibitionist tally on the Eighteenth Amendment, the losses were comparatively steeper in the West and South than in the North, so that the northern states

[8] Even in 1928 the position of any outspoken wet was recognized to be precarious; Thomas B. Love could argue forcefully against nominating Smith, "a man who cannot be elected because . . . the saloons are closed and the women are voting." Love to W. P. Smith, November 24, 1922, Love Papers. In 1928 Pierre S. DuPont gave $50,000 to the Democratic National Committee, $32,000 to the AAPA; John J. Raskob, $110,000 and $17,000; Arthur Curtiss James, $25,000 and $12,000; R. T. Crane, $10,000 and $12,500. The whole roster of AAPA members gave less than $100,000 to the Republicans. *Senate Lobby Investigations, 1930* (Washington, D.C., 1931), pp. 4032 ff. Sinclair: *Prohibition*, pp. 269–306.

with higher immigrant populations now provided two-thirds rather than one-half of the wet vote. Similarly, in the Senate the North provided eight out of twenty votes in 1917, but ten out of eighteen in 1929.[9]

Prohibition was a battle the country would soon lose to the city. Walter Lippmann called it "a test of strength between social orders. When the Eighteenth Amendment goes down, the cities will be dominant politically and socially as they now are economically." At one time the prohibition movement had received support from all classes—both urban and rural; by the twenties it was rural and fundamentalist. Throughout the decade the possibility of reversing a constitutional amendment seemed inconceivable; yet the ineffectuality of the Eighteenth Amendment became increasingly obvious. Only the expense, the quality of the intoxicant, and the ease of obtaining it were affected. Gradually, it came to be apparent that prohibition had been the work of organized pressure groups accomplished under the special conditions of the war, and a reaction set in so quickly as to suggest that perhaps it had never commanded the support of the unorganized majority. It was no surprise that among working-class immigrants repeal sentiment was strong. In 1922 only ninety-three of the immigrant workers at the Edison plant in New Jersey cast their secret ballots for strict enforcement, whereas 978 favored light wines and beer and 966 voted for outright repeal. But the dry forces should have been more disturbed by certain published surveys of attitudes on prohibition—surveys that perforce revealed the views of a middle-class America prosperous enough to subscribe to the telephone service of that day. In such a national poll conducted in 1922, while 306,000 people voted for strict enforcement, groups of 326,000 and 164,000 chose between wet alternatives. By the end of the decade, various polls showed that only the South remained deeply committed to prohibition.[1]

[9] *The New York Times,* March 1, 1929, p. 16; Sinclair: *Prohibition,* p. 353.
[1] The poll of telephone subscribers is reported in the *Literary Digest,* LXXIV (September 9, 1922), 11, 14; that of the Edison workers is also in

As time passed, the Eighteenth Amendment became more and more an object of contempt. By 1926 there was plentiful evidence of a reaction against the drys. The wet Senator James Reed, a Missouri Democrat, was appointed to an important Senate judiciary subcommittee that commandeered the embarrassing files of the Anti-Saloon League and released them later to the newspapers; it was found, for example, that in a certain Illinois senate campaign, the League had supported a candidate of questionable integrity against the wet George Brennan. Also in 1926 the wet strategy of repealing state enforcement laws, hitherto successful only in New York and Illinois, won a victory in Montana, where a "baby Volstead" law was repealed by referendum. At least in retrospect, 1926 appeared to one Catholic social critic, John A. Ryan, as the year in which prohibition, proven impracticable, ceased to be in the public interest and therefore lost its "binding force" upon the national conscience. Finally, that year's referendum in New York showed upstate areas to be wet by two to one and the city by seven to one.[2]

By 1928 the defeat of prohibition seemed a distinct possibility; and to that end a group of industrial leaders who sought a lowering of income taxes through the restoration of the tax on alcohol turned their financial support to the Association Against the Prohibition Amendment. Led by Pierre S. DuPont, who once had supported the dry cause, the industrialists swelled the budget of the Association and freed it of its dependence on the brewery interests; in 1928 Fred Pabst, Colonel Jacob Ruppert, and the Schaefer and Kreuger brewing companies together contributed only $7,750 to the AAPA, while the DuPonts and Edward S.

---

the *Digest*, LXXIV (July 29, 1922), 5. By 1926 only two states, Kansas and South Carolina, had prohibition majorities in a nationwide poll. LXXXIX (April 3, 1926), 7–8. The *Digest* polls, according to Claude Robinson, were biased toward the wets: more men than women participated and drys frequently disdained to vote, but invariably similar results appeared in polls conducted by the Hearst syndicate, the New York *Daily News*, and the Chicago *Tribune*. *Straw Votes* (New York, 1932), pp. 145–71. Lippmann: *Men of Destiny* (New York, 1928), pp. 31–2.
[2] Ryan: *Social Doctrine in Action* (New York, 1941), pp. 182–5; *The New York Times*, November 3, 1920, pp. 1, 12.

Harkness gave $108,580. And to the growing unity and financial vigor of the wet forces, Protestant prohibition could not respond by tightening its own organization. For Protestantism carries with it an inherent tendency to splinter, as the controversy then raging between fundamentalism and modernism demonstrated. The *Christian Century* maintained that national prohibition was "in danger of becoming just another aspect of the squabbles of religious sectarianism which divide and thwart the church forces of the nation." The end was not far off; repeal came in 1933.[3]

By 1930 the social movements and strains that had fractured the Democratic party were on the wane. The Klan was dead, and fundamentalism was in precipitous decline. But the final slackening of rural-urban tension came with the failure of prohibition. And in retrospect, the failure seems destined. The hedonism of the decade alone could have defeated the measure. How could drinking be undesirable when movies and books made it a part of adventurous living? And if sex itself was no longer taboo, it appeared ridiculous that liquor should be. At the same time the automobile, the movie house, and the radio, conveying city manners and jokes against prohibition, were bringing the country and the city face to face; they penetrated the isolation of rural America upon which the prohibitionist relied. Prohibition received its greatest setback in the Great Depression, which made urgent the need for an increase in government revenues and the creation of jobs; in the quibblings of the Wickersham Report of 1930 which showed that drinking was common and that it was spreading among women; and in the capitulation of wealthy drys, including S. S. Kresge, William Randolph Hearst, and John D. Rockefeller, the Anti-Saloon League's chief supporter who, in a letter of Nicholas Murray

[3] Fletcher Dobyns: *The Amazing Story of Repeal* (Chicago, 1940), pp. 9, 19–26; *Christian Century*, XLV (January 26, 1928), 103. Key Pittman (a chronic drinker himself) wrote in 1923 that the drys were in a "pathetic condition." Pittman to John E. Robbins, February 23, 1928, Pittman Papers.

Butler of Columbia, advocated repeal to "restore law and stop drinking."[4]

Constantly throughout the decade the conflict over religion, prohibition, and ethnic stock—and the more general clash of city and hinterland that at once gave added force to the specific issues and received much of its identity from them—touched upon politics; it deepened political faction, and was sustained in political quarrel. It was a political event, the National Democratic Convention of 1924, that set the conflict into definite form, assigning the participants and fixing the points of dispute.

[4] Even William Gibbs McAdoo had switched to repeal by 1931. Henry W. Lee: *How Dry We Were: Prohibition Revisited* (New York, 1963), p. 11. *The New York Times,* June 1, 1932, p. 1.

CHAPTER IV

The Election of 1924

The crumbling of the Wilson coalition, and its final defeat in the election of 1920, left the Democratic party with no sure policies or directions. But the next presidential election year, 1924, was destined even in the very fact of intraparty strife to mark the beginnings of a fresh process of self-discovery for the Democracy; and the congressional elections that took place midway between the two presidential contests gave some indication of the new political era upon which the party was entering. In 1922 the big cities, which had remained predominantly Republican in their congressional representation for a period of twenty-eight years, threw their support to the Democratic party. In a few isolated congressional elections prior to 1922, of course, the cities had gone to the Democrats; but after that date, they would never again waver from their Democratic attachments. The urban Democracy was swiftly gaining its strength.

The election of 1922 is significant both in the Democratic showing and in the number of the party's urban successes. Because President Harding, in his overwhelming victory of 1920, had carried many areas never before won by his party, the

Republican Congress occupied a vulnerable position in 1922. Factionalism, Harding's ineffectiveness as a party leader, and the resignation of Will Hays as National Chairman also contributed to Republican weakness; moreover, the party out of power usually picks up seats in an off-term election, and the depression of 1920 to 1922—the worst since the 1890's—had generated dissatisfaction with the politics of normalcy. But the tide of change in 1922 surprised Republicans and Democrats alike. At first it looked as though the Democrats had won the House of Representatives, although in the final count the Republicans retained control by a slim margin. The Democrats gained seventy-eight seats—within a dozen of a majority. In no other off-year election, the only kind with which that of 1922 may properly be compared, did the party out of power enjoy a comparable increase. The only larger House reversal in American history came in 1932 when Franklin Roosevelt carried with him several dozen congressional candidates who had no real expectations of victory.[1]

The character of the new Democratic contingent in the House is of special interest. Since not one House seat changed from Democratic to Republican, Table VI deals exclusively with previously Republican areas captured by Democrats. The chart reveals at least three trends. First, states of the character of Missouri and Indiana showed merely a resurgence of traditional Democratic strength. Second, in certain districts of the West, discontent reminiscent of populism, though now more narrowly centered on agricultural problems, may have sent some radical Democrats to Congress. Third and most important, the big cities —chiefly but not solely in the East where over forty per cent of

[1] On Wednesday, November 8, *The New York Times* ran a banner head-line: DEMOCRATS APPEAR TO HAVE WON HOUSE. William Gibbs McAdoo did not recognize the evolution of Democratic strength in the cities; better aware of the condition of the party in the country at large, he wrote to a fellow Democrat: "We must not assume that the victory means that the people have turned Democratic and will remain so. The fact is that the victory is more anti-Republican than pro-Democratic." McAdoo to Thomas B. Love, November 25, 1922; see also Robert W. Woolley to Love, December 2, 1922, Love Papers.

TABLE VI

Democratic Congressional Gains in 1922*

States	Number of New Democratic Seats
Connecticut	1
Delaware	1
Illinois	4
Indiana	4
Kansas	1
Maryland	2
Massachusetts	1
Michigan	1
Missouri	8
Montana	1
Nebraska	3
Nevada	1
New Hampshire	1
New Jersey	5
New York	13
Ohio	6
Oklahoma	4
Oregon	1
Pennsylvania	7
Rhode Island	1
Tennessee	3
Virginia	2
Washington	1
West Virginia	4

* *Congressional Directory.* Sixty-seventh Congress, 3rd Session; Sixty-eighth Congress, 1st Session.

the shifts occurred—moved strongly toward the Democratic party. Compared with earlier contests, the 1922 elections amounted to a breakthrough for the party in the city. Particularly the new immigrants trooped into the Democracy as never before; twelve of the thirteen new Democratic congressmen in New York came from districts with high percentages of recently arrived foreigners. And not all of these districts had been Democratic prior to the desertion of immigrants from Wilson's party in 1920. In urban areas, particularly in the Northeast and Middle West—Boston, Providence, New York, Jersey City, Harrisburg, Cleveland, Cincinnati, Detroit, Chicago—the party prospered in 1922. More important, throughout the decade urban areas such as these continued to send a heavy preponderance of Democrats to Congress; and from 1928 to 1952 the large urban areas would give a majority of their vote to the Democratic presidential candidate.

The 1922 shifts occurred within an outmoded congressional map that the House had refused to revise according to the census of 1920. These city victories, therefore, not only strengthened immediately the urban voice in the party; they implied the probability of still further change in the structure of the Democracy once congressional representation should be rearranged to reflect demographic reality. Throughout the twenties, in fact, the 1911 distribution remained. Ironically, incumbent Democrats often feared a shift of district lines as much as their opponents, for in the North predominantly Republican state legislatures could be expected to draw up the new district lines. But the failure to remap the districts cheated the Democrats in the growing cities that could have profited from redistribution. When a new plan finally went into effect in 1932, Los Angeles and Detroit alone gained together a total of ten seats.[2]

[2] *New Republic*, XLVII (May 26, 1926), 11–13; *Time*, VII (April 19, 1926), 7–8; *The Commonweal*, VIII (August 8, 1928), 345–6; *The New York Times*, January 4, 1923, p. 18; January 28, 1928, p. 7; March 3, 1928, p. 2; *Congressional Record, House*, October 14, 1921, pp. 6307–49.

٭

As the 1924 election approached, the shadow of scandal lengthened before the Harding Administration—and with its lengthen-
ing the hopes of partisan Democrats expanded. Late in 1923
Thomas J. Walsh, Montana Democrat and chairman of a Senate
investigating committee, began to uncover the spectacular deal-
ings of Teapot Dome and Elk Hills; encouraged also by their
surprisingly vigorous performance in the 1922 congressional
elections, many Democrats counted on public repudiation of
the discredited regime.[3]

But a series of developments shook Democratic confidence.
The death of the unfortunate President gave the Republicans a
mute scapegoat for the "Harding" scandals. Correspondingly,
the narrow rectitude of the new President, Calvin Coolidge,
helped to dissociate scandal and Republicanism. Moreover,
further disclosures revealed that the corrupt interests had been
bipartisan in seeking political favors. Edward L. Doheny, whose
name grew to be synonymous with that of Teapot Dome,
ranked high in the Democratic party of California. Besides contributing heavily to party campaigns, he had served as vice
chairman of the Democratic State Committee, and in 1920 he
had even been advanced seriously as a candidate for the vice
presidency. And there existed between Doheny and other leading Democrats certain business connections that were to prove
embarrassing to the party. In his oil operations, Doheny employed as counsel such members of Wilson's cabinet as Thomas
W. Gregory, Lindley Garrison, Franklin K. Lane, and William
Gibbs McAdoo; Lane and McAdoo had been paid $25,000 a
year for part-time services. Even Senator Walsh, who did most

[3] In mid-1923 Bernard Baruch wrote to Senator Key Pittman: "We have
the next election in the hollow of our hand." May 14, 1923, Pittman
Papers. The *Kiplinger Washington Letter* of April 12, 1924, predicted:
"We think the Republican Party will not be kept in power," and as late as
a month before the convention, the *New Republic* believed that "the outlook for the Democratic Party is more cheerful than that for the Republicans," XXXIX (May 28, 1924), 5.

to expose the indiscretions of the Harding Administration, confessed to a long acquaintance with Doheny.[4]

In January 1924, further evidence of McAdoo's relationship with Doheny discomfited many Democrats who were advancing Wilson's son-in-law as the party's chief contender for the presidential nomination. After McAdoo's resignation from the government in 1918, Joe Tumulty had sent him a warning to avoid association with the already tainted Doheny. Yet in 1919 the former Secretary of the Treasury took on the oil man as a client for an unusually large intitial fee of $100,000, as well as an annual retainer. Not the least perplexing part of the deal involved a $1 million bonus for McAdoo if the Mexican government reached a satisfactory agreement with Washington on oil lands Doheny held south of the Texas border. The bonus was never paid and McAdoo insisted later that it was a casual figure of speech mentioned in jest. At the time, however, he had telegraphed the New York *World* that he would have received "an additional fee of $900,000 if my firm had succeeded in getting a satisfactory settlement"; since the Doheny companies had "several hundred million dollars of property at stake, our services, had they been effective, would have been rightly compensated by the additional fee." In fact, the lawyer received only $50,000

4 Senator George W. Norris, Republican of Nebraska, added his charge that corruption had also been widespread during the wartime Wilson Administration. And it was later revealed that Governor Smith had in 1920 appointed Harry F. Sinclair, another of the corrupt businessmen, to an unsalaried post on the New York State Racing Commission, and that Sinclair had contributed substantially to Smith's campaign. Even in 1928 Senator Arthur Robinson of Indiana, a Republican, assailed the Democratic party and especially members of Wilson's cabinet for having been involved in the oil scandals. Norris to B. F. Eberhart, March 8, 1924, Norris Papers; *The Nation*, CXXVI (March 28, 1928), 334; Joe Tumulty to Smith, March 24, 1928, Tumulty Papers; *America*, XXXIX (April 14, 1928), 1. The involvement of Democrats in the oil scandals has been demonstrated by J. Leonard Bates in "The Teapot Dome Scandal and the Election of 1924," *American Historical Review*, LX (January 1955), 303–22; see also Burl Noggle: *Teapot Dome: Oil and Politics in the 1920's* (Baton Rouge, La., 1962), pp. 152–76, 191, and *The New York Times*, February 9, 1924, p. 1; February 24, 1924, p. 1.

more from Doheny. It also was charged that on matters of interest to his client, Republic Iron and Steel, from whom he received $150,000, McAdoo neglected the regular channels that propriety dictated he use and consulted directly with his own appointees in the capital to obtain a fat refund.[5]

McAdoo's connection with Doheny appeared seriously to lessen his desirability as a presidential candidate. In February Colonel House urged him to withdraw from the race, as did Josephus Daniels, Thomas B. Love, and two important fillers of Democratic coffers, Bernard Baruch and Thomas L. Chadbourne. Some advisers hoped that McAdoo's chances would improve after a formal withdrawal. William Jennings Bryan, who never doubted McAdoo's honesty, thought that the Doheny affair had damaged the lawyer's chances "seriously, if not fatally." Senator Thomas Walsh, who earlier had called McAdoo the greatest Secretary of the Treasury since Hamilton, informed him with customary curtness: "You are no longer

[5] On McAdoo's excellent chances prior to the oil scandals, see Robert Woolley to Senator Carter Glass of Virginia, August 8, 1923, Glass Papers; Gutzon Borglum to Senator Jim Watson, August 8, 1923, Borglum Papers; and for Mississippi Senator Pat Harrison's like view, Frank Robinson to David Ladd Rockwell, November 22, 1923, Thomas B. Love Papers. On the particularly strong commitment of labor to McAdoo, see Love to McAdoo, November 29, 1922, and J. Louis England to Love, October 26, 1923, Love Papers. In 1921 Doheny gave the Democratic party $25,000; in 1920 he had donated money to both parties. Louise Overacker: *Money in Elections* (New York, 1932), p. 153. Tumulty to McAdoo, November 21, 1919, F. Ray Groves to McAdoo, April 30, 1920, and memorandum of April 12, 1930, McAdoo Papers; William Dodd to John Spencer Bassett, Dodd Papers; McAdoo to Bryan, 1924, copy in Underwood Papers; Wilbur Marsh to George White, White Papers; David H. Stratton: "Splattered with Oil: William Gibbs McAdoo and the 1924 Presidential Nomination," *Southwestern Social Science Quarterly*, XLIV (June 1963), 62–75; Morris R. Werner and John Starr: *Teapot Dome* (New York, 1959), pp. 145–6; *The Nation*, CXVIII (March 5, 1924), 244, and (June 25, 1924), 741; *The New York Times*, February 24, 1924, p. 2 (quoting the New York *World*); February 25, 1924, p. 1; February 26, 1924, p. 1; New York *Herald-Tribune*, April 1, 1924, p. 1; New York *World*, June 4, 1924, p. 1; June 6, 1924, p. 10; July 6, 1924, p. 1; W. A. Watkins to George White, February 7, 1921, White Papers; A. J. Findley to John W. Davis, June 7, 1924, Davis Papers.

available as a candidate." Finally, *The New York Times*, itself convinced that McAdoo had acted in bad taste and against the spirit of the law, reported the widspread opinion that McAdoo had "been eliminated as a formidable contender for the Democratic nomination."[6]

McAdoo was unpopular for reasons other than his close association with Doheny. Even in 1918, *The Nation* was saying that "his election to the White House would be an unqualified misfortune." McAdoo, the liberal journal then believed, had wanted to go to war with Mexico *and* Germany, and he was held responsible for segregating clerks in the Treasury Department. Walter Lippmann wrote in 1920 that McAdoo "is not fundamentally moved by the simple moralities," and that his "honest" liberalism catered only to popular feeling. Liberal critics, thinking him to be a demagogue, found instance in his stand for quick payment of the veterans' bonus.

Much of the dissatisfaction with McAdoo on the part of reformers and urban Democrats sprang from his acceptance of Klan backing. James Cox indignantly wrote that "there was not only tacit consent to the Klan's support, but it was apparent that he and his major supporters were conniving with the Klan." Friends insisted that McAdoo's silence on the matter hid a distaste that the political facts of life kept him from expressing, and

[6] For an inside account of the controversy, see the manuscript diary of Breckinridge Long, February 6 to 24, 1924; McAdoo's floor manager at the June convention, Long wrote in his diary on February 13: "As it stands today we are beat." See also the manuscript diary of Colonel Edward House, February 9 and March, 1924. "Is it McAdieu?" asked William Hard in *The Nation*, CXVIII (April 30, 1924) 505–6. Of course, his eastern opponents promoted the view that McAdoo's chances were nil; the *Kiplinger Washington Letter* suggested that the West was not necessarily in agreement. March 1, 1924. Josephus Daniels to John Burke, March 15, 1924, Daniels Papers; Senator Kenneth McKellar to Hugh Humphreys, March 8, 1924, McKellar Papers; William Jennings Bryan to Daniel Cruice [?], n.d., Box 54, Bryan Papers; Thomas Walsh to McAdoo, February 13 and April 3, 1924, Walsh Papers; Daniel C. Roper: *Fifty Years of Public Life* (Durham, N.C., 1941), p. 218; Carter Field: *Bernard Baruch* (New York, 1944), pp. 204–5; *The New York Times*, February 2, 1924, p. 5; February 29, 1924, p. 26.

especially after the Doheny scandal when he desperately needed support. But McAdoo could not command the support of unsatisfied liberal spokesmen for *The Nation* and the *New Republic*, who supported the candidacy of the Wisconsin Progressive Robert La Follette. A further blow to McAdoo was the death on February 3, 1924, of Woodrow Wilson, who ironically had outlived his successor in the White House. Father-in-law to the candidate, Wilson might have given McAdoo welcome endorsement now that the League had receded as an issue.[7]

These handicaps did not deter McAdoo from campaigning vigorously and effectively in presidential primaries. He won easily against minor candidates whose success might have denied him key delegations in the South and West. Oscar W. Underwood of Alabama was no match for McAdoo. Opposed to prohibition and the Klan, the Alabamian failed to identify himself with the kind of progressivism that would have won him some compensating support. Nor was Underwood a real southerner; he had been born in Massachusetts and his father had served as a colonel in the Union army. "He is a New York candidate living in the South," said William Jennings Bryan. McAdoo defeated Underwood in Georgia and even split the Alabama delegation. Whatever appeal Underwood had outside the South the emerging candidacy of Al Smith erased. Henry Ford—"a man who

[7] Thomas B. Love of Texas—though at one time of a contrary opinion—advised McAdoo not to issue even a mild disclaimer of the Klan. Arthur F. Mullen: *Western Democrat* (New York, 1940), p. 242. To Bernard Baruch and others, McAdoo construed his remarks against prejudice at a 1923 college commencement as a disavowal of the Klan. McAdoo to Thomas Chadbourne, March 22, 1924, copy in Baruch Papers. William E. Dodd of the University of Chicago wrote to his father that Wilson had been "counting on" his daughter being in the White House. April 30, 1924, Dodd Papers. *The New York Times*, however, reported a rumor that Wilson had written to Cox, hoping he would again be the candidate in 1924. May 26, 1924, p. 1. *The Nation*, CVII (November 30, 1918), 640; Lippmann: "Two Leading Democratic Candidates," *New Republic*, XXIII (June 2, 1920), 10–11; James M. Cox: *Journey Through My Years* (New York, 1946), p. 324. David Chalmers agrees with Cox that McAdoo's "representatives solicited the Klan votes." *Hooded Americanism* (New York, 1965), p. 204.

praised the old ways while pushing on the new machines"—once seemed to be a genuine threat to McAdoo. Ford did not interfere when his name was entered in the Nebraska primary of October 1923, but no trace of evidence indicates an interest in becoming President. He announced for Coolidge in December and declared himself unavailable as a candidate.[8] In their immediate effects the heated primary contests drew the financial support of the millionaires Thomas Chadbourne and Bernard Baruch (who was indebted partly to McAdoo for his appointment as head of the War Industries Board); and they firmed the resolve of Governor Smith to make a serious try for the nomination, which he had originally sought primarily to block McAdoo on behalf of the eastern bosses. The contests also hardened the antagonisms between the candidates, and cut deeper the divisions within the electorate. In doing this, they undoubtedly retrieved lost ground for McAdoo and broadened his previously shrinking base of support, drawing to him rural, Klan, and dry elements awakened by the invigorated candidacy of Smith. The primaries therefore played their part in crystallizing the split within the party that would rend the Democracy at the forthcoming convention. City immigrants and McAdoo progessives had earlier joined to fight the Mellon tax plans in Congress, since both groups represented people of small means; deeper social animosities dissolved their alliance, and the urban-rural division rapidly supplanted all others.[9]

[8] A Ku Klux Klan newspaper opposed Ford because he had given a Lincoln car to a Catholic archbishop; it flatly rejected Smith as a Catholic from "Jew York"; and it called Underwood the "Jew, jug, and Jesuit candidate." *The New York Times,* October 13, 1923, p. 1; November 4, 1923, pp. 1, 3; December 19, 1923, p. 1. In a 1923 *Literary Digest* poll for the Democratic presidential nomination, Ford ran second to McAdoo. LXXVII (June 30, 1923), 6. Ford drew support from farmers and laborers, as well as from pacifists, prohibitionists, and anti-Semites. McAdoo and his supporters were keenly aware of the Ford movement. McAdoo to Love, June 2, 1923; George Fort Milton to David Ladd Rockwell, December 10, 1923, Love Papers.
[9] Senator Kenneth McKellar of Tennessee wrote to his sister Nellie: "I see McAdoo carried Georgia by such an overwhelming majority that it is likely to reinstate him in the running." March 22, 1924, McKellar Papers.

More directly, the contest between McAdoo and Smith thrust upon the Democratic National Convention a dilemma of a kind no politician would wish to confront. To reject McAdoo and nominate Smith would solidify anti-Catholic feeling and rob the party of millions of otherwise certain votes in the South and elsewhere. To reject Smith and nominate McAdoo would antagonize American Catholics, who constituted some sixteen per cent of the population and most of whom could normally be counted upon by the Democrats. Either selection would affect significantly the future of the party. Now in the ostensibly neutral hands of Cordell Hull, the Democratic National Chairman from Tennessee, party machinery was expected to shift to the victor in the convention, and a respectable showing in the fall election would insure the victor's continued supremacy in Democratic politics.

Despite the strong showing by McAdoo in the primaries, an argument could be made for the political wisdom of a Smith ticket. In the congressional elections of 1922, the biggest gains had come in New York, New Jersey, and other urban areas where Roman Catholicism prevailed. The new strength of the party, these elections seemed to indicate, lay not in the tradi-

---

The *New Republic* pointed out that Smith's drive for the presidency would send many hitherto complacent or indifferent Protestants scurrying into the arms of the Klan. XXVII (March 19, 1924), 87-8. Frank P. Walsh, a New York lawyer, wrote: "If his [Smith's] religion is a bar, of course it is all right with me to bust up the Democratic Party on such an issue." Walsh to Edward N. Nockels, April 12, 1924, F. P. Walsh Papers. For a close account of McAdoo's activities in this period, see Lee Allen: "The McAdoo Campaign for the Presidential Nomination in 1924," *Journal of Southern History*, XXIX (May 1963), 211–28. In another article, Allen shows that McAdoo's Klan-supported victory in the Texas primary "materially aided in [his comeback] following the February crisis." "The Democratic Presidential Primary Election of 1924 in Texas," *Southwestern Historical Quarterly*, LXI (April 1958), 486–9. Baruch to McAdoo, February 27, 1924 and February 28, 1924; and Baruch to David Ladd Rockwell, April 16, 1924, Baruch Papers; Daniel Roper to Thomas B. Love, May 14, 1924, Love Papers; William E. Dodd to Claude Bowers, July 20, 1924, Dodd Papers; Claude Bowers to Samuel Ralston, August 21, 1924, Ralston Papers.

tionalist countryside of Bryan and McAdoo, but in the tenement areas of the city and the regions of rapid industrialization. And, as Franklin Roosevelt wrote to Josephus Daniels, Smith's followers came from states with the big electoral votes that often swing a presidential election—Massachusetts, New York, and Illinois. Yet the strain of anti-Catholicism in America was a threat of proportions that could not easily be reckoned.

The selection of New York as a site for the 1924 convention was based in part on the recent success of the party in that city, where in 1922 thirteen Republican congressmen had lost their incumbencies. New York had not been chosen for a convention since 1868. Wealthy New Yorkers, who had outbid other cities, declared their purpose "to convince the rest of the country that the town was not the red-light menace generally conceived by the sticks." And, though dry organizations opposed the choice of New York, it had won McAdoo's grudging consent in the fall of 1923, before the oil scandals made Smith a serious threat to him. McAdoo's own adopted state, California, had played host to the Democrats in 1920.[1]

From the start, this "little religious war" of a convention was a cartoon stereotype of the issues and animosities it represented. William Jennings Bryan came from Florida in a Palm Beach suit and carried a fan that a columnist described as one of those presented at county fairs by the local furniture store. McAdoo followed shortly afterwards; upon alighting from his train he promptly damned the city in his best populist rhetoric. "This imperial city . . . the city of privilege," he called New York, "the seat of that invisible power represented by the allied forces of finance and industry which, reaching into the remotest corners of the land, touches the lives of the people everywhere." The city—his home for thirty years—was "reactionary, sinister, unscrupulous, mercenary, and sordid . . . wanting in national ideals, devoid of conscience . . . rooted in corruption, directed by greed and dominated by selfishness." As McAdoo's

[1] Henry F. Pringle: *Alfred E. Smith* (New York, 1927), p. 293; O'Keane: *Walsh*, p. 150; *The New York Times*, June 8, 1923, p. 3.

followers arrived, they were treated with a calculated rudeness. To each visiting state delegation a block of the city was dedicated. Texans were aghast to find theirs the block containing St. Patrick's Cathedral. Governor Smith, meanwhile, came down from Albany and stationed himself in a local hotel where he fretfully smoked cigars with Edmond Moore, who had directed Cox's campaign in 1920.[2]

The convention opened at "Tex" Rickard's old Madison Square Garden on June 24. The building itself, shortly to be demolished, had housed Bryan on August 21, 1896, for a speech on the economics of free silver, and it had also been the scene of other Democratic gatherings. It was a red-brick affair with a checkered and fantastic history: in one of its ten-story towers the architect, Stanford White, had been murdered in 1906. It had recently played host to the Barnum and Bailey Circus, the six-day bicycle races, and a number of bizarre athletic events. The tone of the Democratic Convention that followed varied little from that of the Garden's usual fare. At the outset, corpulent Mrs. Josephine Dorman, dressed in red, white, and blue, was carried through the throng on the shoulders of two cowboys wearing sombreros and tortoise-shell glasses, while she screamed "McAdoo!" until her face turned red. Thus, appropriately, began "the snarling, cursing, tedious, tenuous, suicidal, homicidal rough-house in New York," as Arthur Krock termed it, with which a nation listening in to a convention by radio for the first time was entertained and embittered.[3]

To make matters worse, the country delegates displayed an exaggerated sensitivity, especially on the liquor question. When

[2] McAdoo is quoted in the New York *Evening World,* June 23, 1924, pp. 1, 23. He also promised to "remove the influence of invisible Government from the Treasury and Federal Reserve System," repeal the tariff, lower freight rates for farmers and develop foreign markets to absorb their surplus, and protect natural resources, especially water power. Sherwin L. Cook: *Torchlight Parade: Our Presidential Pageant* (New York, 1929), p. 258; *The New York Times,* June 25, 1924, p. 1.
[3] "The Damn Fool Democrats," *American Mercury,* IV (March 1925), 257.

Senator Pat Harrison of Mississippi, the keynote speaker, remarked: "What this country needs . . . is . . . Paul Revere," he
received a round of boos. According to one observer, some of
the disgruntled prohibitionist delegates apparently confused the
speaker's words with the pronouncements they had grimly
suspected they would be hearing: "What this country needs
. . . is . . . real beer." Bryan himself revised a reference to the bier
of President Harding, and McAdoo apologized for eating cake
soaked in sherry. The convention seemed fated to ill harmony:
the Georgia delegation bristled when the band, thinking perhaps
that it was a treasured southern tune, accompanied a Cracker
demonstration with "Marching Through Georgia." As for
Smith's song, "The Sidewalks of New York," Westbrook Pegler
remarked that it had been "inspired by beer"; and he also noted
that Smith's home territory of the East Side was "the best protected bootleg territory in New York today." In point of fact,
Bryan and McAdoo many times had ample reason to complain
about the abundance of liquor made available to distract thirsty
country delegates. McAdoo charged that the Smith men had
kept many of his supporters drunk since they arrived in New
York. And when the Imperial Wizard of the Klan mysteriously
fell ill of ptomaine poisoning, Klansmen from the Texas delegation resolved to burn a cross outside the meeting hall. But the
1200 city police assigned to prevent any disturbance were not in
the mood. One C. Lewis Fowler, a former college president, had
been jailed for selling his anti-Catholic *American Standard*
outside the doors.[4]

[4] On his way to the Vanderbilt Hotel, McAdoo said he was accosted by
two women. "You will not desert us?" one breathed. "No," he replied.
She dropped to her knees in prayer. Quoted in Edwin P. Hoyt, Jr.:
Jumbos and Jackasses (New York, 1960), pp. 315–16. Roper: *Fifty Years
of Public Life*, p. 224; William Allen White: *Politics: The Citizen's Busi-
ness* (New York, 1924), p. 80; Atlanta *Constitution*, June 28, 1924, p. 1;
July 9, 1924, p. 2; Claude Bowers: Oral History Memoir, Columbia
University, 1954, p. 52; *The Outlook*, CXXXVII (July 9, 1924), 386.
    James Cox wrote to John H. Clarke of "a foolish platform given to us
by Hearst, Bryan, and McAdoo." October 1, 1924, Clarke Papers. On
McAdoo's responsibility for the Wilsonian League plank, see Norman H.

Senator Walsh, chairman of the convention—Catholic and dry, a supporter of McAdoo, he was acceptable to both factions —presided over the adoption of the platform. Here the first event of note was a speech and minority report on the League of Nations by Newton D. Baker, who thought of stampeding the delegates with what was indeed an eloquent plea for American entry. The platform itself sidestepped this and most other controversial issues; yet its sympathies were as wide as its recommendations were thin: it deplored child labor, but offered no remedy; neglecting McNary-Haugen or the equalization fee, it pitied the farmer. A measure of radicalism was brought into the platform through the influence of Bryan, a member of the Committee on Platforms and Resolutions, and other progressives; included were peremptory demands out of harmony with the rest of the document: for "strict public control and conservation of all the nation's natural resources, such as coal, iron, oil, and timber . . ."; for federal aid to education, an excess profits tax in wartime, and vigorous prosecution of monopolies; and for laws requiring a popular vote on certain further constitutional amendments and a referendum on entry into any war not begun by "actual or threatened" enemy attack. Bryan called the platform the best the Democrats had ever written.[5]

A crucial moment came with a platform committee report on whether to censure the Ku Klux Klan by name. McAdoo controlled three of the four convention committees, including this one, and the majority report declared against naming the Klan—although all the committee members agreed that the bigotry and intolerance of the Klan should be condemned. Every effort had been made to avoid the necessity of a direct commitment on the issue. According to Mark Sullivan, "The leading Catholics and Jews in the convention and out of it did

---

Davis to Charles Hamlin, September 24, 1924, Hamlin Papers. On Bryan see also Paxton Hibben: *The Peerless Leader: William Jennings Bryan* (New York, 1929), p. 380.
[5] Lawrence Levine: *Defender of the Faith: William Jennings Bryan; the Last Decade, 1915-1925* (New York, 1965), pp. 303-16. *Official Report of the Proceedings* . . . [of] . . . *1924* (Indianapolis, 1925), pp. 228-45, 260.

not want to mention the Klan by name." But the proponents of Smith's candidacy were anxious to identify McAdoo closely with the Klan and possibly to defeat him in a test of strength before the balloting began; the Smith faction, led by George Brennan of Illinois, demanded that the specific denunciation of the Klan uttered by the committee minority become official. Bryan, whose aim was to keep the party together and to maintain harmony among his rural followers, argued that naming the Klan would popularize it, as had the publicity given the organization by the New York *World*. It was also good politics to avoid the issue, Bryan said, since naming it would irredeemably divide the party. Worse still, Bryan believed, denouncing the Klan by name would betray the McAdoo forces, since it had been Smith's strategy to raise the issue. In contrast to Bryan, former Mayor Andrew Erwin of Athens, Georgia, spoke for the anti-Klan plank—but again the band struck up "Marching Through Georgia." In the ensuing vote, the Klan escaped censure by a hair's breadth; the vote itself foretold McAdoo's own defeat in the balloting.[6]

The role of Bryan at the 1924 convention has often been twisted to make him seem a bigot or a charlatan; in truth, his performance has been misrepresented. He delivered an address on social injustice that Elmer Davis called "brilliant." If his speech on the Klan was tempered, it nevertheless represented a sincere repudiation of prejudice, and was fully consistent with the Bryan who in earlier days had praised the appointment to the Supreme Court of Louis D. Brandeis as strongly as he had denounced Henry Ford's use of the fabricated "Protocols of the Elders of Zion." Much to the delight of an audience at the

[6] Bryan himself had introduced a controversial resolution at the 1912 Democratic Convention that denounced by name J. Pierpont Morgan, Thomas F. Ryan, and August Belmont. For the sake of harmony, Brennan had agreed earlier in 1924 to leave the "three little words" out of his state's Democratic platform, but he insisted upon them in New York. The vote, as officially reported, was 541 3/20 to 542 3/20. New York *Herald-Tribune*, June 29, 1924, pp. 1, 2; *Official Report of the Proceedings . . .* [of] *. . . 1924*, p. 333; *Century*, CX (May 1925), 94–100.

Brooklyn Jewish Center, Bryan in 1923 wore a yarmulke while he delivered his speech; at the convention his brother Charles wore a similar black skullcap over his bald spot to avoid catching cold. And Bryan had once noted: "Those who have come into intimate acquaintance with representative Catholics do not need to be informed that they do not concede to the church authorities the right to direct their course in political matters, but many Protestants, lacking this knowledge . . . , have been misled." Not all of Bryan's remarks on religion in his later years are free of intellectual intolerance; some of his pamphlets on fundamentalism are an intellectual disgrace. But it should be remembered that excellent political reasons undoubtedly motivated his position against naming the Klan—a position in which, incidentally, he was supported by the Catholic senator from Montana, Thomas J. Walsh. In fact, amid the different circumstances of the campaign, Bryan altered his stand. In August, after John W. Davis had denounced the nativist group by name, Bryan joined him.[7]

The New York Times, later comparing the vote on the Klan with the vote on the first ballot for President, found a high degree of coincidence between the McAdoo element at the convention and the element that opposed explicit condemnation of the Klan. It could not be doubted that at least in some sense McAdoo was the Klan's candidate. According to Claude Bowers, Daniel Roper of South Carolina (the real force behind David Ladd Rockwell, McAdoo's official campaign manager), jokingly referred to the "three years I have been working for the nomination of such a Klansman and all around rascal as McAdoo." Still, McAdoo's support was by no means exclusively drawn from the order: in Texas, for example, at least two large anti-Klan papers supported him, and in the primaries counties that had opposed local Klan candidates favored McAdoo over Underwood. Senator Thomas Walsh, a Catholic, and Bernard Baruch, a Jew, both supported McAdoo. In a seconding speech

[7] Levine: *Defender of the Faith*, pp. 258, 310; *The New York Times*, December 4, 1923, p. 5; August 30, 1924, p. 4.

for McAdoo, J. F. T. O'Connor of North Dakota explicitly repudiated the hooded order. But if it was only by way of appearance, and the polarities of the moment, that McAdoo was identifiable with the Klan, much of his following had no like fastidiousness. Brennan perhaps did not realize the full impact the Klan vote would have on the convention. He intended that it should harden feeling against McAdoo, and it did; but just as surely, even before the balloting began, Brennan had by his own strategy killed all hope of nominating Al Smith.[8]

The balloting for President began on June 30. McAdoo and Smith had each evolved a strategy to build up his total slowly: Smith's trick was to plant his extra votes for his opponent, so that McAdoo's strength might later appear to be waning; the Californian countered by holding back his full force, though he had been planning a strong early show. But by no sleight of hand could the convention have been swung around to either contestant. With the party split into two assertive parts, the rule requiring a two-thirds majority for nomination crippled the chances of both candidates by giving a veto each could—and did—use. McAdoo himself wanted to drop the two-thirds rule, but his Protestant supporters preferred to keep their veto over

[8] According to Richard C. Bain, all but one of Smith's first-ballot supporters favored the minority plank, while McAdoo supporters earned a +.63 correlation with the majority plank. See the statistical technique used in *Convention Decisions and Voting Records* (Washington, D.C., 1960), p. 225. For evidence of the Klan's considerable attachment to McAdoo, see Herbert Bayard Swope to Bernard Baruch, October 25, 1923, Baruch Papers; W. J. Vollor to Frank P. Walsh, June 9, 1924, and Kevin Kane of East St. Louis, who insisted to Walsh that "the only ones who are shouting McAdoo are those who wear the hood and sheet"; June 17, 1924, Walsh Papers. In Georgia, Texas, and some other states the Klan officially ordered its membership to support McAdoo. Atlanta *Constitution*, April 27, 1924, p. 1; July 1, 1924, p. 9; July 7, 1924, p. 1. Charles C. Alexander: "Secrecy Bids for Power: The Ku Klux Klan in Texas Politics in the 1920's," *Mid-America*, XLVI (January 1964), 18. Klan strength in the various states is estimated in *The New York Times*, July 1, 1924, p. 3. Love to Thomas L. Chadbourne, May 8, 1924; Love to McAdoo, September 6, 1923, Love Papers; Bowers to Samuel Ralston, August 21, 1924, Ralston Papers; Long Diary, March 15, 1924, Long Papers; *Official Report of the Proceedings* ... [of] ... *1924*, pp. 188–9.

a Catholic candidate; and the South regarded the rule as a protection of its minority interests. The deadlock that developed might as well have been a political contest between the Pope and the Imperial Wizard of the Klan, so solidly did the Catholic delegates support Smith and the Klansmen support McAdoo. At no point in the balloting did Smith receive more than a single vote from the South and scarcely more than the twenty from the states west of the Mississippi; he never won more than 368 of the 729 votes needed for nomination, though even this performance was impressive for a Roman Catholic. McAdoo's strength fluctuated more widely, reaching its highest point of 528 on the seventieth ballot. Since both candidates occasionally received purely strategic aid, the nucleus of their support was probably even less. The remainder of the votes was divided among dark horses and favorite sons who had spun high hopes since the Doheny testimony; understandably, they hesitated to withdraw their own candidacies as long as the convention was so clearly divided.[9]

As time passed, the maneuvers of the two factions took on the character of desperation. Daniel Roper even went to Franklin Roosevelt, reportedly to offer Smith second place on a McAdoo ticket. For their part, the Tammany men tried to prolong the convention until hotel bills should mount beyond the means of the outlanders; the Smith backers also attempted to stampede the delegates by packing the galleries with noisy rooters. But the rudeness of Tammany, and particularly the booing accorded to Bryan when he spoke to the convention, only steeled the resolution of the country delegates. McAdoo and Bryan both tried to reassemble the convention in another city, perhaps Washington, D.C., or St. Louis. As a last resort, McAdoo supporters introduced a motion to eliminate one candidate on each ballot until

[9] Tammany forces tantalized favorite sons with hints of support later should they remain in the race. *Century*, CX (May 1925), 97. Lee N. Allen: "The Underwood Presidential Movement of 1924," unpublished doctoral dissertation, University of Pennsylvania, 1955, p. 239 and *passim*; Atlanta *Constitution*, July 1, 1924, p. 1; *Kiplinger Washington Letter*, June 13, 1924; Frank R. Kent: *The Democratic Party* (New York, 1928), p. 484.

only five remained, but Smith delegates and those supporting favorite sons managed to defeat the McAdoo strategy. Smith countered by suggesting that all delegates be released from their pledges—to which McAdoo agreed on condition that the two-thirds rule be eliminated—although Smith fully expected that loyalty would prevent the disaffection of Indiana and Illinois votes, both controlled by political bosses friendly to him. Indeed, Senator David I. Walsh of Massachusetts expressed the sentiment that moved the Smith backers: "We must continue to do all that we can to nominate Smith. If it should develop that he cannot be nominated, then McAdoo cannot have it either."[1]

On the sixty-first inconclusive round, the convention set a record for length of balloting. In the ensuing days the major candidates held a series of conferences to break the stalemate. After the eighty-second ballot, the convention adopted Smith's resolution to nullify all pledges. On the next round McAdoo led Smith by only fifty votes; on the eighty-seventh the count stood at 361½ for McAdoo, 333½ for Smith; and on the ninety-ninth McAdoo led by a bare one and one-half vote margin. Finally resolved to drop out while he was still a shade ahead, the Californian halfheartedly accepted Smith's suggestion that both withdraw their candidacies; the New Yorker, however, maintained his strength on the one-hundredth ballot, with a count of 351½.

It had seemed for a time that the nomination could go to Samuel M. Ralston, an Indiana Senator and popular ex-governor. Advanced by the indefatigable boss Tom Taggart, Ralston's candidacy might look for some support from Bryan, who had written that "Ralston is the most promising of the compromise

[1] Senator James D. Phelan of California, among others, complained of "New York rowdyism." Phelan to George L. Duval, July 21, 1924, Phelan Papers. Breckinridge Long wrote in his diary that Smith had been drunk when McAdoo tried to compromise with him. October 17, 1924. Harry L. Watson to William Watts Ball, July 12, 1924, Ball Papers; *Official Report of the Proceedings* . . . [of] . . . *1924*, pp. 748–9, 754–5, 783, 816–17; New York *Evening World*, July 7, 1924, p. 1; *Christian Science Monitor*, July 5, 1924, p. 11.

candidates." Ralston was also a favorite of the Klan and a second choice of many McAdoo men. In 1922 the Indianian had made an attack on parochial schools that the Klan saw as an endorsement of its own views; and he won several normally Republican counties dominated by the Klan. Much of Ralston's support came from the South and West—states like Oklahoma, Missouri, and Nevada, with their strong Klan elements. McAdoo himself, according to Claude Bowers, said: "I like the old Senator, like his simplicity, honesty, record"; and it was reported that he told Smith supporters he would withdraw only in favor of Ralston. As with John W. Davis, Ralston had few enemies, and his support from men as divergent as Bryan and Taggart cast him as a possible compromise candidate. He passed Davis, the almost consistent third choice of the convention, on the fifty-second ballot; but Taggart then discouraged the boom for the time being because the McAdoo and Smith phalanxes showed no signs of weakening. On July 8, the eighty-seventh ballot showed a total for Ralston of ninety-three votes, chiefly from Indiana and Missouri; before the day was over, the Ralston total had risen to almost 200, a larger tally than Davis had ever received. Most of these votes were drawn from McAdoo, to whom they later returned.[2]

Numerous sources indicate that Taggart was not exaggerating when he later said: "We would have nominated Senator Ralston if he had not withdrawn his name at the last minute. It was as near a certainty as anything in politics can be. We had the pledges of enough delegates that would shift to Ralston on a certain ballot to have nominated him." Ralston himself had wavered on whether to make the race; despite his doctor's stern

[2] Ralston, commenting on the Klan issue, believed that it would set a bad precedent to denounce any organization by name in the platform. Ralston to Fred Van Nuys, May 21, 1924; see also Bowers to Ralston, May 24, 1924, and June 21, 1924, Ralston Papers. Bryan to John J. Centz, March 21, 1923, Bryan Papers; McAdoo to Love, September 18, 1923, Love Papers; Chalmers: *Hooded Americanism*, p. 167; Hoyt: *Jumbos and Jackasses*, p. 315; *The Outlook*, CXXXVII (June 18, 1924), 267; *The New York Times*, June 24, 1924, p. 1; June 30, 1924, p. 12; Bain: *Convention Decisions*, p. 224.

recommendation not to run and the illness of his wife and son, the Senator had told Taggart that he would be a candidate, albeit a reluctant one. But the 300-pound Ralston finally telegraphed his refusal to go on with it; sixty-six years old at the time of the convention, he was to die the following year.[3]

TABLE VII

The Last Ballots of the 1924 Democratic Convention

Ballot	McAdoo	Smith	Underwood	Davis	Meredith	Walsh
100	190	351	41	203	75	52
101	52	121	229	316	13	98
102	21	44	307	415	66	123
103	Davis by acclamation					

The very last ballots of the convention suggest some interesting possibilities about the nature of the conflict. Table VII shows that Senator Underwood, a wet, and Senator Walsh, a Catholic,

[3] After the convention, Ralston's doctor wrote to the Senator: "In my deliberate judgment, after having given the matter very careful consideration, you did the only wise thing possible. . . . Foreseeing what was liable to happen, I urged you many months ago not to allow yourself to be nominated." Dr. Sterling Raffin to Ralston, July 22, 1924. But Ralston had written to Taggart on June 19: "If . . . the Convention should turn to me, I shall do all in my power to bring success to our party this fall." In reality, he had been very indecisive; in August he told Senator Pat Harrison: "On more than one occasion, I said to you that I had never made up my mind I should want the nomination to come to me. In making that statement, I spoke truthfully. . . ." August 1, 1924. "I am very conscious," wrote the modest Ralston, "of not being in the presidential class." Ralston to Thomas C. Rye, May 12, 1924, Ralston Papers. See also the Atlanta *Constitution*, July 6, 1924, p. 12, and Sexson E. Humphreys: "The Nomination of the Democratic Candidate in 1924," *Indiana Magazine of History*, XXXI (March 1925), 1–9. Taggart's remark is in an unpublished biography of the Indiana boss by A. C. Sallee, Indiana State Library.

together received 327 votes on the one hundred and first ballot, as opposed to Smith's 121. The total for the three candidates, all wet or Catholic, was 448—far greater than Smith's highest vote. Walsh, for instance, received some of the McAdoo votes that are susceptible of being traced. Apparently the objection to Smith was broadly based; it was a resistance more to the whole complex of urban attributes he represented and of which his religion and stand against prohibition were only parts, while the Catholicism of Walsh and the anti-prohibitionist position of Underwood stood in isolation, free of larger contexts.[4]

The nomination, all honor stripped from it, finally went to John W. Davis, a compromise candidate who won on the one hundred and third ballot after the withdrawal of Smith and Mc-Adoo. Davis had never been a genuine "dark horse" candidate; he had almost always been third in the balloting, and by the end of the twenty-ninth round he was the betting favorite of New York gamblers. But, as Charles Hamlin wrote in his diary, Davis "frankly said . . . that he was not seeking [the nomination] and that if nominated he would accept only as a matter of public duty." For Vice President, the Democrats nominated Charles W. Bryan, Governor of Nebraska, brother of William Jennings Bryan and for many years editor of *The Commoner*. Bryan received little more than the necessary two thirds vote, and no attempt was made to make the choice unanimous: boos were sounding through the Garden. The incongruous teaming of the distinguished Wall Street lawyer and the radical from a prairie state provided not a balanced but a schizoid ticket; and because the selection of Bryan was reputed to be a sop to the radicals, many delegates unfamiliar with Davis' actual record came to identify the lawyer with a conservatism in excess even of that which he did indeed represent.[5]

The significance of Davis' victory was that it was also a tacti-

---

[4] Walsh was offered the support of the organized drys in the closing ballots. Justin Steuart: *Wayne Wheeler, Dry Boss* (New York, 1928), p. 220. *Official Report of the Proceedings . . .* [of] . . . *1924*, pp. 974, 979.
[5] Wilbur Marsh wrote to George White that there had been a Davis movement at San Francisco in 1920 "of pretty good sized proportions." October

cal victory for the Smith forces over those of McAdoo. For though a West Virginian by birth, Davis had the support of urban politicians, and as a Wall Street lawyer—he had been partner in a distinguished law firm that from 1889 to 1892 included Grover Cleveland—he had a certain symbolic connection with the forces of urbanism. The shift of votes from the city areas to Davis did not occur until the very last ballot, since Davis was their second choice after Underwood. Indeed, the attempt of some urban leaders to nominate Underwood probably sent some McAdoo delegates to the support of the less objectional Davis—particularly southerners reassured by his West Virginia background. But long before, frequent reports had appeared that Smith, Roosevelt, Taggart, Edmond Moore, George White (an old friend of Davis), Wilbur Marsh, Key Pittman, and James Cox were all "talking Davis." George Brennan, the Illinois boss, particularly backed him.[6] At the same time, strong anti-Davis sentiment developed in the McAdoo camp, where Senator Carter Glass of Virginia was the reserve candidate.

10, 1923, George White Papers. William Jennings Bryan threatened to desert Davis unless a westerner were placed on the ticket. Robert Woolley, manuscript memoir, Chap. xxxii, pp. 10–11. *The New York Times,* July 2, 1924, p. 4; Hamlin Diary, February 5, 1924.

[6] Moore to White, August 13, 1923; Marsh to White, October 16, 1923, and September 23, 1926; White to Davis, March 27, 1924, and White to Fred C. Martin, May 10, 1924, George White Papers; Samuel Ralston to Henderson S. Martin, May 2, 1924, Ralston Papers; Maurice P. Murphy to the Honorable Joseph B. Shannon, June 18, 1924, copy in Ralston Papers (July 1924); Norman Davis to Senator Key Pittman, July 18, 1924, and Samuel W. Belford to Pittman, July 28, 1924, Pittman Papers; Grady Miller to Bush Binley, July 28, 1924, copy in Joseph T. Robinson Papers; William Allen White: *Politics: The Citizen's Business,* p. 95; New York *World,* July 9, 1924, p. 1; Chicago *Daily Tribune,* June 21, 1924, p. 1; Humphreys: "The Nomination of the Democratic Candidate," pp. 1–8; *The New York Times,* April 16, 1928, p. 6. To all of these sources showing strong urban support for Davis can be added the *Kiplinger Washington Letter,* which observed that the "program of the anti-McAdoo leaders is to push the Al Smith boom as far as it will go, then try to transfer it to John W. Davis. This has been their real plan all along." June 27, 1924; see also May 16, 1924, and June 13, 1924.

Claude Bowers reported that McAdoo "looks upon Davis as the tool of his Wall Street enemies." Bryan was particularly distressed by the possibility that Davis might be the Democratic candidate; he stated to the Mississippi delegation the same sentiments that had influenced his shift from Champ Clark to Woodrow Wilson in 1912: "The Convention must not nominate a Wall Street man."[7] When Davis was nominated, Smith appeared before the meeting to congratulate the candidate, while McAdoo was conspicuously absent. Months later after he returned from a European trip, McAdoo let it be known that he could not support the nominee.

In his acceptance speech Davis made the perfunctory statement that he would enforce the prohibition law; but his conservatism prejudiced him in favor of personal liberty and home rule and he was frequently denounced as a wet. After the convention Davis tried to satisfy both factions of his party, but his support came principally from the same city elements that had backed Cox in 1920. Frank Hague of New Jersey replaced Bruce Kremer of Montana, McAdoo's floor manager, as a vice chairman of the party. Those McAdoo men who remained in the party organization worked badly with Davis' eastern headquarters in New York. McAdoo himself failed even to reply to Senator Key Pittman's request from Davis headquarters that the Californian speak in the campaign, and some of McAdoo's followers actively supported La Follette or Coolidge in 1924 and Herbert Hoover in 1928. Daniel Roper wrote to Thomas B. Love of Davis' "bad environment." In the sense that the Davis

[7] New York *Herald-Tribune*, June 2, 1924, p. 2; Bowers to Samuel Ralston, June 21, 1924. In another letter to Ralston, Bowers added that "the Catholic bloc [was] unquestionably in league with the Reactionary or Wall Street bloc throughout." July 10, 1924. Later in the campaign Bowers wrote to Ralston that he was "afraid that [Davis] has been captured too much by this eastern crowd." August 28, 1924, Ralston Papers. *The New York Times*, July 2, 1924, p. 1. Actually Davis practiced law in New York for only three of his twenty-five professional years. *The New York Times*, May 3, 1924, p. 1; July 2, 1924, p. 3.

victory was also a Smith victory, the 1924 convention was a prelude to the victory of Smith at Houston four years later. Davis himself served as a Smith delegate in 1928.[8]

Even before the Democratic convention had ended, a third-party candidate had intruded into the balance of political forces —a candidate whose radical stance would serve as a foil as much to the conservatism of Davis as to that of Coolidge. The decision of Senator Robert La Follette of Wisconsin to run for President in 1924 gave the campaign a unique flavor, spicing it with a fresh and pungent radicalism that attempted to bring together the strength of factory and farm.

The new party movement had its impetus in 1919 when J. A. H. Hopkins, earlier a prominent Bull Mooser, organized the Committee of Forty-Eight as a progressive political action group. The work of political mobilization begun by the committee was taken up in 1922 by two conferences of progressives in Chicago, where La Follette established his position as head of the young movement. The majority of participants at the second meeting were trade union officials; the delegations included William Green of the United Mine Workers and Sidney Hillman of the Amalgamated Clothing Workers. A quarter of the delegates came from the Non-Partisan League, the Farmer-Labor party, and Morris Hillquit's flexible new Socialist party, while individual farmers and labor spokesmen comprised the remainder of the progressive conclave. Although majority sentiment for independent party action did not crystallize in Chicago, the dream of a monolithic new liberal party, reawakening the spirit and power of the insurgents of 1912, captured the loyalty

[8] The dry leader Wayne Wheeler complained of Davis' "constant repetition of wet catch phrases like 'Personal Liberty,' 'illegal search and seizure,' and 'home rule.'" Steuart: *Wayne Wheeler*, pp. 225–6. Another Smith man, James W. Gerard, served as treasurer of the party. Both Love and Roper supported Hoover in 1928. *Official Report of the Proceedings . . . [of] . . . 1924*, pp. 1012 ff.; *The New York Times*, November 7, 1924, pp. 1, 3; personal interview, Warren Kiplinger, September 8, 1964; New Orleans *Item*, August 26, 1928, p. 7; Roper to Love, July 3, 1924, Love Papers.

of many delegates who subsequently turned away from the major parties in 1924.[9]

Out of the Committee of Forty-Eight, some earlier organizations formed by La Follette, and the Chicago conventions grew the Conference for Progressive Political Action; and in 1924 the CPPA sponsored the Progressive party. La Follette had told reporters the previous summer that there would be no need for a third ticket unless both parties nominated reactionaries. Then came the Doheny scandals; and as for a time it seemed likely that the scandals would eliminate McAdoo, who was popular among railroad unions and other labor groups, the way was paved for the party which was launched in June of 1924. It was the dream of the Progressives that they might replace the Democrats, and thereby bring a clearer ideological alignment to American politics.

As Progressive candidate for President, La Follette became leader of the first formal prominent alliance in American political history between members of organized labor and farm groups, and of these with Socialists and independent radicals. Even the American Federation of Labor, although weakened by a precipitous decline in its membership since the war, gave La Follette mild backing and so officially supported a presidential candidate for the first time. The Progressive vice presidential candidate was Senator Burton K. Wheeler of Montana, only one of many Democrats who abandoned the chaos of their own party for the crusading vigor of La Follette's, and found there an idealism and dedication unparalleled within any of the other major political organizations of the 1920's.

At the foundation of La Follette's program was an attack on monopolies. His Socialist supporters took this as an attack on the capitalistic system in general; to non-Socialists, including the Senator himself, it signified a revival of the policy of trust-busting. The Progressive platform also called for government

[9] *Century,* CX (May 1925), 94–100; Kenneth MacKay: *The Progressive Movement of 1924* (New York, 1947).

ownership of water power and a gradual nationalization of the railroads. But the election did not become a pure test of his program. La Follette was criticized for his pacifism by the patriots of the Klan, and for his radicalism by both of the major party candidates. Labor was not strong enough to contribute heavily to its champion's campaign. Yet Daniel Tobin of the Teamsters spoke for a significant portion of organized labor when he rejected the Democrats for being "just as reactionary" as the Republicans; and the commendation of the AFL must have been of some aid to the Progressive candidate. Most of all, La Follette suffered from a host of election technicalities. In California, for example, he was forced to run as a Socialist; in Florida, he failed to meet the state election requirements—the submission of petitions signed by twenty-five voters in each of fifty-four counties; in Ohio, the exclusion of La Follette poll-watchers invited fraud. But the five million votes he actually received in the election—despite the candidate's age, sixty-four, his stand against prohibition, his antiwar record, his opposition to the Klan, his history of serious illness, and the rise in wheat prices over the summer—were a personal tribute to the senator and a sizable endorsement of his reform and isolationist views.[1]

Of the three presidential candidates, La Follette, Davis, and Coolidge, Davis had the most trouble in casting an appealing

[1] Senator Wheeler explained his defection in his autobiography: "When the Democratic Party goes to Wall Street for a candidate, I must refuse to go with it." *Yankee from the West* (New York, 1962), p. 249. In an examination of the La Follette candidacy, it should be remembered that the most halcyon days of Republican prosperity had not yet been reached; unemployment, in fact, was higher in 1924 than at any time between 1923 and 1929. United States Bureau of the Census: *Historical Statistics of the United States, Colonial Times to 1957* (Washington, D.C., 1960), p. 73. La Follette, running in California on the Socialist party ticket, received there four times as many votes as Davis; and La Follette also ran ahead of the Democrat in forty-seven out of forty-eight California counties. Yet William Allen White thought that "La Follette lost about forty per cent of his normal vote because of the Klan." White to Oswald Garrison Villard, October 19, 1924, White Papers. MacKay: *The Progressive Movement of 1924*, pp. 180 ff.; Samuel Lubell: *The Future of American Politics* (New York, 1952), p. 140.

image; to many voters, he appeared to be merely a shadow of the conservative Coolidge. "The framework of his mind was formed in West Virginia [his birthplace]," wrote Walter Lippmann in "The Setting for John W. Davis," an article in the *Atlantic Monthly*. "It is that of the traditional Democrat with the Jeffersonian distrust of centralization, the parochial dislike of bureaucracy, and a strong prejudice in favor of home rule." Lippmann concluded that Davis' nomination reflected confidence in his character rather than studied agreement with his views. Born on Jefferson's birthday, Davis had signed "The American's Creed," a clear affirmation of Jeffersonian principles widely circulated by businessmen in 1924; it included the maxim, paraphrasing Jefferson, "that government is best which governs least." As a member of the House Judiciary Committee, Davis had, it is true, written the final drafts of the anti-injunction and anticonspiracy features of the Clayton Act; but this and similar acts of duty as Solicitor General need imply no commitment further than that of loyalty to the administration, and indeed trust busting itself was in the grain of Jeffersonian decentralization. Just before the campaign of 1920, Wilson had said of Davis that he was "a fine man, but he is a formalist. If you want a standstill, he is just the man to nominate." And it was in character for Davis when he appeared among the conservative backers of the Republican Alf Landon in 1936.[2]

When Davis implied that he would not repudiate his friends to win the presidency, it was widely concluded that he had somehow endorsed his firm's clients, notably J. P. Morgan, and of course the name of Morgan evoked distrust among progressives and opponents of Wall Street. Davis, moreover, had recently managed to get an increase in rates for the New York Telephone Company. In several law cases, Davis had sided with management against hard-pressed unions, which made Samuel

[2] Henry D. Clayton wrote of Davis: "He helped me to formulate the conspiracy, injunction and contempt proceedings of the Clayton Act." Clayton to William B. Wilson, October 10, 1924, W. B. Wilson Papers. *Atlantic Monthly*, CXXXIV (October 1924), 530–5; Homer Cummings File of Ray Stannard Baker Papers, May 31, 1920.

Gompers skeptical of Davis as a friend to labor. In truth, the Democratic nominee had also defended the American Federation of Labor and had protected the right of West Virginia coal miners to strike. Apparently he took his clients without bias; but the impression persisted of Davis as a markedly conservative candidate.[3]

During the campaign Davis found the nominee of the Progressive party more distasteful than the more formidable and conservative Republican opponent. Although La Follette's program was for the most part fairly moderate, and the Wisconsin statesman rejected Communist support, he preached what to the lawyer Davis was a dangerous doctrine: the weakening of the power of the Supreme Court. La Follette, disgusted by judicial nullification of important labor laws, proposed that Congress might nullify a decision of the Court by passing a law a second time—a scheme different in design from that later advanced by Franklin Roosevelt, but similar in purpose; herein, Davis believed, the Progressive candidate had posed the most important issue of the campaign. In attacking La Follette, Davis ignored the sense of William Jennings Bryan's advice to stay clear of states that looked safe for the Progressives.[4]

As for Davis' campaign technique, Colonel House caught its flavor when he confided to his diary:

[3] Davis' statement is quoted in Theodore A. Huntley, *The Life of John W. Davis* (New York, 1924), pp. 133–4. Davis' record as advocate for management in labor cases did not escape the editors of *The Nation*. CXIX (August 20, 1924), 176. See also James Derieux to W. W. Ball, May 15, 1924, Ball Papers, and Samuel Gompers to William B. Wilson, August 6, 1924, Gompers Papers. Fellow-lawyer Frank P. Walsh wrote: "In my opinion, the most reactionary man in that Convention was the nominee, Mr. John W. Davis." Walsh to William Zimmerman, July 21, 1924, F. P. Walsh Papers. In a letter to Breckinridge Long, George Fort Milton speaks of the candidate's failure to answer the prevailing question: "How does Davis feel about Wall Street?" August 13, 1924, Long Papers; see also Hiram Johnson to Charles H. McClatchy, July 10, 1924, Johnson Papers. Matthew Page Andrews to Davis, January 9, 1924, and William J. Barker to Davis, August 24, 1924, Davis Papers.
[4] In a speech in Wilmington, Delaware, Davis pictured La Follette as "rawhead and bloody bones." John H. Holt of Huntington, West Vir-

Frankly, I am disappointed in him as a candidate. . . . I have tried to stir him to action and to make his speeches more forceful and pertinent to the trend of the times. He was candid enough to say that he had been all his life trying to eliminate his emotions from his briefs and addresses to the courts and that it was impossible at this late date to put this quality in his speeches for political effect.

Franklin Roosevelt dismissed Davis as an orator: "His little speeches are always charming and beautifully expressed." Tall, dignified, and manly, Davis lacked not conviction itself, but the oratorical fire and intensity with which to give conviction verbal form. Late in August of 1924, Claude Bowers wrote to Ralston of Davis' shortcomings as a candidate. "The moment I touched on politics," Bowers wrote, "he [Davis] seemed shy and embarrassed." Then Bowers proceeded to relate a story—no doubt overdrawn—about Davis: "I was in Spellacy's room [Thomas Spellacy, in charge of Eastern campaign headquarters in New York] when a delegation of Tammany Irishmen . . . came in to offer their services. . . . They were of the laborer type. After while [*sic*], to my surprise the door opened and Davis came in. . . . Everyone rose and Davis passed down the line shaking hands in a manner almost too dignified and gentlemanly, saying nothing. Then, evidently embarassed [*sic*] and at loss as to what was expected of him, he turned and looked at them in silence.

" 'These men are here to help elect you,' said Spellacy.

" 'Strength to their arms,' said Davis.

"Then he seemed at the end of his rope for a minute after which he added: 'We want every man in the boat and every man with an oar!'

"Then after another long period of silence which was finally interrupted by Spellacy with the astounding suggestion made

ginia, to Davis, October 1, 1924, Davis Papers. Russell B. Nye: *Midwestern Progressive Politics* (East Lansing, Mich., 1951), pp. 330–1, 338–9; Belle and Fola La Follette: *La Follette*, II, 1128; Bryan to Davis, September 29, 1924, Davis Papers.

almost impatiently and of course out loud:—'Tell them that you are an organization man.'

" 'Oh yes, I am an organization man,' said Davis.

"After that he turned to speak to a correspondent of the Boston *Globe* and the thing was over."[5]

But colorless as the West Virginian's candidacy must be judged, it had the strength of integrity. At Sea Girt, New Jersey, he joined his voice to La Follette's in explicit denunciation of the Klan. As Colonel House noted, Coolidge, who would not repudiate the organization, remained the only contestant likely to receive its substantial support.[6]

Davis' campaign was destined to failure. The candidacy of an alleged extremist awakens latent conservatism in an electorate, and this tendency usually benefits the current officeholder; and in an era dominated by one political party, that party tends to attract the new voters, especially when the minority party does not sharply differentiate itself from the majority. Neither Davis nor Frank Polk and Lincoln Dixon, his managers, took issue with the Republicans. And Clement L. Shaver, Davis' new Democratic National Chairman, was charged by one observer with having "none of the qualifications of a leader." Shaver, a little-known lawyer and coal-mine operator from Lost Creek, West Virginia, was as interested in Indian lore and fishing as in politics.

[5] Robert Woolley of Democratic National Headquarters criticized Davis for not being a "flaming crusader." Woolley to Davis, October 7, 1924, Davis Papers. House Diary, October 15, 1924; Franklin Roosevelt to Glenn Frank, August 12, 1924, Roosevelt Papers; Bowers to Ralston, August 21, 1924, Ralston Papers.

[6] The significance of Davis' condemnation was in his naming of the Klan; this had been the critical point at the Democratic convention. After William Jennings Bryan supported his disavowal of the Klan, the candidate regularly made digs at the order. Chalmers: *Hooded Americanism*, p. 214. Claiming credit for having defeated Smith in New York, Hiram Evans of the Klan surveyed the field and pronounced Coolidge the "safe" candidate. House Diary, November 14, 1924; *The New York Times*, June 30, 1924, p. 1; November 10, 1924, p. 1; *World's Work*, LV (January 1928), 10; Benjamin H. Avin: "The Ku Klux Klan, 1915–1925: A Study in Religious Intolerance," unpublished doctoral dissertation, Georgetown University, 1952, p. 27.

Though he had served as Democratic chairman of West Virginia, Shaver was an amateur: in September he told reporters that as matters then stood Davis was licked, but that the tables would turn. Shaver had only one wish for 1928: "If we could take Secretary of the Treasury [Mellon] away from the Republicans, we could win easily." Shaver's wife was an ardent prohibitionist, and her fanatical statements on the subject served to embarrass her husband and his party. When a reporter asked him in 1928 why his wife had endorsed Hoover, he replied: "Are you married?"[7]

But in the final analysis it was the convention itself, and the intraparty divisions that the convention both symbolized and widened, that spelled the doom of the Democratic party in the presidential election. One Minnesotan wrote to Roosevelt: "We defeated ourselves in New York in June." Davis himself recalled:

They got into that North-South fight, at the end of which time the nomination wasn't worth purchase by anybody. They had to put a name on the ticket, and so they turned and put mine on. . . . Every time I'd reach out into the Eastern group personalized by Al Smith, the McAdoo group would run away from me. Then when I'd reach out and try to get the McAdoo group somewhere back into the corral, the Smith group would run away from me.[8]

[7] *Time* spoke of Shaver as the "alleged ineffectual Chairman of the Davis campaign." IV (September 29, 1924), 5. Key Pittman indicted the entire campaign staff: "From the chairman down most of them are incompetent and inexperienced." Pittman to William McKnight, October 23, 1924, Pittman Papers. For chairman, McAdoo had suggested Thomas L. Chadbourne; Smith, Thomas J. Spellacy. So Davis picked the inoffensive Shaver. Angus Campbell *et al.: The American Voter* (New York, 1960), pp. 156–8; *Mirrors of the Year* (New York, 1928), p. 126; *The New York Times,* June 26, 1928, p. 6; Julia Landers to Davis, November 14, 1924, Davis Papers; Breckinridge Long, manuscript diary, September 19, 1924; Robert Woolley, manuscript memoir, Chap. xxxii, pp. 18-19.

[8] H. H. Gillen to Franklin Roosevelt, December 30, 1924, Roosevelt Papers; see also Newton W. Powell to Davis, November 11, 1924, Davis Papers; Davis: Oral History Memoir, Columbia University, 1954, p. 149.

Calvin Coolidge, meanwhile, ran on a platform written almost wholly by monotonously conservative Republicans: Ogden Mills of New York, William Vare of Pennsylvania, Martin Madden of Illinois, and Reed Smoot of Utah. The President's technique was to destroy issues by ignoring them. The most ingenious argument the Republicans devised to injure Davis (whom they usually chose to overlook) was evolved by George Harvey in an article in the *North American Review*. La Follette's candidacy, Harvey maintained, would capture enough electoral votes from the other two parties to throw the presidential choice into the House, then marginally Republican. Democratic and Progressive Representatives would together prevent the selection of a President, while in the Senate, a coalition of Democrats and progressive Republicans would choose Charles W. Bryan as Vice President; and in the absence of a presidential choice, Bryan would succeed to the highest office. So argued Harvey, and the Republicans clinched this point with many voters by skillfully portraying the competent Charles Bryan as a sort of half-witted brother to the allegedly dangerous silver-tongued orator. Even those who could not understand the Republican reasoning might respond to their bizarre slogan: "A vote for La Follette is a vote for Bryan and a vote for Davis is a vote for Bryan. A vote for Coolidge is a vote for Coolidge."[9]

The 1924 election demonstrated again the chronic weakness of the Democratic party on the executive level. Coolidge won 382 electoral votes, leaving Davis with 136 in twelve states and La Follette with Wisconsin's 13. Coolidge received 15,719,921 popular votes (54.0 per cent); Davis, 8,386,704 (28.8 per cent); and La Follette, 4,988,398 (17.2 per cent). Coolidge won the eastern states and all of the West except Wisconsin. The farm states had worried the Republicans, but victory there had been

[9] George Harvey: "The Paramount Issue: Coolidge or Chaos," *North American Review*, CCXX (September 1924), 1–9. Numerous correspondents of Davis confided their fear of Charles Bryan; see, for example, Thomas W. Gregory to Davis, November 8, 1924, and James O'Donnell, November 19, 1924. See also typescript of a news conference of Nicholas Murray Butler, October 12, 1924, Davis Papers.

assured by a moderate rise in agricultural prices prior to the election. Yet the congressional returns did not sustain the appearance of Democratic decline so vividly suggested by Davis' paltry popular vote. The regular Republicans gained only twenty-one votes in the then closely divided House of Representatives. There was another somewhat encouraging sign: on the basis of counties, an important unit in party management, the Republican party showed itself weaker than in 1920 and the Democratic party stronger. Davis led in 1279 counties, a gain of 183 over Cox's in 1920, while Coolidge carried 377 counties fewer than did Harding.[1]

In the cities the voting strength of the Democrats on the presidential level was at an ebb, as it was to be in the countryside in 1928. But the Republicans also declined in the largest cities, to the advantage of La Follette. In that year the Progressive candidate won 23.6 per cent of the vote in the ten major cities, compared to his national average of 17.2 per cent. These industrial areas between Chicago and Boston went largely to Smith in 1928, but it was La Follette, not Smith, who first won the workingmen from the Republican party in great numbers. And these same workingmen, largely immigrants in the cities, had voted Republican or Socialist in their protest of 1920, or had not yet participated in any American election. The Progressive party seems to have functioned for many voters as a way station between the Republican and Democratic parties.[2]

[1] United States Bureau of the Census: *Historical Statistics*, p. 691; United States Department of Agriculture: *Yearbook of Agriculture, 1928* (Washington, D.C., 1929), pp. 686, 714, 957; Chester C. Davis to George Peek, November 8, 1924, C. C. Davis Papers; Edgar Eugene Robinson, *The Presidential Vote, 1896–1932* (Stanford, 1934), pp. 23–4.

[2] In Illinois La Follette drew most of his strength from Harding's supporters of four years before, who could well have been ethnic voters temporarily alienated from the Democracy; most of La Follette's votes went to Smith in 1928. The authors of a recent study argue that third parties prepare the way for major periods of political realignment, that the road to the Roosevelt coalition of 1936, in other words, begins in 1924. Duncan MacRae, Jr., and James A. Meldrum: "Critical Elections in Illinois: 1888–1958," *American Political Science Review*, LIV (September 1960), 674–7. Of the 230 counties that voted Republican in 1920 and

The nature of the La Follette vote is particularly revealing of the forces at work in the 1924 election. Upon which party did the Progressive candidate make heavier inroads? One might observe that fifty-eight per cent of the La Follette counties had been part of the Wilson coalition of 1916; but the Democrats in

TABLE VIII

A Comparison of the 1924 Congressional and Presidential Vote

	Dem.	Per Cent	Rep.	Per Cent	Prog.	Per Cent
House	10,676,076	42	14,818,143	58		
President	8,386,704	29	15,719,921	54	4,988,398	17

that year won normally Republican areas. The election of 1920 caught the party at its weakest point in decades. An examination of the nationwide vote in 1924 for the House of Representatives should be more telling; this more than any other constant would represent the normal Democratic and Republican strength in that year. Even these figures do not tell the full story: there is often a sectional discrepancy between presidential and congressional voting, and perhaps one party consistently received more support on one level than on another. Still the comparison, expressed in Table VIII, is a better gauge than any other election

Progressive in 1924, fifty-one moved to the Democratic column in 1928 rather than back to the GOP. (The Democratic support for La Follette does not appear in a county comparison with 1920, since much of that vote was urban and since almost every midwestern county had been Republican in that year.) A *New York Times* analyst concluded: "The prevailing opinion of political experts was that the great body of Democratic voters in the cities, mostly workers, had deserted their party's presidential candidate to vote for the Wisconsin Senator." September 16, 1928, III, 1.

figures, and it tends to confirm the statement of Major George
L. Berry, the main organizer of the Democratic Labor Committee in 1924: "La Follette's entry . . . will injure the cause of
the Democratic Party infinitely more than it will the Republican
Party." For while the Coolidge vote fell only three per cent

TABLE IX

*Percentages of 1924 Presidential and Congressional Vote
by Sections**

	Congressional Vote		Presidential Vote		
Section	DEM.	REP.	DEM.	REP.	PROG.
I New England, North Atlantic	39	61	26	61	12
II Southern and Border	60	40	57	37	6
III Middle West, Western Middle West	36	64	23	56	21
IV Far West	32	68	16	53	31

* Section I includes those states that Edgar E. Robinson designates as New England and North
Atlantic; II, South Atlantic, East South-Central, and West South-Central; III, East North-Central
and West North-Central; IV, Mountain and Pacific. *The Presidential Vote, 1896–1932* (Stanford,
1934), *passim*.

below the Republican House vote, that of Davis dropped fourteen per cent below the Democratic figure for the House.[3]

[3] Miss Ruth Silva reaches a similar conclusion. *Rum, Religion, and Votes:
1928 Re-examined* (University Park, Pa., 1962), p. 10. See also MacRae
and Meldrum: "Critical Elections in Illinois," 677. The figures in Tables
VIII and IX are computed from *Statistics of the Congressional and Presidential Election of November 4, 1924* (Washington, D.C., 1925); Berry
to Senator Lee Overman, August 2, 1924, Overman Papers.

In what sections of the country did the Democrats lose most heavily to the Progressives? Table IX divides the country into sections patterned on those in Robinson's *Presidential Vote*. In New England and the North Atlantic states, La Follette appears to have drawn almost all of his support from Democratic congressional voters; most of these states included heavily industrial areas, where labor supported the Progressive candidate. In the southern and border states, La Follette obtained his small vote almost equally from the two parties. In the Middle West and Western Middle West he drew somewhat more heavily from the Democrats than from the Republicans, and in the Far West he raided a large vote from both parties, but proportionately much more from the Democrats.

Fortunately for the Democrats, the Progressive party proved to be a short-lived organization. The American Federation of Labor organ, *American Federationist,* deserted La Follette, saying that "the launching of third-party movements has proved wasted effort. . . . Experience therefore has taught labor that to be successful politically it must continue in the future, as in the past, to follow its nonpartisan policy."[4] And La Follette's death in 1925 helped seal the fate of the insurgent party—and incidentally raised the question of to what extent the radicalism of his movement may have been merely a response to his personal magnetism.

In 1924 the Democratic party was in a ruinous condition; and a good part of its difficulty lay in its very fabric, whose poorly assimilated strands of city and country tore apart in open disintegration in the convention at New York. The party incorporated the extremities in the country's population, gaining its greatest support in wholly rural districts and in the most metropolitan of cities.[5] The Republicans, on the other hand, drew their following from the more numerous districts nearer the middle of the spectrum. Even though the peculiar challenge of

[4] XXXI (December 1924), 989–90; XXXII (January 1925), 55.
[5] Arthur Holcombe: *The Political Parties of Today* (2d edn.; New York, 1925), p. 418.

the Progressives soon passed, the Democratic party was left with its most fundamental problems. To recover its soundness it would have to shape both a program and an identity that would capture at the same instant both sets of voters upon which it relied.

CHAPTER V

Franklin D. Roosevelt and Party
Organization in the Twenties

The administrative structure of the national Democratic party
in the twenties was ill devised to offset those forces that were
working toward the party's disintegration. Possibly a national
political party should not be considered a continuing organization at all but merely a succession of hierarchies, each called into
being for victory in the next election. But in the decade before,
the firm hand of Woodrow Wilson had for a time molded the
party into a strong and active unit. Under the President's guid-
ance, William Gibbs McAdoo in particular gave vigor and
progressive direction to the national party offices. But the same
malady that in Wilson's second term weakened the executive
branch of the government infected the party framework as well,
and disorder spread throughout the Democratic echelons. Con-
trasting the state of the party offices in earlier days to their condition late in 1924, a reporter observed that "the Democratic
National Headquarters in Washington are as Romish catacombs
or Pompeiian atriums, elegantly preserved but destitute."[1]

[1] William Hard: "The One-Party System," *The Nation*, CXIX (December 24, 1924), 703.

In the twenties authority itself was decentralized, since the party had no President who could use his office to discipline a following. The political contenders strongly backed for each coming presidential nomination shared and divided party leadership, which after the 1924 convention fell in large part to the man who became the party's choice. It was he who then chose the chairman of the national committee, shaped party policy, and controlled the meager patronage. Between campaigns the unsuccessful candidate of the preceding election normally assumed the role of titular leader, if he were thought to be available as a candidate in the next presidential race. But Cox and Davis had been defeated too decisively and Smith was too controversial to assume any substantial authority.[2]

Since the party could not look to one political leader for direction, it had to depend on its chairman and national committee, who together performed a number of functions vital to party unity. They carried the financial burden of the presidential campaigns; they provided the press with propaganda; they staged the national conventions; they even managed, so National Chairman Cordell Hull indicated, to gain the cooperation of the congressional and senatorial election committees. "Their work and ours," declared Hull at a meeting of the National Committee in 1924, "has [*sic*] been virtually merged now with the most satisfactory results."[3]

[2] Paul T. David *et al.* discuss the repositories of authority in a party out of power in *The Politics of National Party Conventions* (Washington, D.C., 1960), pp. 75–110. According to the authors, the structure of the party out of power is neither "as strong, as clear, nor as far advanced" as that of the ascendant party (p. 107). See also Richard F. Fenno, Jr.: *The President's Cabinet* (New York, 1959), p. 179. The work of political scientists is particularly valuable here inasmuch as the official Democratic party records of the 1920's were destroyed in 1946. The Democratic women's organization did issue a forerunner to today's *Democratic Digest*, but *The Bulletin*, which first appeared in 1922, restricted itself to folksy criticism of the Republicans and to news of Democratic women. Richard Linthicum helped edit the short-lived *Wilsonian*, which appeared in 1922 with articles by George Creel and Joe Tumulty. Some other fugitive literature survives.
[3] *Official Report of the Proceedings of the Democratic National Convention* . . . [of] . . . *1924* (Indianapolis, 1925), p. 1092.

Real leadership, however, was beyond the reach of the committee. Composed of over fifty members—more than one hundred after the addition of female representatives in 1920—it was too large for effective work. Worse still, its membership was chosen by the states, and hostile rural delegates sometimes tried to sabotage the urban national chairmen. The committee gathered only when its chairman called a meeting, and would usually meet for the purpose of turning over to the chairman, whom it did not select, the task of campaign management. The national headquarters was completely beyond the control of the committee. The chairman was potentially an effective force in the out-party leadership vacuum, but in the twenties he received no salary and did not even work full time for the party. Except for the years 1921 to 1924 when Cordell Hull took command, the committee was under the direction of a succession of chairmen, none of whom performed the work that could have been accomplished. John J. Raskob actually wielded his chairmanship not as an instrument of party harmony but as a tool of the anti-prohibitionist faction. Al Smith, who was to do much to strengthen the electoral base of the party, summed up the whole matter with pardonable exaggeration when he complained that "it has been the habit of the Democratic party to function only six months in every four years."[4]

The strife between the urban and rural factions was most intense during the chairmanship of George White. Thomas B.

[4] The backgrounds and campaign activities of White and the other national chairmen of the twenties are described in the respective election commentaries. The national chairmen from 1916 to 1932 and their home states were: 1916–19, Vance C. McCormick of Pennsylvania; 1919–20, Homer Cummings of Connecticut; 1920–1, George White of Ohio; 1921–4, Cordell Hull of Tennessee; 1924–8, Clement L. Shaver of West Virginia; and 1928–32, John J. Raskob of Maryland.

Roosevelt described headquarters as "two ladies occupying one room in a Washington office building." William N. Chambers: *The Democrats, 1789–1964* (Princeton, 1964), p. 76. MS of radio address, January 16, 1928, Smith Papers; Fred L. Israel: *Nevada's Key Pittman* (Lincoln, Neb., 1963), p. 45; William R. Palmer to Franklin Roosevelt, December 7, 1928, Democratic National Committee Papers.

Love, Robert Woolley, and other McAdoo supporters, who controlled as much as two-thirds of the National Committee, tried early in 1921 to unseat White. Love and a majority of the committee members petitioned the chairman to call a meeting in March, but White's tenure was guarded by Cox, Palmer, Underwood, and Pittman, all of whom opposed McAdoo. And Bernard Baruch of New York City, a major benefactor of the party, also wanted to give White a chance. Timely donations of money from Thomas Fortune Ryan and a telegram that Baruch sent to the committee may have been influential in prolonging White's stay in office. In the summer of 1921 Cox announced his continued support of White, but by this time Baruch and his fellow financier Thomas L. Chadbourne joined in the movement to retire the national chairman. A meeting of the National Committee was called for September 21, 1921, and when it was apparent that anti-White forces had obtained enough proxies to unseat him, White resigned on September 20. Early in 1921 White had been receiving general support from urban leaders and a few important congressmen. But rural opposition—particularly strong in the National Committee where each state elected two members—determined his defeat. It must be said, however, that no matter what his affiliations White would have found his tenure under attack. In the 1920 campaign he had not been able to overcome the severe disadvantages under which his party labored, nor was he successful after the election in getting the party out of debt—here his troubles were increased by the illness of Wilbur Marsh, the party treasurer who was too sick early in 1921 to answer letters from creditors.[5]

[5] See Bernard Baruch, telegram to White, February 9, 1921; Norman Mack to White, November 15, 1920; Senator Andrew Jones to White, February 9, 1921; White to Jones, February 15, 1921; White to Arthur Krock, February 22, 1921; White to Charles E. Morris [Governor Cox's secretary], January 18, 1921; White to Frederick C. Martin, December 27, 1920; White to Wilbur Marsh, February 5, 1921, April 27, 1921, January 16, 1925, April 3, 1925; White to John W. Davis, November 4, 1921; White to Edmond Moore, November 4, 1921; George White Papers. *Literary Digest*, LXVII (February 19, 1921), 17–18; *The New York Times*, February 9, 1921, p. 15.

It was clear enough that White opposed the choice of Cordell Hull, who finally took over the chairmanship late in 1921. But Hull was sufficiently a compromise choice that White, in a letter to Edmond Moore, could describe him as "free from any domination from McAdoo." And although the prohibitionist Hull, a Tennessean, was viewed by many Democrats as closer in background to McAdoo than to his opposition—Hull had exhibited a slight preference for the former cabinet member at the 1920 convention—Carter Glass and other McAdoo men had first attempted to secure the appointment of Breckinridge Long of Missouri, Robert Woolley of Washington, D.C., or Daniel C. Roper of South Carolina; only after the failure of these candidates had McAdoo acquiesced in the choice of Hull.[6]

The selection of Hull as chairman made the party organization for the moment an effective body and a force for harmony. Hull, who later said he "took charge of the Democratic Party when it was at its lowest ebb," left the party treasury with a surplus of $30,000, after having paid off a debt of almost $300,-000. The Tennessean made many sacrifices in serving the party: in the early months of his tenure he used his own Liberty Bonds as security for party loans and personally countersigned notes for thousands of dollars. Later, he began to request bimonthly reports on political conditions in key states. Among others, Senator Samuel M. Ralston of Indiana commended Hull, praising the "high degree of efficiency" he brought to the chairmanship.[7]

[6] For the effort to remove White, see Senator Carter Glass to Robert Woolley, August 23, 1921; Woolley to Glass, September 21, 1921; Bernard Baruch to Glass, September 22, 1921; Glass to White, August 23, 1921, Box 165, Glass Papers. See also William E. Dodd to Jouett Shouse, November 15, 1921, Dodd Papers; Breckinridge Long manuscript diary, November 1, 1921; Robert Woolley to Thomas Love, November 30, 1920; Daniel C. Roper to Woolley, July 5, 1921, Woolley Papers, and Chap. xxxi, p. 23, Woolley's unpublished memoir. *The New York Times*, January 21, 1921, p. 3; January 25, 1921, p. 17; February 5, 1921, p. 10; February 7, 1921, p. 15; February 9, 1921, p. 15; February 10, 1921, p. 4; October 25, 1921, p. 17; Louisville *Times*, November 2, 1921, p. 1.

[7] Until John J. Raskob initiated his large-scale financial operations, the national Democratic party prudently avoided spending itself into bankruptcy on hopeless campaigns. Before 1928 the party debt never went over

The tenure of Hull was indicative of the growing concern of congressional Democrats—for whom Hull, formerly a senior member of the House Ways and Means Committee, was a leading spokesman—over the plight of the party organization. And when Hull was succeeded by the undynamic Clement Shaver of West Virginia, Democrats of the House and Senate increasingly stepped in to fill the breach in the national organization. William Oldfield of Arkansas, the Democratic whip and chairman of the 1924 House campaign, was put in charge of national campaign planning. In 1926 Oldfield directed all activities of the congressional campaign from the House and Senate Office Buildings, where he was assisted by a steering committee composed of Democrats from both Houses. When a party is out of power in the White House, congressmen normally serve as party spokesmen by virtue of their offices.[8]

It was during the chairmanship of Clement Shaver that the party machinery of the National Committee came nearest to a complete halt. Party headquarters became virtually inactive between 1925 and 1927, little headway was made against a substantial debt; but Shaver cut the organization to the bone in order to raise money. Though a party publication, the *National Democrat*, appeared in 1925 under the editorship of Frederick W. Steckman, the organ was soon discontinued; it failed, according to Joe Tumulty who helped to finance it, because of "con-

---

about $400,000, but by the end of that campaign Raskob had incurred a debt of about $1,550,000. Gerard was chairman of the party's finance committee in 1920, Jones in 1924, and Lehman in 1928. Hull: *Memoirs*, I (New York, 1948), 116; Ralston to Hull, July 24, 1924, Ralston Papers; Hull to Thomas B. Love, July 27, 1923, Love Papers; George White to J. Henry Cooke, January 30, 1924, George White Papers; Bascom N. Timmons: *Jesse H. Jones* (New York, 1956), p. 148; James W. Gerard: *My First Eighty-Three Years in America* (New York, 1951), p. 308; Allan Nevins: *Herbert H. Lehman and His Era* (New York, 1963), p. 106; *The New York Times*, November 1, 1921, p. 3; June 7, 1925, p. 1; June 12, 1926, p. 2; March 8, 1928, p. 1; Herbert H. Lehman to John J. Raskob, April 30, 1928, December 30, 1928, and June 11, 1932, Lehman Papers; Raskob to Frank J. Donahue, June 25, 1929, Raskob Papers.
[8] The changes in congressional campaigning are described in *The New York Times*, February 2, 1926, pp. 1, 6; July 11, 1926, p. 24.

flicting interests and diverging viewpoints." And the publisher, J. W. Elrod, was exposed as a former editor of the *Fiery Cross,* an Indianapolis Klan magazine, and as "chief lookout" for the Klan at the 1924 political conventions. In "about '26 or '27," recalled Florence Harriman, "the Democratic Party didn't have enough money to keep a headquarters. The Women's National Democratic Club had to take all the archives and put them in the attic of their Club House. The Committee even kept their desks there, because they couldn't afford to have an office." Yet, ineffective as he was, Shaver did help to pave the way for the candidacy of Al Smith. Formerly the campaign manager for the conservative urbanite Davis, Shaver was supported in his tenure by many wealthy eastern contributors whose adherence to the party Shaver's presence strengthened. Even though not an outright partisan of Smith, Shaver was known to be cool to McAdoo, and his appointment and long tenure alike were indicative of a fall in McAdoo's fortunes after 1924.[9]

For McAdoo's career was distinctly in an eclipse. At a time of increasing conservatism he was in some ways a conspicuous progressive; in 1928, moreover, he would be sixty-five, quite old for a presidential candidate. He lost the support of his wealthy urban friends Baruch and Chadbourne, as well as that of his mentor Daniel Roper, all of whom turned to other candidates; Baruch said after 1924 that he would never again participate in nominating battles. In addition, one of McAdoo's staunchest backers, Thomas B. Love, was experiencing his own troubles in Texas politics. When McAdoo's remaining followers attempted early in 1926 to replace Shaver with Edwin Meredith of Iowa or even the conservative J. Bruce Kremer of Montana, they had not the power to effect their will. Late in 1927 the Californian finally terminated his presidential bid; in a letter to the editor of the Chattanooga *News,* George Fort Milton, who had been

[9] *The New York Times,* July 12, 1925, pp. 1, 5; Arthur Schlesinger, Jr.: *The Crisis of the Old Order* (Boston, 1957), p. 273; MS of radio address by Alfred E. Smith, January 16, 1928, Smith Papers; Alfred Rollins, Jr.: *Roosevelt and Howe* (New York, 1962), p. 221.

McAdoo's publicity director in 1924, he explained that he wanted to avoid a repetition of the "disastrous" fight at the 1924 convention. Yet he had not resigned from interest or involvement in nomination politics; in a speech at Richmond, Virginia, early in 1928, he sharply attacked the candidacy of Smith.[1]

With the dimming of McAdoo's chances, Governor Smith's star brightened when in 1926 he and the whole New York Democratic ticket won a statewide victory. Even before that election it had been reported that Bernard Baruch was financing George Peek, the agriculturalist, in an effort to convert a crucial bloc of western farmers to the McNary-Haugen Bill—and ultimately to the Democratic nominee. By 1928 Smith led the field as clearly as had McAdoo before the oil scandals of the early twenties, and the triumph of Smith ushered in a new era for the national organization.[2]

In the hands of Smith and National Chairman John J. Raskob, the party structure took on fresh power and unity. Its unity was now, however, that of exclusion, for Raskob preached repeal and Al Smith to such an extent and in such fashion that the headquarters could be said to speak only for a sector of the party. Raskob spent about a million dollars of his own personal fortune to produce a tightly knit and intent party headquarters. He did set up an executive committee under the direction of Jouett Shouse and during the depression appointed Charles Michelson director of publicity with a full staff and a quarter of a million dollars to attack Hoover. Thanks to Raskob's generos-

---

[1] *The New York Times,* January 18, 1926, p. 3; January 21, 1926, p. 6; February 2, 1926, pp. 1, 6; January 30, 1927, p. 1; January 3, 1928, p. 1. Margaret Coit: *Mr. Baruch* (Cambridge, Mass., 1957), p. 372.
[2] Against the financial forces of the East, McAdoo was now powerless; Wilbur Marsh, the former party treasurer, wrote to George White in 1926: "There is one thing you can depend upon. Governor Smith can have a campaign fund, the like of which no democrat [*sic*] has ever had before." Marsh to White, April 18, 1926. White to Marsh, January 16, 1925; April 3, 1925; Marsh to White, February 28, 1925, George White Papers; Peek to Gilbert N. Haugen, April 9, 1926, Chester C. Davis Papers; Jerry C. Bryan to Clement Shaver, November 19, 1927, in Elbert Thomas Papers, "Political Information, 1927."

ity, the Democratic party had a permanently functioning national headquarters years before the Republican party did. But Raskob's circle could not address the economic hardships that beset the country after 1929 as eloquently and sincerely as could Franklin Roosevelt, the country-based aristocrat who had twice nominated Smith for the presidency. To Roosevelt belonged the future of the Democratic party.

While Democrats in Congress, unsure of their aims and their philosophy, were slipping into an ill-defined conservatism that presented no clear alternative to the well-articulated conservative policy of their Republican opponents, this important and relatively progressive Democrat was thinking hard and shrewdly about the organizational troubles of his faltering party. Late in 1924, Roosevelt prepared a circular letter dealing with the plight of the Democracy and the means to reform, and sent it to some three thousand Democrats, including all the delegates who had attended the prolonged convention of that year. He suggested to his correspondents several revisions in party structure: that the national committee or its executive machinery be made to function continuously and come in closer touch with state organizations; that publicity be extended and a sound financial base be obtained for the party; and that party leaders representing different regions meet more frequently. Roosevelt urged his readers to reply to his circular letter, for he wished to discover "what seems [*sic*] to be the common meeting points of Democratic minds from the North, South, East and West."[3] And, of course, he also wished to remind the party members of his own existence.

The answers Roosevelt received are interesting both in their analysis of Democratic organization and in their probings into the most fundamental weaknesses of the party. On the whole the respondents were pessimistic. One sardonic letter set down four rules for future conventions to ensure the continued failure to which the party seemed to have committed itself: change the two-thirds vote needed for nomination to three-fourths or nine-

[3] Quoted in Frank Freidel: *Franklin D. Roosevelt: The Ordeal* (Boston, 1954), p. 201.

tenths; hold the convention in Maine or Vermont; make the Alabama law apply everywhere, so that no delegate might vote for anyone except a favorite son; nominate no man unless his aspirations were approved by all former candidates.[4]

Upon one point the letters were in substantial agreement. They recognized that the basic cause of the party's decline was the growing disunity within its ranks. They were speaking, of course, of the social and religious antagonisms that had seized upon the Democracy; but Roosevelt's correspondents conceived these same conflicts in sectional as well as social form, and described a party splintered into three sectional components: an urban Northeast—conservative, as most of Roosevelt's correspondents viewed it; a conservative rural South; and a somewhat radical and predominantly rural West. Gavin McNab, an important California Democrat, charged that "the Democratic party is not, and under these circumstances, cannot be, affirmative. Nor can it be truly national."[5]

Many delegates who responded to Roosevelt's letter urged that Democrats in the future simply evade the dangerous issues of prohibition and the Klan, as these had been evaded by the Republicans. But such advice may have had mixed and partially defensive motives, for it came almost invariably from dry states where the Klan was strong, notably Arizona, Colorado, Georgia, and Texas. Some correspondents blamed the party politicians for the divisive effects of the Klan and prohibition; it was argued that the convention fight over the Klan had materialized only because of the selfish ambitions of the candidates, while the controversy over prohibition had emerged after relentless prodding by dry and wet fanatics. Suggestions were made that

[4] Robert Prescott to Franklin Roosevelt, January 29, 1925, Roosevelt Papers.

[5] Compare the septuagenarian Herbert Hoover's analysis of the Democratic party of the twenties: an ultraconservative South, city machines bent on plunder, and semi-socialists and fanatical agrarians. *The Memoirs of Herbert Hoover. II: The Cabinet and the Presidency, 1920–1933* (New York, 1952), 33–4. McNab to Roosevelt, January 16, 1925, Roosevelt Papers.

McAdoo and Smith, the personalities who represented the divergent wings of the party, be eliminated from future consideration for the presidency.

There were echoes of 1918 when western correspondents ascribed the troubles of the Democracy in great part to the eminent position of the South within the party. In the twenties the South appeared to take on a coloration even more conservative than the rest of the nation, as the tradition of southern populism disappeared or transfigured itself into the Klan; and progressive western Democrats were unhappy in their forced union with southern reaction. Despite its own strains of anti-Oriental feeling, moreover, the West was hardly prepared to sympathize with a southern racism that in the 1920's was resurgent in the Klan and in new policies of discrimination. The Californian Gavin McNab coupled southern racism to southern reaction when he observed that the "presence of the Negro has necessarily given a certain cast to Southern minds and prevents, to some extent, [the South's] complete union of thought with the rest of the nation on some governmental problems"; and McNab found the static South to be a questionable political partner to the rest of socially mobile America.[6] In fact, the popularity of La Follette's Progressive party in western Democratic territory illustrated that Democrats in the West would continue restive under conservative leadership, northern as well as southern.

The replies confirmed Roosevelt in his conviction that the Democratic party needed basic structural reform. He called for a national conference, to meet in Washington, D.C., to consider plans for making the National Committee a permanently operating organization. The suggestion won the backing of many

[6] McNab to Roosevelt, January 16, 1925, Roosevelt Papers. An Iowan reminded Roosevelt in 1929 of the continuance among middle westerners of the anti-southern feeling that had injured the Democrats in the 1918 election: "It is the prejudice against the Southern Democrats that has made this Middle West country overwhelmingly Republican." John J. Sullivan to Roosevelt, December 4, 1929, Democratic National Committee Papers.

Democrats, including Thomas J. Walsh, highly respected as a convention moderator. More generally, the idea of strengthening the Democratic organization gained great currency, as was indicated when Colonel Edward House persuaded Bernard Baruch, John W. Davis, and others to meet for the purpose of setting up an organizational framework for the 1926 congressional election. But plans for a national party conference fell through. They were destroyed not only by Shaver's lack of cooperation but also by calls from McAdoo and the Bryans for a new alliance of the West and South against the East, and the refusal of this wing of the party to participate wholeheartedly.[7]

Although his scheme of a national Democratic gathering never came to fruition, Roosevelt himself conferred with many Democrats as he traveled between his Hyde Park home and Warm Springs, Georgia, where he continued to recuperate from the poliomyelitis that had struck him in 1921. And at the smaller conferences and dinners Roosevelt's plans were given weighty consideration. Yet in spite of the New Yorker's good intentions, T.R.B. of the *New Republic* was probably not wide of the mark when he suggested that "the way to promote harmony in the Democratic party is to keep the leaders apart, not bring them together."[8]

While Roosevelt was taking his own increasingly active measures to strengthen the Democracy, other forces even more significant were at work for the rejuvenation of the party. The death of La Follette in June of 1925 had silenced talk of a permanent third party, and the liberal journals and newspapers began again to consider how to make the major parties more progressive. Much of their advice was directed at the Democratic party, and the day would come when the friendship of

---

[7] Louis Howe to Roosevelt, n.d., and Howe to Roosevelt, February 20, 1925, Roosevelt Papers; Alfred B. Rollins, Jr.: "The Political Education of Franklin Roosevelt, His Career in New York Politics: 1909–1928," unpublished doctoral dissertation, Harvard University, 1952, I, 793–4, 798; *New Republic*, XLIII (June 3, 1925), 46; *The New York Times*, March 21, 1925, p. 12; February 1, 1926, p. 1.

[8] XLIII (June 3, 1925), 46.

the liberal journals would be an asset to the Democrats. Further-more, in the 1926 election the Republicans retained control of the Senate by only a single vote margin.[9]

This last represented the backwash of Harding's lopsided victory of 1920, which had carried Republicans into office in normally Democratic states; for of 34 senators whose terms expired in 1926, 27 were Republicans and the remaining 7 Democrats were southerners. At least 18 of the Republican seats would have had to be classified as doubtful, and in the election most of these passed to the Democrats. But the precariousness of the Senate division after 1926—48 Republicans to 47 Democrats—does illustrate that the Democratic donkey, as in every other off-year race since 1906, was capable of delivering a spirited kick. The party, moreover, continued to gain in urban strength—the strength upon which its future successes would in large measure lie. In the 1926 election, as in 1922, the Democrats made House gains in urban areas of the country, gaining 3 seats in New York City, 1 in Newark, 2 in Chicago, 1 in Denver, 1 in Baltimore, and 1 in St. Louis; in the Senate, the Democrats won new seats in Massachusetts and New York, as well as in other traditionally Democratic states.[1]

Meanwhile, the circular letter of 1924 and the call for a national conference were enhancing Roosevelt's prestige within the party. Alfred Rollins, Jr., writes that Roosevelt's activities

[9] See, for instance, the *New Republic*, XLIII (June 24, 1925), 124; see also Julius Pratt to William E. Dodd, June 24, 1920, and Dodd to W. E. Chenery [of *The Survey*], June 16, 1920, Dodd Papers.
[1] The western Republican progessives won even more stunning victories in 1926, defeating loyal administration candidates in the primaries; it was not the revival of Democratic strength but the threat of the independents of his own party that most dismayed the Coolidge Administration. Of Smith Wildman Brookhart's victory, one columnist wrote: "If Iowa had tumbled a ton of dynamite down on the dome of the national Capitol, it could not have produced a greater explosion in Washington." Quoted in Malcolm Moos: *The Republicans* (New York, 1956), p. 359. *Congressional Directory*, Sixty-ninth Congress, 1st Sess.; Seventieth Congress, 1st Sess.; W. F. Ardis to Richard H. Lee, April 1, 1926, McKellar Papers.

helped little to clarify a national Democratic position, for he dealt in "slogans and easy compromises."[2] But with a seemingly offhand thoroughness, the country gentleman from Hyde Park, aided by Louis Howe, went about his task of building his own political reputation. He kept his name before the public by giving aid to various causes, from the Boy Scouts to the Cathedral of Saint John the Divine. His pet project was the Woodrow Wilson Foundation, which he served as chairman. Periodically he issued statements, and always he continued a voluminous correspondence that enabled him to stay in touch with his acquaintances from the Wilson Administration and the 1920 presidential campaign. And from the replies to his circular letters Roosevelt discovered what kind of man the rank and file would most readily accept as party leader.

Throughout the twenties, Roosevelt took a cautious stand somewhere between the two factions of the Democratic party. His connections with the city Democrats were at first tenuous, but they became numerous and strong. Rarely an ally of Tammany Hall while state senator, indeed an outspoken critic of one of Charles Murphy's senatorial candidates, he had nevertheless done patronage favors for Tammany during the war, had spoken at the Wigwam, and was photographed with its chief in 1917; and he had been acceptable to Murphy as candidate for the vice presidency in 1920. Though one writer describes Governor Smith's speech seconding Roosevelt in 1920 as "reluctant," the former vice presidential candidate served as a manager for Smith in 1924 and replaced him as governor of New York in 1928. At the 1924 convention it was Roosevelt who, after eighty-seven ballots, united the delegates as author of a message of sympathy to President Coolidge on the death of his son; and it was also the upstate New Yorker who made the offer of Smith's withdrawal from the convention if McAdoo should withdraw also. Roosevelt early realized how inextricably his own political future was bound to Smith's. The governor would have to have

[2] Rollins: *Roosevelt and Howe*, p. 222.

his own day in the sun before Roosevelt's ambitions could be fulfilled; and until 1928 at least, victories for Smith counted also for Roosevelt.[3]

Even clearer were Roosevelt's attachments to the country. In 1911 he had led a group of New York State Democratic Assemblymen in opposition to Tammany, and in 1914 he had aligned himself with William Gibbs McAdoo in a faction within the Wilson Administration. He voted for McAdoo on most of the roll calls in the 1920 convention, but by 1924 he had deserted McAdoo in the Californian's bid for the presidential nomination. Temporarily retired from politics because of his paralysis, Roosevelt by 1924 was harassing the party regulars of New York City as he had earlier in his career—he openly switched to Governor Smith when the oil scandals appeared to implicate McAdoo; and the sudden death of Boss Murphy of Tammany on April 25, 1924, allowed him to strengthen his commitment to Smith. Yet Roosevelt still declined to cut the ties that bound him to the rural interests; even after 1928, the upstate country squire made promises not to abandon prohibition. After becoming governor of New York in 1929, he carefully edged Smith out of his future. Roosevelt's spectacular success in 1932 testified in part to his judgment in remaining not wholly committed to either the urban or the rural faction of the party.[4]

In the mid-twenties a Tennessean wrote Roosevelt: "I believe your nomination would come nearer to uniting the Democratic party than [that of] any man in America." Though at the 1924 convention he had placed Smith's name in nomination, Roosevelt emerged from that convention a widely popular national figure. If McAdoo and Smith should deadlock again in 1928, Roosevelt would be a logical compromise candidate. And in considering whether to run for governor of New York in 1928, he

[3] Rollins: "The Political Education of Franklin Roosevelt," p. 656; *Official Report of the Proceedings* . . . [of] . . . *1924*, pp. 852–3, 888.
[4] Rollins: "The Political Education of Franklin Roosevelt," pp. 737, 739; Arthur Link: *Wilson: The New Freedom* (Princeton, 1956), p. 171; Roosevelt to John K. Sague, March 1, 1920, and Roosevelt to Donald V. Stephens, June 16, 1924, Roosevelt Papers.

surely knew to what destination that office had been a well-traveled path. As a Democrat, moreover, Roosevelt was wedded to a party sufficiently loose in structure, divided in composition, and unattached to ideology to provide an open field for fresh ideas and fresh leadership. As Arthur Holcombe observed in mid-decade: "Ambitious and realistic politicians, who aspire to bring about a realignment of parties in national politics, should find a more promising field for their operations on the Democratic side than on the Republican."[5]

[5] H. H. Gouchenour of Greeneville, Tennessee, to Roosevelt, January 8, 1924, Roosevelt Papers; Freidel: *Franklin D. Roosevelt: The Ordeal*, p. 169; Holcombe: *The Political Parties of Today* (2nd edn.; New York, 1925), p. 419.

CHAPTER VI

The Congressional Democrats

Who were the congressional Democrats in the 1920's? In the Senate they were almost entirely men who had served under Woodrow Wilson. The 54 Democrats who sat in that body between 1920 and 1928 had served an average of 17 years, and the median term of service was 16 years. Only a handful were newly elected during the twenties—not enough to alter the make-up of the Senate Democratic leadership. In addition, most of the Democratic senators, never fewer than 60 per cent, came from the southern and border states. Included among these southerners were both progressives and conservatives, men who had urged Wilson further into the realm of new legislation and still others who had acted as a brake upon the administration. In the House a majority of Democrats also were holdover southerners from the Wilson era; Finis J. Garrett of Tennessee was the minority leader, John Nance Garner of Texas was the ranking member of the Ways and Means Committee, and William Oldfield of Arkansas served as party whip. In both the Senate and House important committees and other party posts were dominated by southerners, but a greater proportion of

Democratic House than Senate members came from the eastern urban areas where the party was gaining. In 1931, after the Democrats gained control of the House, some urban Democrats were awarded key committee positions in recognition of their growing numbers.

Despite its minority status in the national legislature, the Democratic party was in a not unenviable position. Throughout the decade Republicans as well as Democrats were severely factionalized and particularly in the crucial political battleground of the Senate; a clash between eastern conservatives and western progressives damaged the relationship between the White House and Republicans in Congress and thereby weakened the party's hold upon legislation. The Democratic party, moreover, had a much stronger and initially more vigorous membership in the Congress than its desperate presidential totals would indicate. Table X illustrates the strength of the party, particularly in off-year elections, in the state houses as well as in Congress. "When it comes," wrote Walter Lippmann, "to electing Governors, Senators, Congressmen, Mayors and the like, the Democrats are very much stronger than they are in Presidential elections. The record shows clearly that only rarely do the Democrats succeed in making a national showing equal to the sum of their local victories. They are a party which is much stronger in its parts than as a whole. . . ."[1]

Yet in the Congress as in the nation at large, antagonisms between city and country prevented a united Democratic party from flourishing. This division is revealed in the votes on the sectional issues of McNary-Haugen and Muscle Shoals, and, in 1919, on the Volstead Act. During a discussion of government

[1] Edgar Eugene Robinson wrote in 1920 that "the growth of definiteness of division within the Republican party membership in Congress has been one of the outstanding developments of the past two decades." *New Republic*, XXIV (November 3, 1920), 239. George H. Mayer: *The Republican Party, 1864–1964* (New York, 1964), p. 394; Andrew Sinclair: *Prohibition: The Era of Excess* (Boston, 1962), pp. 21–3; Mark Sullivan to Joseph M. Dixon, April 10, 1923, Sullivan Papers; Lippmann: *Interpretations, 1931–1932* (New York, 1932), p. 256.

ownership of Muscle Shoals, nativist Senator Dial of South Carolina blamed his party's ills specifically on its immigrant faction:

TABLE X

Party Strength in Percentages: Elections of 1920 Through 1930*

	House	Senate	Governor
1920	R70	61	56
	D30	39	44
†1922	R52	54	46
	D48	46	54
1924	R57	59	44
	D43	41	56
†1926	R55	52	50
	D45	48	50
1928	R62	59	56
	D38	41	44
†1930	R49	51	38
	D51	49	62

* United States Bureau of the Census, *Historical Statistics of the United States* (Washington, D.C., 1960), p. 691; *World Almanac* (New York, 1920–1928).
† Off-year elections.

We have infected ourselves and our party with political miasma and pestilence, brought here from fetid and sickening atmospheres of the old countries. We have permitted the great Democratic Party to be degraded and used by a small alien faction. . . . The Democratic Party must declare whether it will serve high, straight, outspoken American Democracy or some kind of shambling, bastard, shame-faced mixture of so-called Democracy and alien-conceived bolshevism or socialism or hell broth of all.[2]

The philosophy of the congressional Democrats underwent a transformation between 1921 and 1928. In the first two Congresses, a formidable alliance developed between the minority Democrats and a vigorous group of western progressive Republicans; in its handling of the administration's domestic program, this bipartisan bloc thoroughly frustrated President Harding and on numerous occasions stymied his successor, President Coolidge. William Jennings Bryan called the Congress elected in 1922 "the most progressive . . . we have had in years. . . . The Democratic Party in that Congress made the most progressive record that the Democratic Party had made since I have been acquainted with politics." The election returns of 1922 seemed a mandate for reform; and Bryan favored a permanent alliance of Democrats with progressive Republicans. But after the disastrous 1924 election, the older congressional Democrats specifically blamed their party's poor showing on its flirtation with radicalism, and many of the newer urban Democrats had no special attachment to the principles of the Republican insurgents. As a result, after 1924 Democrats more and more followed the lead of Coolidge and the Republican majority, and they nearly severed their relations with the western radicals.[3]

The shift in sentiment is apparent in an examination of vot-

[2] Dial's speech, later stricken from the galleys of the *Congressional Record,* is quoted in *The New York Times,* January 4, 1925, p. 18.

[3] When the Democrats in 1925 voted with the insurgents against confirming a Coolidge cabinet appointee, they staunchly denied engaging in an alliance. *The New York Times,* March 19, 1925, pp. 20, 25. *Official Report of the Democratic National Convention . . .* [of] *. . . 1924* (Indianapolis, 1925), p. 531; *The Nation,* CXVIII (June 18, 1924), 697, 701; *The New York Times,* March 10, 1924, p. 1; November 20, 1924, p. 1; January 6, 1925, p. 27; March 19, 1925, p. 20; November 6, 1925, p. 27; December 19, 1925, p. 1; December 20, 1925, p. 1; January 13, 1926, p. 1; February 1, 1926, pp. 1-2; February 2, 1926, pp. 1, 6; May 10, 1926, p. 11.

ing; but care must be taken in such an analysis. Finding the key vote on any given bill may itself be a delicate process; often a motion to recommit, rather than the final roll call, is the critical test on a bill. Then, too, the motive behind a vote may be obscure. A congressman may try to placate some of his constituents by voting for a measure he in fact opposes if he is sure it is destined for burial; or he may dissent in the final conference report after having supported some parts of a bill. Whole tallies may be unreliable if a party is committed to a similar goal but through different means, or in its voting one party may be trying to embarrass the other. And many votes, particularly in the House, go unrecorded under the pressure of time, or because it is cumbersome and expensive to print them; finally, the members by common consent may agree not to publish a roll call. Even the definition of progressive is often different in succeeding generations; for present purposes we can consider as progressive or liberal a measure so designated in the political rhetoric of the times.

The evolution during the decade of a congressional tax policy reveals a conservative trend among House and Senate Democrats. The progressivism of the Democrats in Congress during the early twenties set itself against the administration view. In his message to the Sixty-seventh Congress (1921–3), Andrew Mellon, the Republican Secretary of the Treasury, advocated repeal of the excess profits and estate taxes and reductions of levies on incomes, especially surtaxes on large incomes, to be replaced by levies on items as diverse as automobiles and bank checks. The excess profits tax was removed by a narrow margin in both Houses; most Democrats wanted to keep the tax, but its prospective demise had received the approval even of *The Nation* and James Cox had spoken against it in the 1920 campaign. Many Democrats, however, apparently favored high taxes upon the wealthy, for the rest of Mellon's program met firm opposition, especially in the Senate. Senator Furnifold Simmons, minority spokesman of the Senate Finance Committee, protested that under Mellon's program "the corporations and the ultra-rich" would pass their taxes on to the less fortunate. Senate Democrats contributed 22 of their 36 votes to pass a bill raising the tax to 25 per cent on gifts over $100,000; no Democrats opposed the rise, which was later dropped in conference. But the main issue concerned the setting of a surtax on incomes over $500,000. The administration proposed a gradual reduction from 65 to 25 per cent. The radical Senate Republicans, supported by 24 Democratic votes—or two thirds of that party's contingent, and again with no Democrats in opposition—wrote their own tax bill and forced on the administration a 50 per cent surtax on high incomes and a slight increase in corporation taxes to make up for the elimination of the tax on excess profits. Ninety-nine per cent of the 116 House Democrats who voted concurred in the high surtax. It was hardly a triumph for the conservatives whose candidate had won an overwhelming victory in the 1920 election.[4]

The next Congress, in which Democrats were more numerous, showed still greater resistance to Mellon's proposals. When Mellon called for a sharp decrease of the federal estate tax and reductions for all incomes, surtax rates to be lowered to 25 per cent in the highest bracket, Democrats and insurgent Republicans in both the Senate and House joined ranks against the Mellon program. Henry T. Rainey, a Ways and Means Committee Democrat, called it a "rich man's bill." The Senate by a vote of 43 to 40—29 Democrats contributing to the victory—maintained the surtax on high incomes at 40 per cent and reduced it substantially on small and middle incomes. "We may even have to go higher [than 40 per cent]," Simmons warned, "to satisfy our allies [the radical Republicans]." All but six

[4] After Mellon's defeat *The New York Times* stated that "militant progressivism is in control in Congress, and the Republican party is without direction in its most important legislative policies. . . ." October 20, 1921, p. 14. See also September 28, 1921, p. 1; October 1, 1921, p. 15; October 23, 1921, p. 14; October 27, 1921, p. 21; November 8, 1921, pp. 1, 7. A correspondent of Senator Pat Harrison complained about two parties, each ruled by "half a dozen radicals." J. H. Weston to Harrison, January 5, 1924, Harrison Papers. *Congressional Record, Senate,* October 22, 1921, p. 6648; November 7, 1921, pp. 7486–7; *House,* August 20, 1921, p. 5358.

Democrats in the House, where a published roll call was omitted on the proposal, were reported to favor the higher surtax figure advanced by Representative John Nance Garner, a leading opponent of Mellon's plan. About 31 Senate Democrats aided the passage of amendments opening income tax returns and claims for abatement or refund of taxes to public inspection. Congress further thwarted the administration by raising estate taxes from 25 to 40 per cent and levying a gift tax; the progressive Republican-Democratic coalition forced each of the two proposals to be adopted by common consent in the Senate, and in the House Democrats contributed most of their votes for them. William Gibbs McAdoo congratulated the Democratic legislators for standing firm on taxes; Judge Gary of United States Steel observed that "the worst thing we have at the present time is our American Congress."[5]

The 1924 election, in which John W. Davis won only 29 per cent of the total vote, demoralized the congressional Democrats. Failing to consider the extent to which the La Follette vote may have been in fact Democratic and liable to return to its allegiance, many of the faithful feared that the Democracy was traveling the road to obscurity. Predictions of like nature had been appearing for some time. In 1914 Edgar Eugene Robinson had observed: "If the decline in Democratic majorities continues in the future as it has since 1896, it is only a matter of time when conviction will overcome habit and the Democratic Party will disappear." The election of 1920 seemed on the surface to mark a further point in the same trend; and after the 1924 election one of Roosevelt's urban correspondents wrote: "The drift to this bad condition began in 1896 and, with

[5] The Democrats had been aided in January 1924 by a crucial rules victory in the House. *Congressional Record, Senate,* May 2, 1924, pp. 7692–3; May 5, 1924, p. 7849; *The New York Times,* December 30, 1923, p. 1; January 7, 1924, pp. 1, 3; January 9, 1924, p. 23; January 14, 1924, p. 1; February 14, 1924, p. 1; February 25, 1924, p. 1; February 26, 1924, p. 1; March 31, 1924, p. 6; April 11, 1924, pp. 1, 6; May 6, 1924, p. 1; May 8, 1924, pp. 1–2; May 11, 1924, IX, 3. Judge Gary is quoted in Randolph E. Paul: *Taxation in the United States* (Boston, 1954), p. 137.

the exception of a slight reaction during the Wilson Administration, has continued to the present time." Herbert Croly in the *New Republic* warned that the Democratic party in America would follow the path of England's Liberal party. Careful observers knew that the two-party system was far from extinct, but the Democrats in Congress were understandably frightened by the immediate prospects.[6]

In the shadow of its overwhelming defeat, the congressional Democracy, particularly in the Senate, for the most part adapted itself to the business temperament of the decade. When Secretary Mellon in December of 1925 recommended a further tax cut of $330 million, the Democrats on the Senate Finance Committee countered with a figure of $500 million. Democrats had earlier proposed great reductions in taxes on middle and lower incomes; but the Senate Democratic program now included an additional $93 million reduction in taxes on corporation capital stock and a further cut of $54 million on surtaxes for men with incomes between $20,000 to $1,000,000—men of moderate means, Senator Simmons of the Finance Committee called them. The last adjustment was "to make businessmen realize that the Democratic Party is not bent on taxing them or their enterprises exorbitantly." The Democratic plan made no mention at all of publicity for income tax payments, or of the gift tax, which was totally abandoned, or of estate taxes, which—with Democratic aid and in direct opposition to a plea from the Progressives—were later cut in half. Though western Republicans in the Senate joined the regulars to defeat key parts of the Democratic proposal, the Democrats' eagerness for tax cuts did cause the administration to make more reductions than it had intended. Charging that a deal had been made between the regulars and the minority party, Senator

[6] O. Douglas Weeks wrote after the election of 1928: "The Democratic party . . . seems to be nationally dead." *Southwestern Political and Social Science Quarterly,* IX (December 1928), 337. *American Journal of Sociology,* XV (November 1914), 334; William Foster to Roosevelt, January 26, 1925, Box 11, Circular Letter, Roosevelt Papers; *New Republic,* XLV (December 10, 1924), 10.

Norris of Nebraska commented sarcastically that the Democrats were entitled to greater campaign contributions for their share in "relieving wealth from taxation." Senator Lenroot of Wisconsin told the Democrats that they were "out-Melloning Mellon"; and Senator Reed, the Missouri Democrat, observed that "the poor old Democratic mule is being led in by the ear and Mr. Mellon's hand holds the ear."[7]

The votes in the Congresses from 1925 to 1928 clearly reflected the shift in Democratic sentiment. In the Sixty-ninth Congress (1925–7), only four out of forty Senate Democrats voted against keeping the maximum surtax at 40 per cent. No more than thirteen Democrats joined sixteen insurgent Republicans who proposed to graduate the rate to a maximum of 30 per cent; ten voted with thirteen western Republicans against the lowering of estate taxes; four, along with nine Republicans, wanted gifts of over $25,000 to be counted as gross income. Mellon's biographer noted: "The great difficulty with this Congress was to restrain its members, who had seen a great light on last election day, from voting a deficit in the treasury." Democrats vied with Republicans in cutting rates. In the House

[7] President Coolidge had entertained Senator Oscar W. Underwood at the White House after the 1924 election, an act viewed by some as evidence of a conciliatory spirit. At first Democrats had been divided over the tax program presented by the Senate leadership, but most of them eventually backed it as a party measure. Senator Pat Harrison opposed both estate and inheritance taxes and stood against any increase in the corporation tax in 1926. Senator Wheeler wrote of Harrison: "The trouble is . . . that the Democratic leader has simply turned the bill over to the Republican side, and the Democrats are now asked to follow the Republican leader." *Kiplinger Washington Letter*, December 12, 1924, and November 8, 1926; Harrison to Carl Marshall, January 23, 1926, Harrison Papers. Comments by Senators Wheeler, Norris, Reed, Lenroot, Norbeck, and others on the Democratic about-face are in the *Congressional Record*, February 3, 1926, pp. 3219, 3221–4; June 15, 1926, p. 11289; February 4, 1927, pp. 2925–31. *The New York Times*, June 15, 1925, p. 14; September 11, 1925, p. 1; November 20, 1925, p. 1; November 26, 1925, p. 1; January 5, 1926, p. 4; January 6, 1926, p. 2; January 11, 1926, pp. 1–2; January 12, 1926, p. 2; January 19, 1926, p. 1; February 2, 1926, pp. 1, 6; February 4, 1926, p. 25; February 11, 1926, p. 1; January 28, 1927, p. 3; February 4, 1927, p. 1.

Democrats were not yet of one mind on the matter of taxes; in 1926 Garner even managed to save the estate tax by reducing its highest rates. But in the first session of the Seventieth Congress—the last to meet before the stock market crashed—almost all Democrats, in company with the United States Chamber of Commerce, continued to clamor for reductions beyond the wishes of President Coolidge. In calling for an immediate reduction of half a billion dollars, Garner and Simmons undoubtedly spurred the speculative fever of the later 1920's. They specifically voted for a further surtax reduction on intermediate incomes and a lowering of corporation and consumption taxes. But except for a reduction in the corporation levy, these last proposals met with slight success, for now the Republican regulars were standing solidly with the western bloc of their party in opposition to cuts. In a crucial test the Republican progressives and regulars voted as a matter of principle to use the tax surplus to reduce the national debt; all but one Democrat opposed the motion, which carried. Later in the sessions heavy Democratic majorities failed to repeal taxes on original issues of capital stock or to lower the stock transfer tax, though the Democrats and Republican regulars defeated a La Follette attempt to publicize tax returns. In the House of Representatives roll calls on tax measures continued to be sparse, but in December 1927, Democrats voted to lower the corporation tax more than Mellon had recommended, though at the same time they voted along progressive lines on some issues. In their efforts to graduate taxes on small corporations they seemed to retain their identity as Wilsonian Democrats.[8]

On another financial issue, the tariff, Democrats in the con-

[8] *Congressional Record, Senate,* February 3, 1926, p. 3221; February 10, 1926, p. 3696; February 12, 1926, p. 3850; February 4, 1927, p. 2931; May 10, 1928, pp. 8279–80; May 12, 1928, pp. 8508, 8518; May 14, 1928, p. 8622; May 19, 1928, p. 9175; May 25, 1928, p. 9854; *House,* December 18, 1925, pp. 1164–5; December 15, 1927, p. 716; *The New York Times,* June 11, 1927, p. 18; October 24, 1927, p. 20; January 29, 1928, p. 1; April 5, 1928, p. 13; April 6, 1928, p. 16; April 20, 1928, p. 9; April 27, 1928, p. 6; May 11, 1928, p. 44; May 26, 1928, p. 1; Harvey O'Connor: *Mellon's Millions* (New York, 1933), p. 140.

gressional sessions of 1921 and 1922 adhered to the traditional philosophy of their party. They stood against the Fordney-McCumber bill, with its high rates in face of the struggling European economy, and termed the bill "irredeemably and universally vicious." Senator Underwood and William Gibbs McAdoo added that the tariff would raise the cost of living at home; other Democrats argued that a high tariff made it difficult for Europeans to repay outstanding loans. But on this issue western and eastern Republicans were of one mind, and the small contingent of Democrats in the Sixty-seventh Congress was powerless to stop them. In the Senate 22 Democrats—16 of them from the South—and only 3 Republicans voted against the bill, and in the House 70 Democrats—61 from the South—were joined in their opposition by 21 Republicans. Only 9 House or Senate Democrats voted for the tariff measure. Until about 1924 Democrats continued their attack on the tariff, but in the later Congresses they tended to be less outspoken on the issue. In the matter of the tariff, the Democratic platform of 1928 was similar in its vagueness to the Republican. Even in 1930, after the onset of the depression, Democratic opposition to the Smoot-Hawley bill was weaker than it had been earlier in the decade.[9]

Upon other issues Democrats in Congress rarely made a united and energetic effort for progressive legislation. Often purely sectional considerations restrained many Democrats from making common cause with progressive Republicans, or even others of their own party. Senator Key Pittman of Nevada observed that during this period "localism had replaced the broad Wilsonian slogans. . . ."[1] On the issue of agricultural reform, for

[9] *Congressional Record, Senate,* June 2, 1922, pp. 7992–5; August 19, 1922, p. 11627; March 24, 1930, p. 6015; *House,* September 15, 1922, p. 12718; May 1, 1930, pp. 8148–9; *The New York Times,* April 4, 1922, p. 19; May 7, 1922, p. 16; June 11, 1922, VII, 1; August 16, 1922, p. 1; *The Nation,* CXIII (July 20, 1921), 61.

[1] Certainly little Wilsonianism was present in Democratic attitudes on foreign policy. G. L. Grassmuck has shown that Democrats were usually less favorable to internationalist legislation than Republicans in the 1920's. *Sectional Biases in Congress on Foreign Policy* (Baltimore, 1951), pp. 32–

example, divisions appeared within the party most notably between South and West but also between city and country.

Agricultural legislation during the twenties may be attributed in considerable part to the American Farm Bureau Federation, which entered politics in May 1921. Under the leadership of its secretary Gray Silver, the nonpartisan Farm Bureau devised an effective method to make its point in Washington: it periodically sent questionnaires on farm problems to its members and distributed the responses to the appropriate congressmen. The work of the Bureau contributed significantly to the formation of a farm bloc in May 1921; it was especially effective in the Senate of the Sixty-seventh Congress, where the bloc was composed of 15 Republicans and 12 Democrats, 9 of them from the South. The Farm Bureau underwent a brief decline when it turned its principal attention from legislation to cooperative marketing; but by 1926, when Chester Gray replaced Silver as secretary and Sam Thompson succeeded O. E. Bradfute as president, it had returned to the legislative field, throwing its full weight behind the controversial McNary-Haugen bill.[2]

In the early days of the Bureau and the farm bloc, Democratic legislators from the South and West worked in substantial harmony with each other and with their Republican colleagues from agricultural areas. But on the question of McNary-Haugen, rural Democrats divided, and their contribution never equalled that of the Republican adherents of the measure. In addition, some of the most powerful opponents of McNary-Haugen were Democrats, including Congressmen James B. Aswell of Louisiana and David H. Kinchelow of Kentucky. When in 1924 the new farm bill came to a vote in the House, it contained provisions that would chiefly benefit wheat and hog growers of the western states. Farm organizations, moreover, gave it

70, 97 ff. Pittman is quoted in Fred L. Israel: *Nevada's Key Pittman* (Lincoln, Neb., 1963), p. 49.

[2] Grant McConnell: *The Decline of Agrarian Democracy* (Berkeley, 1953), pp. 57 ff.; Orville M. Kile: *The Farm Bureau Through Three Decades* (Baltimore, 1948), pp. 92–113; 136–51; *The New York Times,* August 28, 1921, p. 1.

slight support. As a result, a mere 48 Democrats—only 23 from the South, where cotton prices were reasonably high—voted for the bill, as against 107 Republicans, and it failed to pass. In May 1926, a revised and somewhat more feasible McNary-Haugen bill was again defeated in the House but 17 additional Democrats favored the measure. In the Senate, where only 14 Democrats supported the bill when it first came to a vote, its southern supporters were few and unenthusiastic. The objection of the southerners was to the tariff principle bolstered in the bill; cotton, the main southern crop, was exported in much larger quantity than was the agricultural produce of the West, and on this issue the South maintained its traditional antagonism to protection. Senator Carter Glass of Virginia, for example, declared the measure unconstitutional and discriminatory against the South; he suggested that a reduction of the tariff would help the farmer more. When cotton and rice prices declined late in 1926, however, the South did come to favor McNary-Haugen, but only as part of a sectional bargain, in which cotton—included for a time in the first bill—rice, and tobacco were also added to the list of price-supported crops, and westerners gave needed backing to proposals for fertilizer production at Muscle Shoals.[3]

On February 11, 1927, 24 Republicans and 22 Democrats joined to pass a new version of McNary-Haugen in the Senate, and the House followed suit on February 27, 214 to 178, with 113 Republicans, 97 Democrats, and 4 Independents in favor. In each house southern Democrats now gave the bill a heavy majority of their votes. In 1928, after Coolidge had vetoed the bill of 1927, Congress modified it to meet the criticisms of the

[3] *Congressional Record, House,* May 20, 1924, p. 9052; June 3, 1924, pp. 10340–1; May 21, 1926, p. 9862; *Senate,* June 15, 1926, p. 11289; June 22, 1926, pp. 11735–52; June 24, 1926, p. 11872; *Congressional Digest,* I (June 1922), 4; *The New York Times,* February 2, 1926, p. 1; June 25, 1926, p. 1; *North American Review,* CCXXI (1925), 417–30; John D. Hicks and Theodore Saloutos: *Agricultural Discontent in the Middle West, 1900–1939* (Madison, Wisc., 1951), pp. 321–403; Gilbert C. Fite: *George N. Peek and the Fight for Farm Parity* (Norman, Okla., 1954), pp. 64, 67–8, 71, 78, 91.

administration and then adopted it again. On this occasion, when strategy dictated a test on whether to retain the controversial equalization fee, 27 Senate Democrats voted with 19 Republicans to form a margin of 46 to 31; in the House 91 Democrats, along with 94 Republicans, hard-pressed by the White House to vote differently, supported the measure, which was again vetoed by the Republican President. But it was not the Democrats who could claim leadership in the agrarian protest that had crystallized into the battle for the McNary-Haugen scheme; the honor belongs to the progressive Republicans of the West. Many Democrats were chiefly interested only in embarrassing the President.[4]

In the determination of a progressive congressional policy on Muscle Shoals, a hydroelectric project in the northern Alabama basin of the Tennessee River Valley, the southern Democrats played a more important role than they did over the issue of McNary-Haugen. The project had been initiated during the war to insure an adequate supply of nitrates, for which we had previously relied upon Chile. In 1920 Congress shunned the pleas of Bernard Baruch and others to make Muscle Shoals into a government-owned fertilizer plant, and the whole problem was a subject of congressional fumbling for the remainder of the decade.

In 1922 Henry Ford, then alleged to be a Democratic presidential aspirant, made an equivocal but sweeping offer to lease the area from the government and develop it into a great new Detroit for the benefit of the American people. Southern Democrats were sympathetic to Ford's proposal, as they had been to the plan for government ownership, and President Coolidge thought it an excellent idea. But the West was more interested in development of the St. Lawrence Seaway, and only after prolonged agitation by the Farm Bureau did Ford's proposal for cheap production of fertilizer attract widespread support. Ford's bid

[4] *Congressional Record, Senate,* February 11, 1927, p. 3518; April 27, 1928, pp. 6278-9; *House,* August 20, 1921, p. 5358; February 17, 1927, p. 4099; May 3, 1928, pp. 7770-2; *The New York Times,* February 4, 1927, p. 7; February 12, 1927, pp. 1, 5; February 13, 1927, p. 1.

drew opposition, however, both from representatives of the power trust and from progressives who feared the possibility that the project would be exploited in violation of the Water Power Act of 1920 and its real conservationist values neglected. Also, the Teapot Dome scandals made legislators uneasy about government leases, and Ford seemed more interested in cheap electricity than in producing fertilizer. Ford himself added little to his cause when he denounced his opponents as the international Jews of Wall Street. In 1924 a bill embodying the Ford offer passed the House—with 90 per cent of the Democrats supporting it—but not the Senate. Recognizing the fact of congressional deadlock, Ford finally withdrew his offer.[5]

The fight was now joined between Senator Norris, who advocated public operation for flood control and cheap power, and Democratic Senator Oscar W. Underwood of Alabama, who sponsored a plan of the Coolidge Administration for leasing by private power interests. Norris held the spotlight: he hinted darkly of foreign control of the Alabama Power Company, and he exposed an offer from thirteen power companies as being in fact nothing other than the overture of one giant combine dominated by General Electric. Early in 1925 Norris failed in his attempt to substitute his proposal for government ownership; fewer than half of the Democrats supported the Republican Senator. Yet seizing upon a technicality in the conference report of the House and Senate committees, Norris succeeded in dealing to the Underwood measure, which allowed Coolidge to lease the property, a crippling delay. "We defeated [Muscle Shoals] even without a filibuster," he said later, "because it was known and believed by those who were behind the legislation

[5] Urban Democrats claimed that Ford's presidential candidacy was designed to pressure Congress into leasing Muscle Shoals to him. *The New York Times*, November 16, 1923, p. 1. *Congressional Record, House*, March 10, 1924, p. 3927; Preston J. Hubbard: *Origins of the TVA: The Muscle Shoals Controversy, 1920–1932* (Nashville, 1961), pp. 128 ff.; Jerome G. Kerwin: *Federal Water-Power Legislation* (New York, 1926), pp. 270–83; Judson King: *The Conservation Fight* (Washington, D.C., 1959), pp. 100, 103, 116, 124.

that we would filibuster." Senator Robinson, the Democratic minority leader, acidly attacked La Follette's Muscle Shoals plan all through the twenties. But by late 1926 Norris was probably right to observe that "the sentiment of the people is gradually turning our way"—though perhaps the shift in feeling represented chiefly a frustration at the failure of the national legislature to adopt any plan. In 1928 enough southern Democrats, realizing that the only possibility of action lay in the Norris plan, joined with western Republicans to pass a bill for government operation of Muscle Shoals. Twenty-seven Democrats voted Aye as did 21 Republicans, and 121 House Democrats joined 90 Republicans to send the bill to President Coolidge, who gave it a pocket veto. In his fight Norris had received needed support from some Democrats: Wheeler and Walsh of Montana and Dill of Washington, as well as McKellar of Tennessee and other southerners; and sectional needs forced many other Democrats to the progressive side. But as in the battle over McNary-Haugen, western Republicans had provided the initiative and leadership; some Democrats favored both bills for purely partisan reasons. The willingness of southern Democrats to support both private and public power bills indicated that development itself, not the method used, was uppermost in their minds.[6]

Democrats in the big cities seemed no more reform-minded than their rural counterparts. Though the small but expanding contingent of urban Democrats was progressive enough to vote almost solidly in favor of high surtaxes in 1921, and even in 1925 gave a strong majority for a similar motion, the McNary-Haugen bills of the decade never received more than fifteen per cent of the city Democratic vote. The 1928 conference report on Muscle Shoals received the support of only one-half of the urban Democrats. After the Great Depression, that con-

[6] Hubbard: *Origins of the TVA, passim;* King: *The Conservation Fight,* pp. 138, 156, 175; Alfred Lief: *Democracy's Norris* (New York, 1939), pp. 277, 295; *Kiplinger Washington Letter,* December 19, 1924; *Congressional Record, Senate,* January 8, 1925, pp. 1449–50; March 13, 1928, p. 4635; *House,* May 25, 1928, p. 9957; Norris to W. L. Locke, March 12, 1925, Norris Papers, Nebraska Historical Society.

tingent evidently became more radical on public power, giving majority support to a crucial bill in 1931; but they overwhelmingly favored the manufacturer's sales tax as a solution to the financial problems of 1932.[7]

In the 1920 and 1924 elections the AFL and many other labor groups had been able to see little difference between Republicans and Democrats. But in 1926 the mild William Green of the AFL wrote of the House Democratic leader: "Representative Garrett has not lost an opportunity during his long session in Congress to antagonize most bitterly every important measure that has been introduced in that body in the interest of labor. . . . He has used his position as leader of the minority to hamper and discredit bills of great importance to not only the wage earners but the people generally." Yet the organized worker could hardly complain: enjoying prosperous times, labor itself hewed to the conservatism of the decade. Mesmerized by attractive business paternalism, it confined itself mostly to protests against the use of the injunction and to some relatively ineffective lobbying in Washington.

In the late twenties, the viewpoint of the congressional Democrats remained for the most part provincial, divided, and predominantly conservative. Their votes on the tax bills clearly demonstrated their mood; their friendliness toward business was also apparent when in 1926 Democratic leaders attacked Coolidge for spending four times as much money as had President Wilson ten years earlier. By 1928 it had indeed become plain that the congressional Democrats of that day bore little trace of the crusading zeal that had been present during the Wilson Administration. "Congressionally," wrote the farm

---

[7] All 21 members of the Tammany delegation at first declared themselves in favor of the sales tax; on the vote itself they divided themselves 16 for and 5 against. *The New York Times,* March 17, 1932, pp. 1, 4. *Congressional Record, House,* August 20, 1921, p. 5539; March 10, 1924, p. 3927; December 18, 1925, p. 1164; May 3, 1928, p. 7771; May 25, 1928, p. 9957; February 20, 1931, p. 6666; *The New York Times,* March 25, 1932, p. 3.

correspondent Lynn Haines, "the Democratic record is not an asset for 1928"; he complained that the labors of Democrats in the House and Senate recently have not been "constructive or coherent or consistent or courageous." The Democratic record in Congress blended well with its conservative party platform of 1928: in that year the League for Independent Political Action concluded that "today in the United States there is no vital party of opposition. Democrats in the election of 1928 revealed the fact that they have not one fundamental economic issue to distinguish them from the Republicans." But it was not among Democrats alone that the reform impulse had begun to fade. Even the Republican progressives appeared late in the decade as tired liberals drained of their energies. Except on the special issues of Muscle Shoals and McNary-Haugen—and even here the veto had sufficed to stalemate the battle—the conservative Republicans had routed their opposition.[8]

The depression years brought with them an unprecedented challenge to the congressional Democrats. True to their recently deepened conservatism, they were slow to develop programs in alternative to Hoover's. After the 1930 elections, Speaker of the House John Nance Garner and Senate minority leader Joseph T. Robinson joined with Cox, Davis, Smith, Raskob, and Jouett Shouse, head of the Democratic Executive Committee, in assuring the public that Democrats would cooperate with President Hoover and not countenance "dangerous" legislation. Widely applauded by businessmen, the offer, complained the *New Republic,* would insure the failure of progressive legislation. But Hoover, who blamed the Senate for "playing politics at the expense of human misery," was himself too partisan and

[8] Senator Peter Norbeck wrote to a friend: "The *American Mercury* article is making quite a sensation around here because much of it is true." Quoted in Reinhard H. Luthin: "Smith Wildman Brookhart of Iowa: Insurgent Agrarian Politician," *Agricultural History,* XXV (October 1951), 194. *American Mercury,* XVI (April 1929), 385–93; Haines: "Al Smith and Certain Soothsayers," unpublished manuscript in the Chester C. Davis Papers, 1928.

tactless to work with the Democrats; and the leaders, at the behest of Democratic senators, eventually repudiated their statement. Yet the very kind of coalition the liberals feared had already passed the Hawley-Smoot tariff in 1930. According to John Dewey: "The Democratic party . . . was, on the whole, an accomplice to the passage of the bill, passive and even active." Five Democratic votes in the Senate salvaged the measure there; but even more striking is the action of about seventeen Democratic senators who voted for high rates on coal, oil, copper, and lumber. After the tariff vote *The Nation* cynically observed that the Democratic party differed from the Republican "only in that its desire to become the party of privilege has never been satisfied."⁹

The crucial issue before the Seventy-second Congress was that of taxation, for the demand of the economic emergency were draining the Treasury. In January 1932, Senators Robinson and Harrison warned that a radical increase in taxes would be "disturbing to business." Because of his fiery attacks on Secretary of the Treasury Mellon, John Nance Garner was considered by many to be a dangerous radical; but "Cactus Jack," who gave up his official car to dramatize his interest in economy, decided to promote the safe and sane measures of President Hoover. On the critical question of revenue, Garner agreed with Republican leaders to support a manufacturer's sales tax (in the early twenties he had opposed such a tax). His action was an admission of the failure of the Democratic congressional leadership to provide an alternative to the policies of the Republican administration; for example, the Democrats were uninterested in overtures by progressive Republicans who wanted to vote a raise in corporation taxes. The sales tax received enthusiastic

⁹ Of Robinson even Smith wrote: "He has given more aid to Herbert Hoover than any other Democrat." Ray T. Tucker: *The Mirrors of 1932* (New York, 1931), p. 130. *New Republic,* LXV (November 19, 1930), 4–5; (December 17, 1930), 137; (December 24, 1930), 164; LXVI (March 25, 1931), 151; *The Nation,* CXXXII (January 28, 1931), 60; *The New York Times,* March 27, 1932, p. 1; Lippmann: *Interpretations,* p. 136.

backing from the national Democratic organization, and from Senator Robinson, who was preaching radical economies in public expenditures. Robinson's chief fear was the dole, and with his encouragement Senate Democrats contributed about forty per cent of the votes cast against the La Follette-Costigan relief bill late in February. In early March the *New Republic* mourned: "Up to this date we have had the spectacle of the Democratic party in the House and Senate voting with almost complete solidarity in favor of . . . one Hoover recommendation after the other. . . . The plain fact is that the Democratic party is at heart just as conservative as its opponent.[1]

But when finally roused in the spring of 1932 to the worsening crisis, they broke away from the caution of their leaders. There were many House Democrats who considered the sales tax proposed by Hoover and endorsed by the Democratic leadership as both a real and symbolic burden upon the poor—a sort of reverse income tax. Already aroused by Garner's limitation of the debate on the Glass-Steagall bill that made available to business a large quantity of government gold, about fifty Democrats, under the leadership of Robert Doughton of North Carolina, rebelled against the Speaker and managed to defeat the sales tax. In a rapid fire of votes the Democrats substituted a variety of progressive measures, including surtaxes of up to sixty-five per cent; the taxation policy they offered was reminiscent of that in effect during the war years and the early twenties. Later in the session Garner—who on March 29 had roused almost the entire membership to stand in favor of a balanced budget—himself decided to support a massive relief bill, and in the Senate Democrats proposed numerous reforms. At last, it appeared, some of the shackles of economic traditionalism were beginning to fall away from the Democratic party. Skeptics pointed out that even the sales tax revolt was sparked in some measure

[1] *New Republic*, LXVII (June 10, 1931), 97; LXVIII (December 23, 1931), 161–2; (January 20, 1932), 270; LXIX (March 9, 1932), 96; (March 16, 1932), 126; (March 30, 1932), 181.

by the self-interest of important mercantile groups. Yet in the next Congresses the same men who had hedged on ideology for almost a decade would contribute their votes unquestioningly for one advanced scheme after another.[2]

2 Jordan A. Schwarz: "John Nance Garner and the Sales Tax Rebellion of 1932," *Journal of Southern History,* XXX (May 1964), 162–80; Bascom N. Timmons: *Garner of Texas* (New York, 1948), p. 138.

CHAPTER VII

The Brown Derby Campaign

A President must, without compromising his integrity of origin and manner, show that he is broadly representative of the nation over which he has been placed, and toward which he stands in so peculiarly symbolic a relationship. The task of squaring a social, ethnic, or regional with a national identity need not be an overwhelming one: Harry Truman and John Kennedy, both deeply stamped by their divergent breedings and places of origin, succeeded admirably. But some presidential candidates never transcend the political image that served them in local politics. To this category belongs Governor Alfred E. Smith of New York.

In studying the 1928 campaign, analysts have quite properly concentrated their attention upon the scurrilous tactics of Protestant bigots; almost by default, the New Yorker has emerged as a liberal martyr sacrificed to religious prejudice and prohibitionist morality. But this view of Al Smith is more myth than fact. It is now commonly recognized that any study of the 1928 campaign must begin upon the assumption that whatever the more flamboyant issues, economic prosperity probably pre-

destined the success of the party in power. As Richard Hofstadter has observed: "There was not a Democrat alive, Protestant or Catholic, who could have beaten Hoover in 1928."[1]
More serious, however, has been the reluctance to examine the
strategy within the Smith camp—to gauge the response on the
part of the candidate and his lieutenants to the charge that his
background ill fitted him to represent the whole American
people, rural as well as urban, Protestant as well as Roman
Catholic. Such an examination will reveal that Al Smith was less
than successful, and at moments less than tactful, in presenting
his case to that portion of American society which lay outside
his immediate cultural experience.

The failure of Smith to present himself as a national candidate—reflected in his choice of a brown derby as a campaign
symbol—was also a mark of his party's failure to unify itself. In
1928 the Democrats thrust upon the whole nation the same
conflict that had caused them internal chaos four years earlier
in New York. But no longer was Smith's political opposition
solely a fundamentalist rural America under the leadership
of William Jennings Bryan and William Gibbs McAdoo.
While this rural element undoubtedly contributed to his defeat,
Smith now faced in Herbert Hoover a powerful antagonist who
could command the respect of politically sophisticated Americans having little in common with the narrow ruralists of 1924.
And the whole controversy surrounding Smith's candidacy has
since obscured the solid appeal of his opponent almost as much
as it has romanticized the New Yorker himself.

To gain a deeper understanding of the campaign, we may first
call to mind the background of the 1928 Democratic nominee:
his big-city upbringing, and his political rise; and then examine
the campaign itself, in order to discover the kind of presidential

[1] "Could a Protestant Have Beaten Hoover in 1928?" *The Reporter*, XXII
(March 17, 1960), 31. For a sympathetic account of the Smith campaign
written by a warm admirer, see Oscar Handlin: *Al Smith and His America* (Boston, 1958), pp. 125–36; see also Edmund A. Moore: *A Catholic
Runs for President: The Campaign of 1928* (New York, 1956).

image the Smith forces created for their candidate, and the nature of their reply to the assaults of Protestantism, nativism, and rural politicians.

Smith's birthplace, now in the shadow of Brooklyn Bridge, stood in sharp contrast to President Coolidge's homestead in Vermont or Hoover's Quaker village in Iowa. Nor were both of Smith's parents American-born; his father was a native of Manhattan, but his mother's birthplace, according to Smith himself, was in West Meath County, Ireland.[2] Smith's boyhood was shaped to a pattern unprecedented among major presidential candidates. In place of the swimming hole, he had the East River; he attended not the one-room schoolhouse of rural nostalgia but the city's Roman Catholic parochial schools. He married Katie Dunn of the lower East Side, who bore him five children, all of whom attended the same church schools. And Smith's later career as governor in upstate New York never took him far from the mode of life he knew in the city.

Smith was born in 1873; his formal education was ended before he completed the ninth grade when his father died leaving young Al, age fifteen, to help support the family. Graduating, as he later would say, from the Fulton Street Fish Market, where he was a bookkeeper in a commission house, Smith entered ward politics at an age when boys from families of higher income entered college. In 1902 he was elected to the New York State Assembly and served there with increasing prominence until 1915. After distinguishing himself in that year's state constitutional convention, he became Sheriff of New York County and then President of the Board of Aldermen of New York City. Smith went on to win the governorship of New York in 1918. He lost in 1920, but won again in 1922, 1924, and 1926; altogether he served four terms, a record unequalled since the administration of George Clinton. William Allen White stigmatized Smith as a "town-lot Sir Galahad who never fared afield." H. L. Mencken, who voted for and frequently defended him, observed that

---

[2] *The New York Times*, September 2, 1928, p. 2.

Smith's world "begins at Coney Island and ends at Buffalo."[3]

The governor had gotten his political start as the favorite of Charles Murphy of Tammany Hall. But though at first he was of necessity obedient to the political bosses of New York City—his record came under attack from the Citizens' Union of Manhattan—Smith later overshadowed them and developed his own independent Democratic organization. In affairs at Albany Smith depended not primarily on Murphy, but on advisers such as Mrs. Belle Moskowitz and Judge Joseph Proskauer. Mrs. Moskowitz in particular encouraged the governor to promote city welfare legislation that actually helped to diminish the influence of Tammany Hall, since it made voters less dependent on local politicians for favors. The governor also gained considerable power within the increasingly important Democratic machines in Brooklyn and the Bronx. After Murphy's death in 1924, Smith's following was powerful enough to name as his successor George W. Olvany. Yet this victory is itself evidence of Smith's ambivalent relationship toward Tammany bossism; while sufficiently strong and autonomous to be able to dictate terms to the organization, the Smith forces nevertheless found it necessary to support, in Olvany, a man whose ethics seem to have been in the Tammany vein. Smith's own integrity is certain, but he could never shake the stigma of Tammany; it remained a nettle to his rural and small-town opponents. Smith's association with the Wigwam put the Democrats in a defensive position in 1928, much as that in which the Teapot Dome oil scandals had earlier placed the Republicans.[4]

[3] Mencken wrote of Smith still more caustically: "Not only is he uninterested in the great problems facing the nation, but he has never heard of them." *A Carnival of Buncombe*, ed. Malcolm Moos (Baltimore, 1956), p. 143. White is quoted in Henry F. Pringle, *Alfred E. Smith* (New York, 1927), p. 97. Ralph D. Casey: "Scripps-Howard Newspapers in the 1928 Presidential Campaign," *Journalism Quarterly*, VII (September 1930), 228 ff.

[4] Charles Murphy was more sophisticated than some of his outrageous predecessors on Fourteenth Street, but he, too, took enormous sums in the form of "honest graft." Both he and Olvany left estates of over $2 million, although Tammany paid them no salary and they had held no

Smith drank in defiance of prohibition and won for himself the epithet "Alcohol Al." In the summer of 1923 he was presented with a bill repealing the state's prohibition-enforcement law. Franklin Roosevelt advised a veto; instead, the governor—in conformity to his own conscience as well as to the demands of Charles Murphy—signed the bill and issued a declaration that wine and beer should be legalized. When Smith stepped beyond state politics, his stand against prohibition became a major political liability, especially in the South and West. That same year Smith made an off-the-record remark to some newspapermen, which was widely quoted as: "Wouldn't you like to have your foot on the rail and blow the foam off some suds?" Early in 1924, in a letter to Franklin Roosevelt, a nervous Louis Howe remarked: "I took lunch today with some of the Albany boys and they told me in some ways at least Smith is much drier than he used to be. How long he has sworn off for this time, God knows. Let us trust until after the national convention." Even at the Executive Mansion in Albany, Edward Flynn recalled, "a cocktail or highball, in fact, was always available."[5]

The question of Smith's own conduct during prohibition days was to persist. "Does 'Al' drink and does he drink too much?" asked a correspondent of Oswald Garrison Villard, editor of *The Nation*, in 1927. "I am reliably informed," wrote Villard in reply, "that he drinks every day, and the number of his cocktails and highballs is variously estimated at from four

other jobs but that of Sachem. Dennis Lynch: "Friends of the Governor," *North American Review*, CCXXVI (October 1928), 426–7; *Outlook and Independent*, CLII (May 15, 1929), 86, 117. The censures of the Citizens' Union are discussed in "Governor Smith of New York," *World's Work*, XXIX (January 1920), 239; Norman Thomas and Paul Blanshard condemn Olvany in *What's the Matter with New York: A National Problem* (New York, 1932), pp. 52–4. See also "The New Tammany Under George W. Olvany," in William B. and John B. Northrop: *The Insolence of Office* (New York, 1932), pp. 193–203; William Allen White to Edward J. Woodhouse, July 20, 1923, White Papers; *The New York Times*, July 13, 1924, p. 1; July 14, 1924, p. 3; November 27, 1925, p. 1; November 10, 1931, p. 1.
[5] Pringle: *Alfred E. Smith*, p. 138; Howe to Roosevelt, February 25, 1924, Howe Papers.

to eight." The liberal editor was to regret the remark, for it was widely quoted, but later he assured Lillian Wald: "I am certain that it is true, or was true before the campaign began." A friend of William Allen White insisted: "I am told that he drinks regularly. If this is true, how does he get his liquor? He must be either violating the law or knowing that someone else does. If this is true he is not a fit man to be either Governor or President."[6]

The behavior of Smith, in face of national prohibition, during these years prior to 1928 provides one of the more startling instances of an urban provincialism or perhaps a mere personal stubbornness on his part. What was at issue here, of course, is not Smith's legitimate opposition to the prohibition laws but the manner of his opposition. Certainly it would be no great crime for a private citizen to engage in genial defiance of a law that appeared both senseless and obtrusive; Smith regarded the prohibitionist cause, moreover, as a covert attack on the immigrant and his culture, and he thought it hypocritical to camouflage his personal life. But Smith was no private citizen; he was occupant of one important position of public trust and aspirant to another, in which he would become the highest of the sworn defenders of the Constitution, the representative of the whole people. One of the most recent additions to the fundamental national law embodied a principle close to the heart of small-town American Protestantism; and the blatant refusal of Smith to submit to prohibition could be interpreted as a cocky defiance, almost a contempt for that considerable part of the nation that made the law. Having scorned one of our enactments, which of our remaining hopes will this man choose to dash if he becomes our President and representative? So might the query

[6] *The Nation*, CXXV (November 30, 1927), 596. According to Bishop Cannon, the information was supplied to Villard by Henry and Belle Moskowitz. *Bishop Cannon's Own Story*, ed. Richard L. Watson, Jr. (Durham, N.C., 1955), p. 413. Villard to Lillian Wald, June 19, 1928, Wald Papers; T. H. Barrow of Austin, Texas, to White, August 31, 1928, White Papers; Flynn: *You're the Boss* (New York, 1947), p. 66; Cannon to Carter Glass, December 11, 1928, Cannon Papers.

have come from the America that lay west of the Alleghenies and south of Staten Island.

The question of Smith's religion, too, was far from non-existent long before the presidential campaign of 1928. Smith embraced his church, simply and deeply. He took great pride in outward tokens of his faith; in the Executive Mansion in Albany, for instance, he displayed a portrait of Pope Pius XI autographed in 1924. And Katie Smith exhibited on the religious issue a similar openness. In 1925 Louis Howe was fidgeting over the loquacity of the governor's wife, who had just returned from a European trip that included a papal audience. "Mrs. Smith is back from Europe," Howe wrote to Roosevelt:

> and complains to your "Missus" that there were too many ruins in Rome. She is talking too much for Al's good, describing with much gusto and detail their special audience with the Pope and how he referred to Al as his son and the great knowledge he showed in the political campaign. One of her stories is particularly delicious. She says that the Pope turned to McCooey [John H. McCooey, Brooklyn Democratic leader], who was with them and said, "I know how hard you have worked for my beloved son, Governor Smith, but next time you must work even harder." She also is announcing that she brought back a photograph of the Pope personally inscribed "To my beloved son, Alfred E. Smith."[7]

Before 1928, Smith had also become innocently involved in a number of incidents that anti-Catholics could use against him. In 1915 he had offered a highly controversial amendment to the Commissioner of Education at the New York State Constitutional Convention. The measure proposed to strike out of the constitution a clause prohibiting the state from making direct appropriations to denominational schools. Actually, Smith had not pressed his resolution and later explained that he had intro-

[7] During the 1928 campaign, snobbery was unleashed against Mrs. Smith. When complimented by an ambassador's wife on her gown, for example, Mrs. Smith would supposedly reply: "You said a mouthful." Howe to Roosevelt, April 15, 1925, Howe Papers.

duced it to counter another amendment providing for the taxation of church property. Smith's record as governor might have seemed invulnerable to attacks on religious grounds. But his opponents pointed out that New York City, with Smith's approval, paid as much as $4 million in one year to parochial schools. Though a long-standing practice, it rebounded, of course, against Smith.[8]

Joe Tumulty warned the governor in 1927: "You must flatly, once and for all, dispose of the notion that the Pope will be the Colonel House of your administration"; and before the 1928 presidential race got under way, Smith settled to his own satisfaction the "problem" of his religion. He did so by taking advantage of an invitation offered him by Ellery Sedgwick, editor of the *Atlantic Monthly* and a supporter of McAdoo in 1924. Sedgwick had persuaded Smith to clear the air by replying to an Episcopal lawyer, Charles Marshall, who in an article published in Sedgwick's magazine had alleged a conflict between the American Constitution and the "Two Powers" dogma of the Roman Church, and had assembled evidence to try to show that American Catholics would have at best a divided allegiance between church and state. The draft of Smith's reply was written by Judge Joseph Proskauer with the approval of two priests, Francis P. Duffy and Francis J. Spellman; yet the sentiments were patently Smith's own. If religious questions arose, he said, he would follow the dictates of his own conscience. The governor also pointed to his own career as a pragmatic testament that theological controversies did not bind the judgment of Catholic statesmen. In fact, as governor of New York he had approved a bill providing for an extension of the grounds for divorce that the Catholic Church specifically opposed; and he objected emphatically to most forms of public censorship. "I believe," he wrote, "in the absolute separation of church and

[8] *New York State Constitutional Record, 1915* (Albany, 1916), I, 75; *Journal of the State Constitutional Convention of 1915* (Albany, 1916), p. 188. *The Nation,* CXXVII (October 24, 1928), 426.

state. . . ." But other events were to show that ammunition far more powerful than a single magazine article would be necessary in face of the religious issue.[9]

Those voters who were prepared to look beyond Smith's religion and his stand on prohibition to his political and economic philosophy could ascertain that though he had won a well-deserved reputation as a progressive, he was in a deeper and more lasting sense a conservative. Here he contrasted with Bryan, who remained an economic radical to the end. In 1924 Smith promised, if elected President, to reassert states' rights and to halt the expansion of federal taxes, laws, and commissions; "We must stop the dangerous overcentralization of Federal power," he wrote during Coolidge's first year in the White House. As presidential aspirant in 1928, as well as in 1924, Smith chose to advertise himself as a Jeffersonian. He instructed the Houston convention to build a platform on "unflinching application of Jeffersonian principles to the problems of the day." Rexford Tugwell admonished the candidate in the *New Republic:* "Cannot Governor Smith understand that—ridiculous as it sounds—the stronghold of Jeffersonianism has shifted from the South to the Northeast and that its latter day prophet is Coolidge?" The testimony of friends and critics alike suggests that Smith's later opposition to New Deal reform may not have been the about-face that is so often portrayed. Walter Lippmann in 1925 called Smith "the most powerful conservative in urban America." His remark is echoed and expanded upon in dozens of commentaries, including ones by Henry F. Pringle, Robert Moses, Edward Flynn, Mrs. Franklin D. Roosevelt,

[9] Later, Michael Williams, editor of *Commonweal,* remarked on Charles Marshall's letter to Smith and his subsequent book, *The Roman Catholic Church in the Modern State* (New York, 1928): "We called him a variety of names. We accused him of misquotation and bad faith. But the point is we did not reply to his book." *The Commonweal,* IX (January 2, 1929), 251. On Proskauer's role, see his *A Segment of My Times* (New York, 1950), p. 55, and personal interview, January 8, 1963. Tumulty to Smith, March 31, 1927, Tumulty Papers; *Atlantic Monthly,* CXXXIV (April 1927), 540–9; (May 1927), 721–8.

John Gunther, Bernard Bellush, Richard Neuberger, and George Mowry.[1]

Set against all this, to be sure, is a remarkably progressive streak in Smith's thinking. His gubernatorial administration made some major legislative and executive advances in education and factory labor; a "mildly humanitarian" program, the historian George Mowry calls it, but for its own day a very impressive program indeed. And he completely reorganized the state government, following to a certain extent the example of Governor Frank Lowden of Illinois. The reformist and the conservative tendencies in Smith are in any case quite compatible; it is possible to find their common source in his upbringing and early manhood. The city streets had schooled him in the facts of economic hardship and the plight of the ghetto; they had also set him forth upon a self-made career—and the economic individualism of the self-made is a matter of common record.

As a self- made man Smith had experienced in his own person

[1] On Smith's conservatism, see Samuel B. Hand: "Al Smith, Franklin D. Roosevelt, and the New Deal: Some Comments on Perspective," *The Historian*, XIII (May 1965), 365–83; *The New York Times*, June 22, 1924, p. 1; *New Republic*, LIII (February 1, 1928), 285; LIII (May 10, 1928), 302; Norman Thomas: "Letter to the Editor," *The Nation*, CXXVII (September 5, 1928), 226–7; Paul A. Carter: "The Campaign of 1928 Re-examined," *Wisconsin Magazine of History*, XLVI (Summer 1963), 263–72; and Jordan A. Schwarz: "Al Smith in the Thirties," *New York History*, XLV (October 1964), 327–8. A group of remarks about Smith's conservatism is quoted in David Burner: "The Brown Derby Campaign," *New York History*, XLVI (October 1965), 363. See Eleanor Roosevelt: *Autobiography* (New York, 1961), p. 152; Edward Flynn: Oral History Memoir, Columbia University, 1950, p. 5; Pringle: *Afred E. Smith*, p. 237; Walter Lippmann: *Men of Destiny* (New York, 1927), pp. 5–6; Robert Moses: *A Tribute to Governor Smith* (New York, 1962), p. 39; John Gunther: *Roosevelt in Retrospect* (New York, 1950), pp. 249–50; Bernard Bellush: *Franklin D. Roosevelt as Governor of New York* (New York, 1955), p. 97; Richard L. Neuberger and Stephen B. Kahn: *Integrity: The Life of George W. Norris* (New York, 1937), p. 177; Hand: "Al Smith," 368; Martin Feldman: "An Abstract of the Political Thought of Alfred E. Smith," unpublished doctoral dissertation, New York University, 1963, p. ii; Smith: *The Road to Victory* (1924), unpaged.

some of the privations of the urban poor; and this was the grounds of a progressivism that is less moral and evangelistic than practical, addressed to specifics. And because he was a politician, and as long as he remained active in politics on the city and state level, Smith had to take major account of the problems of his constituents, and could not have taken on the hard, arrogant indifference of some of the self-made who go into business; as a politician, moreover, he had the kind of constant contact with the urban poor, at least at second or third hand, that would have kept his sympathies genuinely alive, his memories fresh. And since he was not a businessman, he did not need to undergo those painful encounters with labor unions or socially inspired taxation that can make an entrepreneur, risen from the streets or the backwater farm, turn his back upon those who must continue to endure the hardships he has overcome. The complexity and technical nature of urban problems and the sophisticated structure of the urban political machines also conduce to a pragmatic reform rather than one of an ideological origin. The machine in particular may in its demand for loyalty offset the more humane impulses of its workers and protégés—even if one of its members gets as far up as a legislative seat, he will not find it to his advantage to support clean-government legislation, or to oppose business interests allied to a Tammany.

But Smith's background may have had its even deeper effect. He grew up in the atmosphere of moral conservatism, of endangered values carefully preserved, so vividly portrayed by Oscar Handlin in *The Uprooted;* and his traditionalist attitude toward some issues of social and moral conduct is striking. For all his apparent hostility to the blue-law temperament, he signed the so-called Padlock Bill of 1927, a Draconic measure that would close a theater for one year if any play it presented should be declared indecent by the courts. This came about after he mistakenly attended a Broadway play depicting Lesbianism. He reacted to Edward Bourdet's classic by asking the city police to take action against theaters not only when formal complaints were made, but also to anticipate what productions might be violating the law. His devotion to civil liberties had its limits. The principles he upheld in denouncing the Red-baiting Lusk Committee he abandoned in signing a bill that almost outlawed the Ku Klux Klan. He also refused to speak against a clean literature bill, supported by the Catholic Church, which would place the definition of obscenity in the hands of a jury and declare irrelevant the testimony of literary critics. He was notably hostile to woman suffrage; he relied heavily on the political advice of a woman, it is true, but one who believed in the mental inferiority of her sex. A conservatism of this sort, nurtured within the ordered community, would leave its mark upon economic as well as moral considerations; concretely sensitive to the special economic needs of the community, it would at the same time react instinctively whenever the pace of reform seemed to threaten the traditions and the orthodoxies.[2]

In sum, the man the Democrats nominated in 1928 possessed a peculiar mixture of characteristics, some as yet new to national politics, and some as old as American statesmanship; a breeding and a religion foreign to Jackson, Lincoln, and Theodore Roosevelt; a conservatism cut in part to a conventional American mold.

As the Democratic Convention got under way at Houston in June of 1928, Smith had little competition. Edwin T. Meredith of Iowa had inherited some of McAdoo's strength but died ten days before the balloting commenced; the wet Maryland Governor Albert Ritchie was impeded by the relative obscurity of his name. Cordell Hull of Tennessee and Senator Walter F. George of Georgia were also mentioned as possible nominees. But Senator Thomas J. Walsh, a dry Catholic from Montana, was the only figure other than Smith who might have been a formidable candidate. Democrats remembered Walsh as the in-

---

[2] Miss Paula Eldot will soon publish her doctoral dissertation, which connects Smith's reforms with the New Deal. "Al Smith, Reforming Governor," Yale University, 1961. Mrs. Belle Moskowitz declared her belief in the intellectual inferiority of women at a Columbia University forum held on April 28, 1926. *The New York Times*, April 29, 1926, p. 25. Mowry: *The Urban Nation, 1920–1960* (New York, 1965), p. 55.

vestigator of Teapot Dome and as chairman of the 1924 convention. Because he was a dry, Walsh found himself acceptable as a candidate to the Methodist Board of Temperance, Prohibition, and Public Morals. His supporters urged that he was uniquely qualified to be at once the candidate of the dry, Protestant, rural South and the wet, Catholic, urban North. Unlike Smith, however, Walsh had no large personal following who would support him in the election, and after suffering a severe defeat in the California primary he withdrew weeks before the convention opened. The McAdoo group made a last-ditch effort to stop Smith by supporting Senator James A. Reed of Missouri, who had recently visited twenty-eight states and entered several primaries without winning any. Reed was a former wet, and it was disastrous for the McAdoo element to pin its hopes on him.[3]

Smith and his supporters made a conscious effort at the 1928 Democratic Convention to eradicate the poor impression that lingered in the minds of those who had attended the 1924 conclave in New York. At that time, James J. Hoey, a Smith man, had kept the galleries full of unruly crowds who infuriated the McAdoo and Bryan supporters, and a host of Catholic clergy had by their presence antagonized the rural delegates. After his defeat in the New York convention, Smith had not bothered to hide his resentment. In an address to the convention, he had told the skeptical delegates that New York was the greatest city in the world; the speech had a self-congratulatory and arrogant tone. But in 1928 the Smith contingent had mellowed and matured its tactics. Two upstate Democrats, George R. Van Namee, State Democratic Chairman, and Franklin Delano Roosevelt, led the floor fight for the governor, and the more urban politicians stayed sober and respectable. Senator Thomas J. Walsh remarked that "there was no finer looking, better

[3] Walsh believed that southerners could have escaped the charge of religious bigotry had they supported him against Smith. But in spite of help from McAdoo, Walsh gained negligible southern support. Walsh to Hope Fitzgerald, June 20, 1928, Thomas F. Walsh Papers; McAdoo to Ray Stannard Baker, March 25, 1928, Baker Papers; Thomas B. Love to E. J. Mantooth, June 4, 1928, Love Papers.

dressed, more polite, less demonstrative delegation in the convention than the delegates sent by Tammany Hall." Some New Yorkers carried books of poetry with them, others tomes written in a foreign language. In the selection of the New York delegates, preference had been given to those born in the South. Heeding the advice of Joe Tumulty to "let the demands for your election come from elsewhere in America," Smith made certain that speeches seconding his nomination be representative of all regions. In addition, he had given up his fight for repeal of the two-thirds rule; repeal would have denied the South a veto that its politicians had decided not to use on Smith. Finally, the governor assured the delegates that the lengthy deliberations of the 1924 convention would not recur, and promised to withdraw if as many as ten ballots had to be taken.[4]

At the convention "things went off like clockwork," remarked Franklin Roosevelt. The proceedings that opened on June 26 closed on June 29, and except for a fist fight among the Mississippi delegates and another skirmish over the prohibition plank, the Democrats behaved like an assembly of Republicans. Roosevelt, who one day would bring to the party the surface harmony that Smith had not achieved, nominated the governor as "one who has the will to win—who not only deserves success

[4] In 1924 Franklin Roosevelt had expressed concern at the way delegates from the South and West were treated in New York. *The New York Times*, July 3, 1924, p. 2. A few of the delegates imagined that they had been attending a convention of Catholics in 1924. James W. Orr of Kansas, for example, wrote to Roosevelt: "The Democrats of the 47 states left the New York Convention with the spectacle of Catholic Priests, Bishops, Nuns and Catholic Institutions [*sic*] parading the aisles of the Convention." December 17, 1924, Roosevelt Papers. Claude Bowers wrote to Senator Samuel Ralston of "priests by dozens on the floor . . . once as many as 40." July 10, 1924, Ralston Papers. Smith's speech to the 1924 convention is in *Official Report of the Proceedings of the Democratic National Convention* . . . [of] . . . *1924* (Indianapolis, 1925), pp. 1012–15. *The New York Times*, December 9, 1927, p. 20; March 1, 1928, p. 1; June 8, 1928, p. 2; July 5, 1928, p. 18; *The Outlook*, CIL (July 4, 1928), 374–7; Tumulty to Smith, March 23, 1927, Tumulty Papers; Norman Mack to Alfred E. Smith, September 30, 1926, Mack Papers.

but commands it. Victory is his habit—the happy warrior, Alfred E. Smith." Although street-corner evangelists predicted that God would intervene to avert the catastrophe, and a local Baptist church held all-day and all-night fundamentalist prayer meetings, it was to no avail; the governor of New York was nominated when Ohio switched its vote at the end of the first ballot. The delegates refused to name him by acclamation, but it was an impressive victory, astounding in contrast to the previous convention. Smith was joined on the ticket by Senator Joseph T. Robinson, an Arkansas dry. A southern seminary head described the pairing of Smith and Robinson as an attempt to carry fire and water in the same bucket. Robinson—who earlier had been reported "unalterably opposed" to Smith's candidacy —was the first southerner, aside from Woodrow Wilson, to have a place on the national ticket since the Civil War.[5]

A fortnight before Smith won the Democratic nomination, Herbert Hoover was awarded that of the Republican party. A great success in far-flung engineering projects, Hoover had gone on to acquire an even wider reputation as a result of European relief work. And in bringing to several high federal posts, during and after the Great War, a vision and an administrative skill acquired in big business, he won solid acclaim as a progressive. Beginning in 1921 Hoover served as Secretary of Commerce, strengthening his department so that its many functions

[5] Roosevelt's nominating speech is in the *Official Report of the Proceedings of the Democratic National Convention* . . . [of] . . . *1928* (Indianapolis, 1928), p. 104. Joseph Proskauer claims to have written this speech. Personal interview, January 8, 1963. Roosevelt had used the epithet "Happy Warrior" in nominating Smith four years before; the name was applied to Theodore Roosevelt in a speech F.D.R. heard at Harvard. *Official Report of the Proceedings* . . . [of] . . . *1924*, p. 128. Roosevelt remarked on the convention to Sara Delano Roosevelt; quoted in Alfred B. Rollins, Jr.: "The Political Education of Franklin Roosevelt, His Career in New York Politics: 1909–1928," unpublished doctoral dissertation, Harvard University, 1953, II, 844. New York *Herald-Tribune*, June 20, 1928, p. 6; June 24, 1928, p. 3; *The New York Times*, February 11, 1928, p. 3; June 28, 1928, p. 3; October 29, 1928, p. 2.

visibly served the business community. On the important issue of prohibition, his background was that of a teetotaler, although in early June 1918, he had urged Wilson to veto the wartime prohibition act. On the religious question, Hoover occupied unassailable ground. "By blood and conviction," the Quaker candidate could say in 1928, "I stand for religious tolerance both in act and spirit." He spoke during the campaign neither of Smith's religion nor his affiliation with Tammany. And while the jovial Smith permitted countless photographs of himself with a cigar in one hand and his brown derby in the other, the meticulous Republican candidate refused even to allow pictures to be taken while he smoked a pipe. By any measure, Hoover's candidacy seemed ideal for the Republicans.[6]

In his speeches during the 1928 campaign, Hoover gave body to the promise of his wartime career. Far more than Smith, the Republican candidate looked forward to a material fulfillment for America: to the day, when, in the words of his acceptance address, "poverty will be banished from this nation." Hoover continued: "There is no guarantee against poverty equal to a job for every man. That is the primary purpose of the economic policies we advocate." In the same speech, delivered at his alma mater, Stanford University, Hoover called for a shorter work-day and greater purchasing power for labor, for ending the abuse of the injunction, and for collective bargaining; more public works, greater educational opportunity publically financed, and the spending of "hundreds of millions" of dollars for farm relief. A week later he declared against the national-origins principle of the immigration law, complaining of its favoritism toward Great Britain and Ireland, and still later he called for a "humanizing" of the law. While endorsing a limited number of reforms, Smith in his acceptance speech complained of the proliferation of government agencies and their rising

6 *The New York Times*, August 12, 1928, p. 2; George Peek to John J. Raskob, September 11, 1928, Chester C. Davis Papers; *Kiplinger Washington Letter*, March 5, 1924; Hoover: *The Memoirs of Herbert Hoover. II: The Cabinet and the Presidency, 1920–1933* (New York, 1952), 208.

costs; insisted that "Government should interfere as little as possible with business" and at the same time noted that a few corporations were making outrageous profits; advocated putting the tariff on "a strictly business basis"; and called for "fearless application of Jeffersonian principles." Neither candidate sought any general revision of taxes.[7]

Only on the matter of public power did Smith appear more progressive than Hoover. But as Norman Thomas, the Socialist candidate, put it: "He [Smith] accepts Hoover's general philosophy and reduces the battle between them to the comparatively insignificant question of power at Muscle Shoals and Boulder Dam." Elsewhere, Thomas criticized Smith for not having carried out his earlier proposals for regulating utilities. Hoover, on the other hand, tried to stand by his commitment not to let the government compete with private enterprise, but later in the campaign he did agree to public development of Muscle Shoals. And he had been a most active supporter of the proposed St. Lawrence Seaway, Boulder Dam, and the deepening of the Mississippi River. Smith's own willingness as governor to permit utility companies to contract for the transmission of power further narrowed the divergence between the two candidates on the question, yet Hoover condemned Smith's position as one of state socialism.[8]

[7] *Teamster's Magazine*, XXV (January 1928), 10–14; (June 1928), 13; *The New York Times*, August 12, 1928, pp. 1, 3; August 19, 1928, p. 3; August 23, 1928, pp. 2–3, October 17, 1928, pp. 1, 14.
[8] Smith called for a "fair and equal distribution of power through contractual agreements with the district companies." *Campaign Addresses of Governor Alfred E. Smith* (Washington, D.C., 1929), pp. 61–76. In his *Memoirs* Hoover listed development of water power resources as one of the subjects on which there was "no great difference between Governor Smith and myself." *Memoirs of Herbert Hoover*, II, 199. Senator George Norris, a Republican for whom a government program of flood control was of paramount importance, endorsed Smith with considerable reluctance; Norman Thomas sent Norris a list of public power topics on which Smith had never committed himself; and Franklin Roosevelt, Smith's successor in Albany, seemed in the recollection of Norris to be far more opposed to the utilities interests than Smith. Neuberger and Kahn: *Integrity*, pp. 176–7, 220. On the equivocal positions of both candidates, see Judson

On the issue of farm relief, Smith endorsed the "principle" of McNary-Haugen but not the equalization fee, and he was unspecific about possible remedies. During the campaign, Hoover dismissed the whole plan as unpromising—as indeed it was; it had earlier been rejected in the Republican Convention by a vote of 807 to 277. Instead, he proposed a special session of Congress—if the one ending in December 1928, should offer no solution—to set up a Federal Farm Loan Board, which would provide initial funds for a farmer-owned stabilization agency to offset "seasonal" and "periodic" surpluses. Speaking of the farm situation as the "most urgent economic problem in our nation today," Hoover hoped for the achievement of better than pre-war standards of agricultural prosperity, and his acceptance speech impressed Governor Frank Lowden of Illinois, although he still opposed Hoover on the farm issue. Understandably, farm support was divided between the two candidates.[9]

Hoover was more definite and more positive in his formulation of economic policy; he was, indeed, the more explicitly

King: *The Conservation Fight* (Washington, D.C., 1959), pp. 182–5. *The New York Times*, September 23, 1928, pp. 1–2; October 9, 1928, pp. 1–2; October 23, 1928, pp. 1, 3; October 25, 1928, pp. 1, 13; *The Nation*, CXVII (September 5, 1928), 226.

[9] Hoover was not duped by the agrarian myth: although "conscious of sentimental regret for the passing of . . . old-time conditions," he did not suggest a return to a more secure agricultural past. In reality, he said, the past had more toil, lower living standards, less leisure and recreation —"less of the comforts of home, less of the joy of living." *The New York Times*, August 22, 1928, p. 2. But in 1929 Senator George Norris remarked on how far Democratic leaders and his own Senate colleague, Smith Brookhart, had been deceived by what he called the "glittering generalities" in Hoover's campaign speeches. During the campaign Brookhart had reported that according to six congressmen Hoover had urged Coolidge not to veto the McNary-Haugen Bill. Norris to W. L. Locke, April 23, 1928, Norris Papers, Nebraska Historical Society. *The New York Times*, June 12, 1928, pp. 1, 3, 5; June 13, 1928, pp. 1, 9; June 15, 1928, pp. 1, 4, 12; August 12, 1928, pp. 2, 3; August 24, 1928, pp. 1, 3; August 27, 1928, p. 5; September 9, 1928, p. 3; September 20, 1928, pp. 1, 2; September 21, 1928, p. 1; September 22, 1928, p. 3; William T. Hutchinson: *Lowden of Illinois* (Chicago, 1957), II, 605–6; Gilbert C. Fite: *George Peek and the Fight for Farm Parity* (Norman, Okla., 1954), pp. 196–201.

progressive candidate—enough so that Coolidge's Secretary of the Treasury Andrew Mellon fiercely opposed his presidential candidacy. Of sixty-six social workers who responded to a pro-Smith campaign letter from Lillian Wald, forty-five declared for Hoover. Add to this progressivism a personal identity with the business community, a magnificently successful and splendidly humanitarian career, both public and private, and a manner and background appealing alike to urban and provincial voters; the Republican candidate would have presented an awesome challenge to any Democratic opponent.[1]

The conservative—or, at most, thinly progressive—cast of the Democratic campaign was reflected in its programs and personnel. The platform adopted at Houston was significant in its omissions and could be read as a passive endorsement of the status quo. A low tariff, one clearly traditional bulwark of the Democratic party, went unchampioned in a campaign financed by industrialists protected by Republican high tariffs. Reference to the League of Nations and the World Court was also omitted, while regard was paid to the isolationist sentiment of "freedom from entangling alliances." Newton Baker remarked of the platform that McKinley could have run on the tariff plank and Lodge on the one dealing with international relations. The convention gave only vague endorsement to the McNary-Haugen agricultural plan. Finally, the platform stressed economy, protection of states' rights, and "businesslike methods in Government."[2]

[1] *The New York Times*, June 11, 1928, pp. 1, 2; James E. Watson: *As I Knew Them* (Indianapolis, 1936), p. 256; Clarke A. Chambers: *Seedtime of Reform* (Minneapolis, 1963), p. 140.

[2] Smith clearly opposed a lowering of the tariff; see his statement in *The New York Times*, June 24, 1928, pp. 1, 2. Senator James E. Watson, on the other hand, complained that Hoover "was not a good protectionist." *As I Knew Them*, p. 259. Senator Peter Norbeck of South Dakota remarked to George Peek: "I see Mr. Work [the Republican National Chairman] is going to make the Tariff the issue. I do not suppose he read either platform, or he could not have talked that way." July 14, 1928, Chester C. Davis Papers. Clarence H. Cramer: *Newton D. Baker* (Cleveland, 1961), p. 224; Baker to William E. Dodd, November 16, 1928, Dodd

The governor's conservative strain, as well as his stubbornness, also revealed itself in his choice of John J. Raskob as National Chairman of the Democratic party. Raskob, in the manner of a Horatio Alger hero, had been born poor and had risen to the top as a secretary to Pierre S. DuPont; and this background appealed to Smith. In 1919 Raskob had acquired prominence as a business delegate at President Wilson's National Industrial Conference in Washington, where the position of the business representatives for the open shop and against labor's unimpeded right to organize and to bargain collectively brought the meeting to a halt. By 1928 Raskob was vice president of E. I. DuPont de Nemours and chairman of the finance committee of General Motors. He also served as a director of the Bankers Trust, American Surety, and County Trust companies. In the then current *Who's Who* he accurately listed himself as a capitalist; William Leuchtenburg describes him as an "arch reactionary."[3]

Raskob, like Smith, was a devout Catholic and an ardent wet. He had contributed more than a million dollars to the church, and in recognition of loyalty Pope Pius XI made him a Knight of the Order of Saint Gregory the Great. Raskob saw the Pope in 1927 and again in 1928 when the industrialist received a special benediction and was made a private chamberlain in the papal household. George Van Namee, who had served in the complementary position of preconvention manager, was also a Catholic, as were a number of state chairmen, like that of Iowa. As for

---

Papers; *The New York Times,* September 9, 1928, pp. 1, 3; *Official Report of the Proceedings* ... [of] ... *1928,* pp. 186–96.
[3] Roosevelt, Josephus Daniels, Josiah Bailey, and other Democrats saw in the appointment of Raskob a break with the conciliatory spirit of the convention. Roosevelt to Daniels, July 20, 1928, Roosevelt Papers; Daniels to George Fort Milton, n.d., copy in Furnifold Simmons Papers, 1928; Bailey to George Van Namee, July 20, 1928, and Bailey to Joseph Proskauer, July 12, 1928, Bailey Papers; Thomas B. Love to Davis S. Rose, July 21, 1928, Love Papers; *The New York Times,* October 11, 1919, p. 1; October 18, 1919, p. 2; October 20, 1919, p. 1; October 24, 1919, p. 1; October 25, 1919, III, 5; August 8, 1924, pp. 1, 3; *Who's Who in America, 1928–1929,* XV (Chicago, 1928), 1727; Leuchtenburg, *Franklin D. Roosevelt and the New Deal, 1932–1940* (New York, 1963), p. 5.

prohibition, Raskob pronounced it a "damnable affliction," and on receiving his appointment he called it the "chief issue" of the campaign. He was, in a way, a counterpart of the professional dry, for lately he had spent a large part of his time and energy as a director of the Association Against the Prohibition Amendment; and when he took on the job of National Chairman, he did so knowing that the Democratic party would serve the interests of the Association, which he energetically promoted until his retirement in 1932. In 1928 his remarks on the liquor issue were stronger even than those of Smith himself, and on this subject, at least, Raskob's influence surpassed that of Belle Moskowitz, one of Smith's longstanding advisers.[4]

Raskob was not a man to attract either organized labor or the hinterland; and as if this were not enough, southerners could not have found it to their liking that in the 1928–9 edition of *Who's Who* he had listed himself as a Republican. "I do not know Mr. Raskob personally," wrote Walter Lippmann after seeing him in action for three years, "but from watching his brief political career I have the impression that in politics he is an innocent lamb." The choice of Raskob, which was made against the objection of his closest advisers, foreshadowed the way in which in the course of the campaign Smith would react to the charges of his opponents. He seemed determined to flaunt what was most controversial about his candidacy.[5]

The new chairman did bring to the campaign a skill in money raising unprecedented in previous Democratic history, and no

[4] *The New York Times*, April 11, 1928, p. 15; July 12, 1928, p. 1; *Christian Science Monitor*, July 13, 1928, p. 1; Mabel Walker Willebrandt to Bishop Cannon, July 16, 1928, Cannon Papers; Belle Moskowitz to Josiah Bailey, July 26, 1928, Bailey Papers; Nathan Miller to Hoover, July 12, 1928, Hoover Papers.

[5] *The New York Times* intimated that Smith's personal preference for governor of New York was not the popular Franklin Roosevelt but Owen D. Young, Chairman of the Board of General Electric. July 16, 1928, p. 1. *Who's Who in America, 1928–1929*, p. 1927; *The New York Times*, July 12, 1928, p. 1; August 29, 1928, p. 5; Vaughn D. Bornet: *Labor and Politics in a Democratic Republic* (Washington, D.C., 1964), p. 76; Lippmann, *Interpretations, 1931–1932* (New York, 1932), p. 257.

doubt his own enormous wealth and his connections dictated his choice as chairman. Thomas Fortune Ryan, who had made some $200,000,000 in street railway franchises, William Kenny, a wealthy New York building contractor, former Senator Clarence W. Watson of West Virginia, John W. Davis, and other conservatives generously responded to his requests for contributions. In all Raskob's Democratic National Committee disbursed $5,342,000 against $3,529,000 for the Republican headquarters: in 1928, for the second time in American history, the Democrats spent more than the Republicans in the national campaign. Raskob himself underwrote Smith's campaign in the amount of half a million dollars, and gifts to the two parties were roughly proportionate in size, although Hoover's preconvention campaign was clearly financed by smaller gifts than Smith received. Yet the addition of Raskob to the Smith retinue deepened the already existing problems attached to the Happy Warrior's candidacy.[6]

During the convention a measure of peace had been maintained between North and South; the very choice of Houston as the convention city had been aimed at appeasing southern Democrats, for not since 1860 had a Democratic convention met in the South. But even before appointing Raskob, Smith shattered the harmony that prevailed at Houston when he sent an important telegram to the adjourning delegates declaring for "fundamental changes in the present provisions of national prohibition." The statement was taken as a rejection of the more moderate platform plank. Franklin Roosevelt later wrote of that "fool telegram," Josephus Daniels called it "unnecessary and ill-timed," and the Anti-Saloon League reacted by an immediate endorsement of Hoover—the first candidate the League had ever officially supported. Actually, it was not clear what course Smith would pursue with regard to prohibition should he

[6] On campaigns for all levels of government combined, the Republicans continued to outspend the Democrats by about $9 to $7 million. *The New York Times*, May 12, 1928, p. 1; Raskob to Bernard Baruch, November 17, 1928, Baruch Papers; James K. Pollock, Jr.: "Campaign Funds in 1928," *American Political Science Review*, XXIII (February 1929), 63, 65.

achieve the presidency. Walter Lippmann predicted that he would follow a moderate policy of law enforcement; certainly, Lippmann observed, the Democrats could do no worse job of it than the Republicans had beeen doing. To other commentators, "fundamental change" suggested repeal. As the campaign progressed, Smith's meaning became clearer. In August he took an advanced stand when he called for state control of liquor, and later he said he would lead a nationwide fight for a change in the prohibition law.[7]

The good fellowship of the convention was dissolved by the Smith telegram and the Raskob appointment. The campaign would henceforth take on a new tone, but nowhere more emphatically than in the South. Bishop James Cannon, Jr., of the Methodist Episcopal Church, South, and Dr. Arthur J. Barton, Chairman of the Committee on Social Service of the Southern Baptist Convention, met in Asheville, North Carolina, in July to form an anti-Smith group. Cannon in particular worked indefatigably in directing the *ad hoc* association in its mission of defeating the New Yorker; he raised ample funds, some of them donated by the Republican National Committee, to spread propaganda into every area of the South.[8]

Through the Anti-Smith Democrats and other organizations the South was encouraged to refuse Smith its traditional hospitality when he made a campaign trip there—he had first visited the region in April of 1928. Newspapers patronizingly reported that at the town of Biltmore, North Carolina, Smith had said to a cheering crowd: "I hope to meet yez-all personally." In his autobiography, Smith wrote that in Louisville a policeman accused

[7] At the convention a petition had been displayed that purportedly represented 6.4 million southerners opposed to any candidate not fully committed to prohibition. Roosevelt to James C. Bonbright, March 11, 1930, Roosevelt Papers; *The New York Times*, June 30, 1928, p. 1; July 1, 1928, pp. 1, 6; August 22, 1928, p. 1; September 23, 1928, p. 1; September 30, 1928, pp. 1–2; October 12, 1928, p. 1; *Harper's Magazine*, CLVI (January 1928), 133–9.
[8] *The New York Times*, November 2, 1928, p. 24; Rembert G. Smith to Cannon, August 4, 1928, Bishop Warren A. Candler Papers.

him of being drunk, the whole police force was rude, and someone turned the heat too high in the auditorium where he delivered a speech. After a series of discourtesies on October 11,
Smith was "solemn, silent and sullen." It appeared that although
most of the southern politicians had accepted Smith in the convention the majority of voters would not support him. "Of the
Southern delegates who voted for Smith," wrote one observer,
"not one reflected the real wishes of his constituents."[9]

While it was most pronounced in the South, the denominational attack on Smith was national in scope. A large contingent
of ministers, including the popular Billy Sunday, fought Smith
by every means available. Sunday called himself the "Ambassador of God" out "to defy the forces of hell—Al Smith and the
rest of them."[1] A Methodist paper with countrywide circulation
declared: "Governor Smith has a constitutional right to run for
President, even though a Catholic. This we confess. And we have

[9] John E. Sullivan, Smith's physician who accompanied him on the campaign, recalled that when the candidate's bodyguard, William Roy, went
down to the steamroom to see what the matter was, he found a cordon
of policemen protecting the engineers who were stoking the furnace.
Personal interview, March 25, 1963. *Time*, VIII (April 23, 1928), 8; Alfred
E. Smith: *Up to Now* (New York, 1929), pp. 400–1; Stuart Deskins: "The
Presidential Election of 1928 in North Carolina," unpublished doctoral
dissertation, University of North Carolina, 1944, p. 81; Sherwin L. Cook:
Torchlight Parade (New York, 1929), p. 274.
[1] Sunday called Smith's male supporters "the damnable whiskey politicians,
the bootleggers, crooks, pimps and business men who deal with them,"
while the New Yorker's female supporters were "street-walkers." After
the election Vice President Charles Curtis sent Sunday a letter thanking
him for his "valued assistance" and "good work in the South." One of the
most intemperate of the churchmen who opposed Smith came not from
the South but from the Calvary Baptist Church in New York City: in a
speech in Dallas, John Roach Straton announced that "Smith is the
nominee of the worst forces of hell." And in Riverside Park, New York,
Dr. Ed Bywater delivered his popular sermon "To Hell with the Pope."
The New York Times, August 26, 1928, p. 3; September 4, 1928, p. 6;
Memphis *Commercial Appeal*, October 25, 1928, p. 5. William G. Mc-
Loughlin, Jr.: *Billy Sunday Was His Real Name* (Chicago, 1955), p. 285.
The New York Times, September 24, 1928, p. 2; *Book of Horror* (a col-
lection of inflammatory literature used in the 1928 campaign), Columbia
University Library.

a constitutional right to vote against him because he is a Catholic. This we assert." The Moral Welfare Department of the Presbyterian Church of America adopted a resolution denouncing any prospective wet candidate. And the leaders of four million Baptists voted in convention to warn the Democratic party against a Catholic candidate. Dr. Mordecai Ham of the First Baptist Church, the largest in Oklahoma City, made the penalty for voting Democratic clear enough: "If you vote for Al Smith, you're voting against Christ and you'll all be damned." Lutherans were most emphatic in opposing Smith for his religion. Even the Unitarian leader, Dr. Alfred C. Dieffenbach, called to mind the Roman Catholic persecution of Unitarians in other countries and declared that no Catholic should be elected to the presidency. One scholar later noted that "the people seemed to have one thing in their minds—Al Smith's religion."[2]

Such was the denominational opposition to Smith; the nation-wide attack it fostered was in most cases the least fair of the campaign, for it was the most difficult to combat. Smith was accused of all the crimes of the Spanish Inquisition and the medieval popes. Bishop Edwin Mouzon of the Methodist Episcopal Church, South, compiled in the North Carolina *Christian Advocate* a list of "Catholic crimes" in Mexico and England. In the same periodical Mouzon suggested topics for political-religious sermons. In New Jersey a confectioner sent along with his invoices copies of "The Inquisitorial Horrors of the Roman Catholic Church, as Described by an Officer in Napoleon's Army." The fundamentalist *Fellowship Forum* caricatured Smith driving a beer truck bearing the sign "Make America

[2] Bishop Warren A. Candler of Emory University, among others, ventured the hope that his fellow Methodists would not bring their church into politics. Cook: *Torchlight Parade*, p. 274; Wesleyan *Christian Advocate* of Atlanta: quoted in Michael Williams: *The Shadow of the Pope* (New York, 1932), pp. 192, 195; *The New York Times*, May 28, 1928, p. 3; August 17, 1928, pp. 1, 2; August 21, 1928, p. 4; October 3, 1928, p. 3; *America*, XXXIV (October 3, 1928), 654; *The Commonweal*, VIII (October 3, 1928), 654; *Christian Register*, CVII (November 22, 1928), 948–9; William G. Carleton: "The Popish Plot of 1928: Smith-Hoover Presidential Campaign," *The Forum*, CXII (September 1949), 145.

100 per cent Catholic, Drunk, and Illiterate," and another cartoon, showing a buxom woman giving a cup to a reclining cleric, bore the caption "The Pope Converted the Vatican into a House of Ill Fame." The flavor of the *Fellowship Forum* is caught in its advertisement for an "eye-opening" ten-cent pamphlet: "Can a Bobbed-Haired Woman Go to Heaven?" The *Forum* and other such publications gave wide circulation to a spurious Knights of Columbus oath: "I will spare neither sex, age nor condition, and [I swear] that I will hang, waste, boil, flay, strangle and burn alive these infamous heretics [Protestants]; rip up the stomachs and wombs of their women and crush infants' heads against the wall, in order to annihilate forever their execrable race. That when the same cannot be done openly, I will secretly use the poison cup, the strangulation cord, the steel of the poniard, or the leaden bullet [and so forth]."[3]

Senator Thomas Heflin of Alabama delivered some of the most vitriolic anti-Catholic attacks on record. Initially he used the floor of the Senate to denounce Smith and the Pope, and to urge the deportation of all Catholics; but in 1928 he carried his message throughout the country. In that year as before, one of the groups to pay his speaking expenses was the Ku Klux Klan. With Heflin, anti-Catholicism became a mania, growing into a conviction that the Catholics were planning to murder him. The Cincinnati *Catholic Telegram* said of the Alabamian—who slept with a gun under his pillow—that he had "strangely overlooked what is probably the most striking proof of the papal invasion of the United States. The telegraph pole bears the form of the cross from one end of the country to the other. . . . The plan was devised by none but a mastermind."[4]

[3] Mouzon: "The Roman Catholic Question," North Carolina *Christian Advocate*, August 2, 1928, p. 9; *The New York Times*, September 29, 1928, p. 3.
[4] A Holy Name Society sent Heflin a check for $250 "in appreciation of aid to the Catholic church." *The New York Times*, June 20, 1928, p. 5. A fellow senator described Heflin's delusion as "the airiest bubble that

With a co-religionist as a major presidential candidate for the first time in the nation's history, American Catholics were naturally on the defensive in 1928. A study of Catholic periodicals has shown that few openly urged the election of Smith. Many Catholics thought that only when one of their number became President could they achieve full social status in America, and they did not choose to forfeit their opportunity by confirming the fears of Protestants. Ellery Sedgwick of the *Atlantic Monthly* complimented the Catholic clergy on its good manners and restraint. Their discretion in the campaign contrasted with the behavior of many Protestant ministers who chose not to respect the principle for which they spoke, the separation between religion and politics. In Ohio two thousand of them willingly heard Mrs. Mabel Walker Willebrandt, Assistant Attorney General of the United States, urge them to use their pulpits and clerical influence against Smith. A public outburst would have greeted a comparable appeal for Smith before an assembly of Catholic priests.[5]

had ever found lodgment in an empty head." Circular letter of W. Earl Hotales: "Tom Heflin National Legion Secretary," May 5, 1930, Heflin Papers, Howard College [Alabama] Library. The Catholic paper is quoted in *America*, XXXIV (June 9, 1938), 197. For Heflin's harangues in the Senate, see the *Congressional Record, Senate*, May 3, 1928, pp. 7697–700; May 8, 1928, pp. 8050–9; May 11, 1928, pp. 8381–2; May 17, 1928, pp. 8835–42; May 23, 1928, pp. 9542–51; May 28, 1928, pp. 10209–21 and 10283–7. *The New York Times*, June 1, 1928, p. 1; June 16, 1928, p. 1; June 18, 1928, p. 1; September 25, 1928, p. 6. Virginius Dabney: *Liberalism in the South* (Chapel Hill, N.C., 1932), p. 273; *The Commonweal*, VIII (June 20, 1928), 176.

5 Mrs. Willebrandt spoke at the request of the Republican National Committee. "There are 2,000 pastors here," she said. "You have in your churches more than 600,000 members of the Methodist Church in Ohio alone. That is enough to swing the election." *The New York Times*, September 8, 1928, pp. 1, 3; October 25, 1932, p. 15. Moore: *A Catholic Runs for President*, pp. 175–8; Helen M. Matzke: "The Attitude of the Catholic Periodicals in the Election of 1928," unpublished Master's essay, Columbia University, 1929, p. 13; *Current History*, XXIX (December 1928), 377–81.

Could there be a well-founded suspicion of Smith on religious grounds? Some Catholic leaders, it is true, had indicated a willingness to bring the church into politics. In 1922, for example, two priests, John A. Ryan—the New Deal liberal of a later day—and Moorhouse F. X. Millar had published *The State and the Church*, a work that might offend many Protestants too sophisticated to base their thinking upon stories of the inquisitorial atrocities of other lands and centuries. Ryan and Millar used as one of their texts the famous 1895 Encyclical of Pope Leo, which stated in part that "it would be very erroneous to draw the conclusion that in America is to be sought the type of the most desirable status of the Church. . . . She would bring forth more abundant fruits if, in addition to liberty, she enjoyed the favor of the laws and the patronage of public authority." In one of his essays included in the book, Ryan argued that "the State should officially recognize the Catholic religion as the religion of the Commonwealth. . . . Should [non-Catholics] be permitted to practice their own form of worship?" he asked. "If these are carried on within the family, or in such an inconspicuous manner as to be an occasion neither of scandal nor of perversion to the faithful. . . ." Ryan insisted that in America the Church would never be so recognized and that tolerance was a precious part of the American Catholic heritage; but he added that "error has not the same rights as truth."[6]

It was not alone the autocratic remarks of individual priests that antagonized many intelligent Protestants toward the presi-

[6] (New York, 1922), pp. 33–6. *The Manual of Christian Doctrine*, a Catholic text for parochial elementary schools, was scandalous to Ryan; he claimed, hopefully, that "there is no evidence that the section on the relations of Church and State has been taken seriously by the average teacher. . . ." Francis L. Broderick: *Right Reverend New Dealer, John A. Ryan* (New York, 1963), pp. 118–20, 176. In addition, the reproofs the Church offered to liberal American Catholics such as Bishop Keane and Archbishop Ireland seemed to underscore the foreign and autocratic character of the Church. Some Catholic churchmen, it should be noted, had insisted upon the separation of Church and State even if Catholics someday predominate. Robert D. Cross: *The Emergence of Liberal Catholicism in America* (Cambridge, Mass., 1958), pp. 74, 195–205.

dency of a Roman Catholic. The example of several European and Latin American countries, where the Catholic Church had inexorably attempted to control political as well as spiritual affairs, was particularly disturbing. As Catholics became more numerous, might not the same fate befall America? At an International Eucharistic Congress held in Chicago during the summer of 1926, Smith was kept forward as the major lay figure; and before attending the meeting he had held a reception for eight cardinals at City Hall in New York, knelt before two of the visiting prelates, and kissed the ring of the papal legate, Cardinal Banzano. The Vatican itself made known that it would rejoice to see a Catholic President of the United States. Rome, apparently, was interested, and it is not odd that some Protestants—even though the threat of papal control was absurd—believed they had ample reason to take offense at that interest. Smith's unequivocal stand in the *Atlantic Monthly* in 1927 was not enough to dispel these fears.[7]

Here again, the conduct of Smith requires commentary. A Catholic both loyal and stalwart in the assertion of his faith, Smith had before 1928 engaged in many small expressions of his Catholicism remarkable for a hardened politician aiming for national election, and as constitutional delegate and governor had taken political actions perhaps reflective of his religion. During the presidential campaign of 1928 he continued to follow the path he had always trod, making no apparent concessions to the instinctive revulsion shared by much of America against the

[7] Instances were reported of the participation of Catholic churchmen in politics. Bishop Alma B. White: *Heroes of the Fiery Cross* (Zarephath, N.J., 1928), p. 122; Edgar I. Fuller: *The Visible of the Invisible Empire* (Denver, 1925), pp. 40–8; William Hall Allen to William Allen White, July 19, 1928, White Papers, Library of Congress; Caroline I. White to Bishop James Cannon, Jr., August 21, 1928, Cannon Papers. There also were frequent reports of Republicans aiding the anti-Catholic crusade; see, for instance, *The New York Times*, November 2, 1928, p. 24. Smith himself listed the Klan as a Republican ally, saying that it got a great deal of encouragement from Republican leaders. *The New York Times*, October 30, 1928, pp. 1, 4; June 16, 1926, p. 1; June 22, 1926, p. 14; *Christian Register*, CVII (January 6, 1927), 3.

symbols of Catholicism. In September he even volunteered to serve as an acolyte during a New Jersey church service.[8] Smith's conduct on the matter of religion must, it is true, be judged on grounds somewhat different from those by which his defiance of prohibition is tested. In showing at least some respect for the law of the constitution and for that large segment of the people who had called for the prohibition amendment, Smith would have combined good politics with good morals. But with regard to the religious question, morality and political strategy had to diverge; the minutest compromise of religious faith and observance would have been as morally questionable as it would be politically shrewd. Of course, it may be pointed out that the display of an autographed picture of the Pope in Smith's Albany office, for example, falls outside the scope of religious duty. Yet even here, Al Smith's conscience might have equated the least coyness in the affirmation of his faith with moral cowardice.

But all this does not free Smith from the charge of provincialism on the religious issue. For if he could not shirk his religion itself, or modify the slightest symbolic act of allegiance, he could at least have addressed himself more fully to the fears in which so many of his fellow Americans had been reared. Even assuming that the Smith forces may at first have pinned their hopes on the *Atlantic Monthly* article—which the governor had been reluctant to write—and reasoned that further reference on their part to the religious controversy would only more inflame the issue, it should have become apparent during the course of the camaign that nothing could have worsened the situation as it already stood. Smith might have acknowledged the occasional alliance between Latin Catholicism and political tyranny and then pointed to the historical American tradition of religious harmony, as embodied in Lord Baltimore; he and his supporters might even have made explicit contrast between their position, along with the position of countless of their fellow religionists in the United States, and that of Catholic reactionaries; he might have sought out the support of Protestant

[8] *The New York Times*, September 5, 1928, pp. 1, 4.

clergymen or outstanding laymen; he might have increased the Protestant contingent in his campaign committee.[9] In short, Smith might have acted as though he were aware of the anxiety, however silly or bigoted, that was felt by much of rural American Protestantism, as one who shared with it a sense of America's role in preserving religious liberty. A provincial Protestant ruralism and a provincial Catholic urbanism stared at each other in uncomprehending hostility, and with the single exception of Smith's article of 1927, neither attempted to break the impasse with a liberal word or gesture.

The contrast between Al Smith's handling of the religious question and John Fitzgerald Kennedy's is compelling. Smith discussed the issue once during the campaign. In his speech at Oklahoma City he lashed out angrily at a hostile audience, whom he attacked for hiding under the cloak of antiprohibition. He overpersonalized the religious debate and used explosive gesticulations to match his words.[1] Kennedy, on the other hand, spoke often and directly to critics of his religion. "My experience . . . shows it is a matter of great concern," he said. "I am delighted

[9] Senator Burton K. Wheeler, Democrat of Montana, asked that prominent Norwegians and Swedes be enlisted in his state to defend Smith on the religious issue: "The need for that kind of approach ought to be pounded into the heads of those simple-minded people in New York who think the whole world revolves around that section of the country east of the Hudson River. The Smith forces may be playing fine politics as far as the East is concerned, but they did not display very much intelligence thus far with reference to the West in the selection of their advisers." Wheeler to Key Pittman, July 21, 1928, Pittman Papers. Lynn Haines, a journalist who wrote an unpublished manuscript, "Al Smith and Certain Soothsayers," added to Wheeler's criticisms with a warning for Smith: "He must go west—not merely west of Broadway, not west of the Hudson, but west of the Alleghanies [*sic*]. From Ohio west and northwest and southwest, clear to the coast, is electoral territory ripe for Smith conquest. The key to the situation is the great agricultural depression—that plus a fighting progressive slant to the whole campaign. . . . Governor Smith will be nominated; if he goes far enough west of Broadway—in understanding and sympathy and spirit and purpose—he will easily be elected"; Chester C. David Papers. Tom Connally also considered Smith's background "provincial." *My Name Is Tom Connally* (New York, 1954), p. 132.
[1] *Daily Oklahoman*, September 21, 1928, p. 1.

to answer any questions about it. . . . There is nothing improper in discussing it." In a speech to the Greater Houston Ministerial Association, he gave his audience the benefit of the doubt for opposing him. He was specific, moreover, in his remarks about what worried that audience: "No church or church school," he said, should be granted "public funds or political preference." Kennedy asserted his opposition to state control of religion; and on the matter of birth control he promised to follow his own conscience without regard to outside religious pressures. Nor had Kennedy compounded the religious problem by politically amateurish appointments. As National Chairman, for example, he named Senator Henry M. Jackson of Washington, after passing over a prominent Catholic congressman. Undoubtedly, Kennedy had profited from Smith's mistakes, as he had also profited from the liberalization of his church.[2]

Smith's religion did not stand alone as an issue in the campaign; opponents saw it as but one of a complex of characteristics that marked the New Yorker as a personality alien to the American grain. Smith was not merely a wet; he was a "Bowery wet," and his position toward alcohol, like his faith, affronted not only the most ignorant but also Americans of a genteel, middle-class tradition—offended their gentility or their conception of Americanness as much or more than their morals. As a social liability, Smith's wet position vied with a number of mannerisms that stamped him as a Gotham Cockney. Over the radio, then a new and impressive contribution to presidential campaigns, Smith's voice could be heard only with difficulty, for he spoke indistinctly and insisted on dashing from one side of the microphone to the other. His speeches themselves lacked grace and symmetry. He employed "ain't" and "he don't," and changed "work" to "woik"—forms of speech defended by the Johns Hopkins philologist Kemp Malone. His language, gestures, and physical appearance, all of which the new motion-picture newsreels conveyed, stamped him as an intruder in national politics. Even the two spittoons in Smith's Albany office

[2] *The New York Times,* August 29, 1960, p. 1; September 13, 1960, pp. 1, 22.

seemed to speak loudly of his social origins. His eighth-grade education was insufficient, critics insisted, to equip him to face national and world problems, and on more than one occasion Smith himself admitted that he was interested only in the concrete and did not read books. When Smith visited Lincoln's birthplace in Kentucky, he bought a corn-cob pipe at the souvenir stand and immediately stuck it between his teeth. On another occasion, he joked with reporters about the needs of the states west of the Mississippi: "What states *are* west of the Mississippi?" he asked. When he met Babe Ruth, Smith—who had signed bills legalizing boxing and Sunday baseball—remarked: "Say, I read in a paper somewhere that in some place —I think in Pennsylvania—somebody wouldn't let the series be announced on Sunday. Well, I'd like to see that place," mused the Governor, "it must be a hot one." He did not even hesitate to make a potentially abrasive public demonstration of fellowship with Tammany Hall, that embodiment of big-city politics and values. Before the national convention Smith visited Tammany, where, after a two-years absence from the annual ceremonies, he was reinstated as an honorary Sachem. Because Tammany Hall had lasted a century, he said, it must be "all right."[3]

In sum, the matter of Smith's Catholicism, his obliviousness to Tammany's bad name, and his intransigence toward the Eighteenth Amendment blended with other characteristics less explicitly reflective of Smith's political outlook, yet combining to

[3] Mildred Duncan to Lillian Wald, October 22, 1928, Wald Papers; New York *Sun*, August 24, 1932, p. 1; *The New York Times*, November 1, 1928, p. 3; Pringle: *Alfred E. Smith*, p. 338. The various anecdotes are in Cook: *Torchlight Parade*, p. 295; Pringle: *Alfred E. Smith*, p. 97; Geoffrey Parsons: Oral History Memoir, Columbia University, 1949, p. 30; *The New York Times*, October 11, 1928, p. 1—the Babe Ruth story, quoted in the *Times*, appeared as a human interest item at the top of p. 1. *The New York Times*, July 15, 1928, p. 2; October 27, 1928, p. 12. On Smith and Tammany Hall, see the *New Republic*, LVI (October 10, 1928), 188–90, and the more critical article in *The Nation*, CXXVI (June 13, 1928), 659. On his becoming a Sachem, see *The New York Times*, May 15, 1928, p. 1; July 5, 1928, p. 1.

create a total impression of the man. A Florida Democrat told Roosevelt that "the sidewalks of New York didn't synchronize with my thought . . . of the dignity of the job." One woman wrote to Roosevelt:

> There were vast numbers who did not regard him as a fit man, either by birth, culture, dignity, or breadth of vision, to fill the great office of President of the United States. One who had never until middle life traveled beyond the counties of his native state could not possibly have other than a provincial viewpoint. His superficial knowledge of nationwide affairs, hastily acquired, could not give him the understanding or sympathetic outlook necessary in dealing with great national and international problems.

Another correspondent of Roosevelt identified a mélange of reasons for voting Republican; this is one of many "know-nothing" letters written to political figures in 1928:

> Mr. Roosevelt: Birds of a feather flock together, and if you uphold Smith and help him get in it is obvious you are in Tammany's pay. Of course he may be better than the ordinary man but Tammany has not become honest. . . . Everyone knows that Tammany uses Public School surplus to supply parochial schools so god knows what they will do when he gets to be President. . . . If you ever heard the Knights of Columbus oath I am sure you a Protestant would be through with [Roman Catholics]. They say it is all right to steal or cut out the bellies (the exact words used) of Protestants. . . . Why people are saying that he will make us have war with Mexico and he will so he can kill off some Protestants. . . . We can't trust them, don't you know that their church and the Pope come first, and they will be subject as it was to them first, and to America and her ideals second. . . . You ought to know the corruption there is in New York with Smith having a private telegraph wire to Tammany Hall, so of course he'll have a private wire to Tammany if he is made President. . . . An eyewitness saw him carried on the train

dead drunk after his mother's funeral. He'd make a fine President, getting the Protestants drunk like he did when he was speaker or leader of the floor, in Albany, just so they would vote his way. And everyone knows his sons had to get married. And what kind of a woman would that be in the White House. Some difference from Mrs. Coolidge, who is educated and refined and cultured. Mrs. Smith's father was a saloon keeper, and kept Prostitute Houses and yet you'd help those kind of people get in. Well, all I can say is God help you and all of us, if they do get in.

From an American who wants an American President who will protect America's Ideals, first, last, and always.[4]

Even in his choice of an executive committee, Smith displayed a lack of sensitivity toward the touchy social and ethnic issues of the campaign. The selection of Raskob has already been mentioned; the rest of the committee came principally from New York and was largely composed of first- or second-generation Jews and Irish Catholics. Some of them were adept at urban politics and most had no connection with Tammany, but in general they showed the limited outlook of their candidate. One of Smith's closest advisers was James J. Hoey, the man who led the raucous galleries at the 1924 convention as they cheered "Oil! Oil!" to embarrass McAdoo. Joe Cohn of the tabloid New York *Evening Graphic*, Smith's press contact man, was another bad choice; as Smith himself observed in an interview some ten years later, his snappy clothes and overbearing manner made it almost impossible for him to win over conservative, middle-aged newspapermen of the West and South. Conversely, Smith ignored advice from most western and southern Democrats. As early as May 1927, Joe Tumulty had criticized him for failing to consult out-of-state Democrats traveling through New York. Franklin Roosevelt, who was definitely not a member of Smith's inner circle, objected vigorously to the way Smith ran his presi-

[4] G. G. Dodge of Tampa to Franklin Roosevelt, August 20, 1931, Democratic National Committee Papers; Mary Robbins Long to Franklin Roosevelt, February 12, 1929, Roosevelt Papers.

dential campaign, especially to the publicity organization, which he described as a combination of Mrs. Moskowitz and the advertising section of General Motors. On his campaign train Smith took with him Tammany judges and other New Yorkers; the only noneasterners to accompany him for very long were J. Bruce Kremer, the conservative Montanian closely associated with the Anaconda Copper Company, and former Senator Gilbert Hitchcock, who had voted against the prohibition amendment in 1920. Senator Robinson, the southern vice presidential candidate, who considered Raskob's acceptance remarks "inadvisable and unnecessary," did not hear from Smith for almost two weeks after the notification ceremonies.[5]

Are the Smith forces free of responsibility for the misunderstandings and antagonisms of the campaign? In answer, we may first acknowledge that no amount of political skill on their part,

[5] In complaining of Smith's tactics to Harry Byrd of Virginia, Roosevelt said: "Things depend so much on the way they are put." August 20, 1928, Roosevelt Papers. F.D.R. complained bitterly of being treated as "window dressing" in the campaign. Memorandum, April 6, 1938. Elliott Roosevelt, ed. *Franklin D. Roosevelt: His Personal Letters*, II, 771-3. George Peek, managing the campaign in the farm states, explained to one supporter why he was being ignored at Smith's headquarters: "Things are moving so lively with them in New York that it is pretty difficult for me to get anything over to them now about what is to go in Governor Smith's speeches." Peek to Julien N. Friant, October 10, 1928, Chester C. Davis Papers. Even at the Houston convention, Judge Proskauer had allegedly been antagonistic to supporters of Smith from outside the East. *The New York Times*, June 27, 1928, p. 4. In 1928 the national Democratic headquarters and Congressman Oldfield's Democratic National Congressional Committee were transferred to the General Motors Building in New York. Roosevelt to Van Lear Black, July 25, 1928; George Foster Peabody to Franklin Roosevelt, September 11, 1928, Roosevelt Papers; H. D. Carre to Senator Kenneth McKellar, January 26, 1928, McKellar Papers. Joe Tumulty to Alfred E. Smith, May 16, 1927, Tumulty Papers; Robinson to Raskob, August 10, 1928, Robinson Papers; Bascom N. Timmons: *Jesse H. Jones: The Man and Statesman* (New York, 1956), p. 149; Frances Perkins: *The Roosevelt I Knew* (New York, 1946), pp. 52-3; Arthur Schlesinger, Jr.: *Crisis of the Old Order* (Boston, 1957), p. 380; *Time*, VII (October 1, 1928), 12-13; Leona F. Becker: "Alfred E. Smith [Personal interview, May 3, 1937]," unpublished Master's essay, University of Chicago, 1938, pp. 96-7.

no conceivable effort at conciliation, could have obliterated the bigotry with which they had to contend. But it was not bigotry alone that ruled the emotions of the campaign; was there not a legitimate concern, on the part of some of the anti-Smith voters, at the possibility that the kind of America they had known might cease to find its symbol in the Executive Mansion[6] —a concern that need not have been unduly aroused by Smith's candidacy, had he only taken the proper steps to still it? Failing this, a candidate can hardly complain if voters sense the mutual estrangement. And in 1928, a special responsibility rested upon Smith to harmonize his America with that beyond the Hudson. For at that time America had only begun to recognize that the "urban frontier," as well as the rural, had composed the substance of her past; she had not had time fully to absorb that more teeming frontier—of which Smith is today almost a folk hero— into her self-image. Smith might have tried to make 1928 a year of reconciliation between the two American cultures, but to do so he would have had to reach out, beyond the eastern city, to rural and small-town Protestant America, address it and show that he understood its feelings as well as the feelings of the lower East Side and the Bowery.

Instead, he sometimes displayed during his candidacy an exclusionist provinciality unequalled even during the bids of William Jennings Bryan. His taste for the Sunday manner of New York was laudable; his sniping at the Protestant blue laws

[6] Three years prior to the 1928 campaign, Walter Lippmann wrote: "The older American stocks in the South and the West, and in the East, too, are not all Ku Kluxers, and the Governor's more hasty friends show an intolerance when they believe that Al Smith is the victim of purely religious prejudice. Quite apart even from the sincere opposition of the prohibitionists, the objection to Tammany, the sectional objection to New York, there is an opposition to Smith which is as authentic and, it seems to me, as poignant as his support. It is inspired by the feeling that the clamorous life of the city should not be acknowledged as the American ideal. . . . The Ku Kluxers may talk about the Pope to the lunatic fringe, but the main mass of the opposition is governed by an instinct that to accept Al Smith is to certify and sanctify a way of life that does not belong to [their America]." *Men of Destiny*, pp. 8–9.

of small-town Pennsylvania was not good politics. His identification with the sidewalks of New York was of course legitimate; his reluctance to campaign in the South—against the advice of his strategists[7]—and his jocular reference to "the states
west of the Mississippi" made him doubly vulnerable to the
charge of remaining a provincial New Yorker. To oppose prohibition was his prerogative; flagrantly to defy it was not. In
fact, it may be suggested that had Smith entered the White
House, rural America—and genteel urban Protestants as well—
would have had as much cause to suffer a sense of alienation
from the Presidency as would H. L. Mencken, for example, at
the election of Bryan. Smith was at once a victim of prejudice
and of his own clinging loyalty to his special environment. In
1932 he blamed his defeat on "bigotry"; but in an interview in
May of 1937, he admitted that he had lacked a sensitivity to
the social and cultural condition of those Americans he should
have addressed.[8]

[7] *The New York Times,* June 15, 1926, p. 3; August 18, 1928, p. 2; August
21, 1928, pp. 1, 2; August 30, 1928, p. 1; October 9, 1928, pp. 1, 2; October
10, 1928, p. 2.
[8] *The New York Times,* October 26, 1932, p. 15; Becker: "Alfred E.
Smith," p. 162.

CHAPTER VIII

The Composition of the 1928 Vote

The presidential election of 1960, in which a Catholic faced a Protestant for the second time in American history, prompted new interest in the 1928 election and led to an extensive reexamination of the earlier contest. But only one point seems to have been established with finality: that in 1928 Hoover would have won over any Democratic candidate. No Democrat, whatever his faith and whatever his political program, could have vanquished the party that was presiding over the feverish prosperity of the later twenties.

While historians have recently come to assign to prosperity the central role in the defeat of Smith, they have been less successful in evaluating the importance of the more spectacular issues of religion and prohibition; yet the weighing of these two factors as elements in the defeat of Smith has been a preoccupation of political commentators since 1928. One of the first attempts at an analysis of the election was a contemporary article written by William Ogburn and Nell Talbot, who concluded that prohibition was by far the more influential of the two issues. The authors had contrived a rather cumbersome method by which to measure statistically the relative importance of major issues in the election; but since their investigation is confined to the Smith vote and takes no account of the vote for Hoover, it in fact does not take wholly into consideration the anti-Catholic and antiprohibitionist sentiment. Other objections may be raised against the study: the authors accepted as a definition of "urban" the census bureau's misleading standard of 2,500 people; they used "foreign-born" as an all-inclusive term, and thereby ignored crucial differences in nationality; the 1920 Democratic vote, which Ogburn and Talbot set against that of 1928, was almost the worst example of "party regularity" available; for some states they measured the "wetness" factor by the slanted *Literary Digest* figures; finally, their study is limited to 173 counties chosen at random in eight states and the same statistical weight is given to each county, regardless of population.[1]

Other statistical studies of the 1928 election present contradictory findings. The most ambitious, Miss Ruth Silva's *Rum, Religion, and Votes: 1928 Re-examined* (published in 1962), concludes that Smith's membership in the Democratic party was a greater liability to him than his membership in the Roman Catholic Church and that like religion, the vote for liquor had virtually no impact on Smith's strength at the polls in 1928. The major flaw in Miss Silva's admirable pioneering work is that the Davis vote of 1924 is taken as a standard measure of Democratic strength, while it was in fact the nadir of Democratic power. This study, which is also limited to the Smith vote, needs some correction on other points: it is based on a state-by-state approach and fails to contend with possible interaction among discrete factors, it relies on the untrustworthy government census of religious groups made in 1926, it projects backward a 1934 vote on the Eighteenth Amendment for use in analyzing the 1928 vote, and it fails to take into account the strength of party organization, which may have been an important determinant of Smith's vote in the cities. Two state analyses have been made.

[1] Ogburn and Talbot: "A Measurement of the Factors in the Presidential Election of 1928," *Social Forces*, VIII (December 1929), 175–83.

One, an account of the Democratic vote in Missouri, contends that both Catholicism and repeal were important correlates of the Smith vote, but that non-Catholics were relatively unaffected by the religious factor. The other, based on the Democratic tally in Pennsylvania, finds only Catholicism to correlate with the Smith vote.[2]

The belief persists among many historians that prohibition—insofar as it can be separated from the Protestant churches—overshadowed religion as an element in the Hoover-Smith contest. In 1958 one writer asserted that "prohibition was not a straw man. . . . To millions of Protestants prohibition was . . . an issue of transcendent importance. . . . When Protestants said they opposed Smith because of his wetness, they meant precisely what they said.[3] Unquestionably, some of the professional prohibitionists—and some politicians, too—thought of nothing else; but other dry leaders were Protestant ministers for whom Catholicism was the historic enemy. More important, what of the less fanatical and more numerous drys, the rank and file of the Protestant churches? It was the mass of these voters to whom Reinhold Niebuhr referred after the election when he said that the real issues of the campaign "were hid under the decent veil of loyalty to a moral ideal —prohibition." Niebuhr argued that "there will . . . be many who will hide anti-Catholic sentiment behind their opposition to his [Smith's] prohibition views. This is certainly true in the South, where there are more dry voters

2 Ruth Silva: *Rum, Religion, and Votes: 1928 Re-examined* (University Park, Pa., 1962). See the review of Miss Silva's book by a government statistician, Philipps Cutright of the Social Security Administration, in the *American Sociological Review*, XXVIII (June 1963), 484–5, and that by Edmund A. Moore in the *American Historical Review*, LXVIII (April 1963), 840–1. Richard A. Watson: "Religion and Politics in Mid-America: Presidential Voting in Missouri, 1928 and 1960," *Mid-Continent American Studies Journal*, V (Spring 1964), 33–55; Lola S. Hobbs: "A Catholic Runs for President: 1928 in Pennsylvania," unpublished Master's essay, Pennsylvania State University, 1961, pp. 24–6. See also Harold F. Gosnell, who holds that the prohibition issue was not important. *Machine Politics: Chicago Model* (Chicago, 1937), p. 111.
3 Robert M. Miller: *American Protestantism and Social Issues, 1919–1939* (Chapel Hill, N.C., 1958), p. 51.

than teetotalers." Moreover, the number of people who drank but felt a stake in Protestantism was considerable. The secret ballots and magazine polls that were indicating a sharply waning support for prohibition provide some evidence to back up Niebuhr's charge that in 1928 the issue had become a polite veneer spread over the unsightly reality of anti-Catholicism.[4]

That prohibition was of transcendent importance in 1928 appears, in fact, most dubious, and especially in the light of evidence recently accumulated illustrating the vital role religion may play for American voters. When a Roman Catholic candidate has run for office, there has apparently emerged both a Catholic and an anti-Catholic vote. The most authoritative of the many studies indicating the significance of religion in American politics—one conducted by the Survey Research Center of the University of Michigan[5]—investigates the election of 1960 and finds that in some areas as many as forty per cent of the Democratic Protestant voters who regularly attended church threw their vote against Kennedy, and the incidence of defection was highest among the most constant of churchgoers. At the same time, claimed the Michigan survey, Kennedy received more consistent Catholic support than had any recent Democratic presidential candidate. After examining both the Protestant and Catholic vote, the authors judged that religion had deprived Kennedy, on balance, of approximately 2.2 per cent of the two-party

---

[4] Reverend Bob Jones, the ardent prohibitionist, said he would rather see a saloon on every corner or a "nigger" as President than a Catholic in the White House. Gustavus Myers: *History of Bigotry in the United States* (New York, 1943), p. 326. Scott McBride, Superintendent of the Anti-Saloon League, intimated that regardless of whether the Democrats should adopt a dry plank he would vote for Hoover if Smith were nominated, as did Mrs. Booe, President of the WCTU. San Antonio *Express*, June 19, 1928, p. 4; *The New York Times*, January 10, 1928, p. 16; *World Tomorrow*, XI (December 1928), 493; *Christian Century*, XLV (September 13, 1928), 1107–8; Andrew E. Lee to George Peek, November 17, 1928, Chester C. Davis Paper. See Chap. iii, footnote 1. p. 99.

[5] Angus Campbell *et al.*: *Elections and the Political Order* (New York, 1966), pp. 78–124.

vote. Outside the South the faith of the Democratic candidate gained him about 1.6 per cent of the vote, and in the South it lost him roughly 16.5 per cent.[6]

That in 1960 religion could still constitute so imposing a political force suggests its importance in the earlier election. For in 1928 Catholics were at a cruder stage of assimilation into American society; and their own parochialism rivaled that of their Protestant foes. In 1928, for example, many Irish and Italian election districts in New York that had shown no comparable political homogeneity in any previous presidential election gave Smith all but two or three per cent of their vote. And, of course, the Catholic support of Smith in 1928 may have been a response to the anti-Catholicism of the campaign as well as a positive affirmation of religious solidarity.

There is therefore reason to believe that religion outweighed prohibition as an election issue. Senator George Norris of Nebraska stated the case emphatically: "The greatest element involved in the landslide was religion. Regret it and conceal it as we may, religion had more to do with the defeat of Governor Smith than any other one thing." Bishop Mouzon, a leader of the anti-Smith Democrats in the South, admitted that "Whatever else may appear above the surface, this [religion] is in the deep undercurrent of our thinking." Among those who believed religion to have been a more influential issue than prohibition

---

[6] Campbell *et al.: Elections and the Political Order*, p. 83. Catholic support, of course, aided Kennedy in the most crucial states, and probably his minority group status won him some compensating Jewish and Negro support. Other studies of voting along religious lines include John H. Fenton: *The Catholic Vote* (New Orleans, 1960); Peter H. Odegard, ed.: *Religion and Politics* (New York, 1960); Louis Bean: *How to Predict Elections* (New York, 1940), pp. 99–104; David H. Gold: "The Influence of Religious Affiliation on Voting Behavior," unpublished doctoral dissertation, University of Chicago, 1953; Madge M. McKinney: "Religion and Elections," *Public Opinion Quarterly*, VIII (Spring 1944), 110–14; Scott Greer: "Catholic Voters and the Democratic Party," *Public Opinion Quarterly*, XXV (Winter 1961), 611–25; and Andrew R. Baggaley: "Religious Influences on Wisconsin Voting, 1928–1960," *American Political Science Review*, LVI (March 1962), 66–70.

were Smith himself, his running mate, Robinson of Arkansas, Senators Kenneth McKellar of Tennessee, Thomas P. Gore of Oklahoma, James A. Reed of Missouri, and Key Pittman of Nevada, Mark Sullivan, Bernard Baruch, James Cox, Harold Ickes, Wilbur Cash, and many others. Even Dr. Arthur J. Barton, speaking as a member of the Anti-Saloon League, said in Birmingham that religion was a more important concern than prohibition, and warned that America might come under the domination of a foreign religious "sect." Before the election *The New York Times* had predicted that Smith would lost a million votes on account of his religion; later, the paper commented on the returns: "Most of [the votes] were cast against the Democratic candidate because he is a Catholic; the rest were because he is an antiprohibitionist." "Without doubt," pronounced *Time*, "the religious question was foremost."[7]

Prohibition and religion together constituted the most flamboyant issues of the campaign. The final tally, however, reflects a conjunction of these with a number of other concerns; and a more satisfactory understanding of the election requires a closer scrutiny into the nature of the campaign and vote among several regions and classes. This inquiry must be tentative, for in the final analysis the motives of an electorate are hidden—perhaps even from itself. During the campaign it had become clear that so abstract a consideration as the image of the presidency played a key role in turning many Americans against Smith. It is this

[7] Norris is quoted in the Charlotte *Observer*, November 10, 1928, p. 5; Mouzon in *The Commonweal*, VIII (October 3, 1928), 541. Robinson to Pittman, November 21, 1928, Robinson Papers; McKellar to James D. Phelan, November 10, 1928, McKellar Papers; Gore to John J. Raskob, December 15, 1928, Gore Papers; Pittman to Franklin Roosevelt, November 13, 1928, Roosevelt Papers; Lee Meriwether: *Jim Reed, "Senatorial Immortal"* (Webster Groves, Mo., 1948), pp. 176–7; *La Follette's Magazine*, XX (December 1928), 181, 185; Sullivan to Bernard Baruch, February 28, 1928, and Baruch to Winston Churchill, September 6, 1928, Baruch Papers. The opinions of Cox, Ickes, Cash, and others are noted in Andrew Sinclair: *Prohibition: The Era of Excess* (Boston, 1962), pp. 301–2. *The New York Times*, December 23, 1927, p. 12; July 10, 1928, p. 1; November 7, 1928, p. 24.

reason that helps to explain, for example, why Smith as governor was able to carry New York State by a substantial margin only to lose it by a landslide in the presidential contest. Still, a formal investigation of some of the returns has its value.

In the South, where in 1928 there was massive defection from the Democratic party, an uneven decline in Democratic strength had been under way for some time. The beginnings of the textile industry in the cities of that section created business groups for whom the high-tariff Republican party had its attractions; guardians of free enterprise would give ear to Hoover's assertion that Smith preached "state socialism." "In Georgia, in North Carolina, in Alabama, in fact all through the South," commented *The Nation*, "the industrial development has been enormous. The manufacturers and the managers of mills and factories and many of their employees have become Republicans because they felt it was to their financial interests to do so." Smith, after all, had earned much of his reputation by sponsoring labor reforms. The Republican inroads had come first in Florida, where an influx of northerners was rapidly building a two-party system. Between 1916 and 1924 the Republican vote in that state had doubled; and it doubled again between 1924 and 1932, in spite of the depression. In Texas also the Republican vote was on the increase during the twenties. Other states, such as Virginia, North Carolina, and Tennessee, had long registered strong Republican minorities. In 1920 Tennessee had even given the Republican candidate its electoral vote, while the border states of Kentucky, West Virginia, Maryland, and Oklahoma also voted for Harding.[8]

8 According to the 1927 manufacturing census, the South's share of the cotton textile industry was, by yardage, sixty-seven per cent. "The community acknowledged the standing of the industry," writes a labor historian, "by yielding to its management the decisive voice in shaping southern affairs." Irving Bernstein: *A History of the American Worker: The Lean Years* (Boston, 1960), pp. 2–3. Dewey M. Grantham, Jr., observed that "it was becoming easier [in the twenties] to think of Republican affiliations in a region so strongly committed to the gospel of business expansion and economic diversification." *The Democratic South* (Athens, Ga., 1963), p. 66. *The Nation*, CXXVII (November 21, 1928), 537;

The election of 1928 simply introduced new and more power-ful factors to widen a small but already discernible crack in the South. Al Smith's stand against prohibition ended an alliance between the drys and the Democrats that had prevailed in the region for decades. The region was strongly susceptible to the religious issue; the loss of southern clergymen was a major handicap, for in the South the churches wielded great power. Sporting Al Smith barber shops and Herbert Hoover butcher stores, the South in 1928 enjoyed its first real presidential cam-paign since Reconstruction. Even that part of the region which had most clearly represented the "Solid South" nearly went Republican; the popular vote in the eleven former Confederate states from Virginia to Texas was 47.8 per cent for Hoover and 52.2 per cent for Smith. The border states of Oklahoma, Kentucky, West Virginia, Maryland, and Delaware gave Hoover 60 per cent of the vote and Smith only 40 per cent.

But in 1928 the overriding political concern throughout much of the South was not prosperity, nor religion, nor prohibition; it was, as usual, loyalty to the Democratic party—and beyond, of course, loyalty to the racial commitment ingrained in the southern Democracy. In 1928 the claims of the party that sym-bolized regional tradition and white supremacy clashed for a moment with the claims of Protestant Anglo-Saxonism. "South-erners were frankly skeptical," according to an observer of the campaign, "of maintaining white supremacy in a two-party system." Throughout the southern countryside the strength of the Democratic presidential vote varied directly with the ratio of Negro to white. The New York *World* observed that in 1928 this pattern held true on the statewide level; that it held on a local level as well, V. O. Key carefully verified in his *Southern Politics*.[9] Counties such as those composing "Little Dixie" in

New Republic, XLVII (August 4, 1926), 296–7; Deskins: "The Presidential Election in North Carolina," *passim; Literary Digest*, IC (November 24, 1928), 8–9.

9 "The Democratic solidity of the several [southern] states," noted the *World*, "varies directly with the proportion of Negroes in the population; and the Solid South—what is left of it—was not voting against the Eighteenth Amendment. It was still voting against the Fifteenth." Quoted

Missouri, once containing a large Negro population though
now preponderantly white, also remained loyal to Smith; so did
counties in the Ozarks and elsewhere that had been settled by
emigrating white families from slaveholding areas. Democrats
spread unlikely stories about Hoover courting Negro girls while
directing flood relief in 1927, and dancing with a Mary Booze,
a colored Republican committeewoman, in Mound Bayou, Mississippi. They observed that Hoover had abolished segregation
in the Department of Commerce. Southern Republicans in turn
tried to portray Smith as a liberal on the race question: pictures
of him dictating to a Negro secretary were widely circulated,
and in Maryland Senator Millard Tydings charged that Republicans hired drinking Negroes to ride through the East Shore area
in cars emblazoned with Smith signs.[1]

But if the campaign disrupted the Democratic party in the
South, it invigorated the party in other areas. Among these were
a number of farming regions.[2] In the twenties the farmers had

in the *Literary Digest*, IC (November 24, 1928), 8. V. O. Key: *Southern
Politics in State and Nation* (New York, 1949), pp. 318–29.

[1] In some states, such as Mississippi, the Republican organization was con-
trolled by Negroes. *The Independent*, XXX (March 10, 1928), 227. Senator
Heflin's ravings against Smith in the Senate often settled down eventually
on the Negro issue; see, for example, the *Congressional Record, Senate,*
May 3, 1928, pp. 7698–9. Heflin defined the issues as "Race, Rum, Roman-
ism, and Raskob." On racial appeals, see Herbert Hoover to Henry W.
Anderson, October 11, 1928; Lizzie Bankhead Hotchkiss to Hoover,
Box L/512; Eugene P. Booze to Hoover, October 22, 1928, Hoover Papers.
Frank Mitchell: "Embattled Democrats: Missouri Democratic Politics,
1919–1932," unpublished doctoral dissertation, University of Missouri,
1964; John H. Fenton: *Politics in the Border States* (New Orleans, 1957),
p. 10; Paul Lewinson: *Race, Class, Party: A History of Negro Politics and
White Suffrage in the South* (New York, 1932), p. 180; Hugh D. Reagan,
"Race as a Factor in the Presidential Election of 1928 in Alabama," *Alabama Review*, XIX (January 1966), 5–19.

[2] In contrast to the farm revolt, labor had no major grievance in 1928.
Most AFL leaders preferred Smith, whose labor record in New York was
longstanding and impressive, but some important unionists, including John
L. Lewis, William L. Hutchinson, and Daniel Tobin, endorsed Hoover.
"It is noteworthy," Vaughn D. Bornet writes, that "union leaders who
came to the support of Smith in the campaign seldom, if ever, attacked
Hoover." *Labor Politics in a Democratic Republic* (Washington, D.C.,

suffered more perhaps than at any time in the recent past, and the prolonged agricultural depression was wearing down their patience with Calvin Coolidge. By the summer of 1928 the prices of wheat, corn, and wool had reached their lowest point in two years, and there was no fortuitous rise before the election, as there had been in 1924. At the Houston convention, a number of farm leaders, angered at Coolidge's vitriolic opposition to the McNary-Haugen bills and at the silence of the Republican platform upon the scheme the bills had embodied, were officially welcomed into the fold by Clement Shaver and Jesse Jones. Hoover's long residence in England was also a count against him with isolationist midwesterners.

The agricultural leaders George Peek and Chester C. Davis, who had helped Senator McNary to draft the farm bill, were sent into their native territory as early as the spring of 1927 to direct the Smith campaign; there they were aided by grants from the New York Democratic headquarters totaling more than half a million dollars. Both men were well aware of Smith's hesitation to commit himself on the farm problem, particularly the controversial McNary-Haugen plan for which he had declared himself "in principle"—then repudiated as it had been worked out in the three congressional bills of 1924, 1927, and 1928. Peek and particularly Davis recognized that Republicans had actually suggested proposals more specific for the solution of the farm problem than had the Democrats. Yet they also believed that the Democrats would be more likely to experiment with McNary-Haugen, since the Republican administration had fixed upon its party a policy of opposition to the plan. And they thought that Hoover, from his Food Administration days onward, had shown little genuine concern or understanding for the farmer. During the summer and fall Davis and Peek contributed all their energies to the campaign, particularly in

---

1964), pp. 132–3, 163, 166–7, 236. Organized labor was not only divided but weak and cautious, having lost almost forty per cent of its membership during the past decade. Bernstein: *The Lean Years*, pp. 96–104. Donald Richberg to Martin F. Ryan, June 4, 1928, and B. M. Jewell to D. B. Robertson, July 16, 1928, Richberg Papers.

the ten states in which the combined votes of John W. Davis and La Follette would have comprised a majority in 1924.[3]

The work of the two agricultural spokesmen, and the desertions of a few important Republican officeholders, such as Governor Frank W. Murphy of Minnesota, and Governor Adam McMullen and Senator George Norris of Nebraska, resulted in a degree of Democratic success in the 1928 presidential returns. "Republican majorities in most of the farm states from Illinois to Montana," wrote Gilbert Fite, "were drastically reduced." And reduced they were in some Protestant as well as in numerous Catholic rural counties; and as Fite shows, most of the 1924 Progressive vote went to Smith rather than to the Republican party from which a considerable part of the Progressive electorate had been drawn in that area. "The significant fact," Fite concluded "is that the drift was Democratic in a substantial number of farm states as early as 1928."[4] If Smith had been a

[3] Peek confessed that "it may be true that we do not know what the Democratic administration would do for agriculture, but on the other hand there is probably some hope in that direction and none with Hoover." Peek to S. P. Bush, July 19, 1928, Peek Papers. Gilbert C. Fite: "The Agricultural Issue in the Presidential Campaign of 1928," *Mississippi Valley Historical Review*, XXXVII (March 1951), 659-60, 662, 664. Fite in his book on Peek refers to Hoover as an "arch enemy of American agriculture." *George N. Peek and the Fight for Farm Parity* (Norman, Okla., 1954), pp. 125-30. Bernard Baruch, in a letter to Smith, also noted that "the farmers look upon Hoover as their arch enemy." July 3, 1928, Baruch Papers. The manuscripts in the new Hoover Library may alter this view of his farm policies. United States Department of Agriculture, *Yearbook of Agriculture, 1928* (Washington, D.C., 1929), pp. 686, 714, 959; *The New York Times*, August 3, 1928, p. 1; August 4, 1928, pp. 1, 4; James K. Pollock, "Campaign Funds in 1928," *American Political Science Review*, XXIII (February 1929), 66.

[4] Senator Peter Norbeck observed: "It was not the strength of the Republican position and Mr. Hoover that entirely account [*sic*] for victory —it was fully as much the weakness of the opposition." Norbeck had earlier written to Peek that "Smith with the Tammany connections and New York residence seems so remote and unpromising." Norbeck to Mrs. E. R. Doering, November 9, 1928, Norbeck to Peek, July 14, 1928, Peek Papers. Chester C. Davis, in a memorandum written two weeks before the election, named the religious factor as the chief obstacle to a Democratic success. September 15, 1928, Chester C. Davis Papers.

candidate more personally appealing to the prairie voter, the Democratic showing might have been still more impressive.

The sign of new life in the Democratic party was as visible in the Far West as in the Northeast and farm belt. In the Pacific states, where the La Follette vote had cut deep into the Democratic vote, that party's share of the two-party vote jumped from 28 per cent in 1920 and 16 in 1924 to 42 in 1928. In the Mountain states the increase was only slightly less. No issue such as that of peace restored the balance between the parties struck in the West in 1916, but the Democratic identity was apparently progressive enough to retrieve some of the Far West's radical vote lost to third-party candidates in 1920 and particularly in 1924.

More important than these gains, however, was the expansion in the urban Democratic vote. And because of its effect upon Democratic fortunes in the cities the candidacy of Governor Smith, regardless of his personal shortcomings as a campaigner, was undoubtedly a significantly healthy event in the evolution of the Democracy. Smith won the nation's two most urbanized and most Catholic states, Massachusetts and Rhode Island, where a slump in textile production also played a part. Throughout the new America of the metropolis, the immigrant, and the Catholic Church the story was the same. Because of Smith's remarkable performance in these areas, Walter Lippmann wrote that the chief result of the Smith candidacy was the reconstruction of the Democratic party and its liberation from Bryan and the South. The Smith victory was not a conversion of Republicans; that party apparently had used up its male voting potential in the cities in 1916 and its female potential in 1920. It was not that Hoover lacked urban support: on the contrary, he won more urban votes than any former Republican presidential candidate, building his strength on old-stock and Negro communities strong in the cities. But in metropolitan America taken as a whole, the Democrats gained more.[5]

[5] Carl Degler has shown that in 1928 Democratic strength in cities with a high population of foreign stock expanded enormously, while in preponderantly old-stock urban centers it fluctuated little in comparison with

The massive immigration of 1900 to 1914 was apparently pay-
ing dividends in votes in 1928. Part of the explanation for Smith's
strength in the immigrant cities, however, was an apparent rise
in voting among Roman Catholic women, a phenomenon that
Samuel Lubell has noted. In Boston it is possible to measure
the voting by sex of those ethnic groups that appear in large
numbers in unpublished government lists of 1930 census reports.
Unfortunately, the largest Roman Catholic group—the Irish—
no longer appear markedly as "foreign-born" in the 1930 census.
Within heavily Italian census tracts, however, we find the voting
precincts where female registration rose by twenty-nine per
cent, and precincts identified as strongly Irish by names appearing on voting lists show a comparable rise in registration of
women. But in another section of the country there were other
women of conservative tradition who, hitherto reluctant to assume the prerogative of the vote, were drawn to the polls by the
angry issues of 1928. In the South as well as in the Northeast the
total vote rose so sharply, as Table XI indicates, as to suggest a
considerably increased participation by women.[6]

1920. And in cities of native population outside the South, the Republican
vote showed no comparable rise. It must be observed, however, that this
analysis has only limited value, since 1920, when the immigrant disaffected
more sharply from the Democratic party than at any other presidential
election in this century, is the worst year to choose for a comparison of
urban voting. Degler: "American Political Parties and the Rise of the
City: An Interpretation," *Journal of American History*, LI (June 1964),
50–9. Samuel J. Eldersveld analyzes the expanding political strength
in urban areas since 1920 in "The Influence of Metropolitan Party
Pluralities in Presidential Elections Since 1920," *American Political Science Review*, XLIII (December 1949), 1189–1206, and "A Study of
Urban Electoral Trends in Michigan, 1920–1940," unpublished doctoral
dissertation, University of Michigan, 1946. The Republican National
Chairman, Dr. Hubert Work, had earlier designated the East as the
battleground of the campaign. *The New York Times*, August 26, 1928,
p. 5. *Yale Review*, XVIII (September 1928), 18–27.
[6] Lubell: *The Future of American Politics* (New York, 1952), p. 40. The
reluctance of women in southern and border states to vote had been for
several years a matter of concern to Cordell Hull and other national
chairmen. A rise in female registration in predominantly Catholic New
York City is noted in *The New York Times*, October 11, 1928, p. 2, and

The unusually high 1928 presidential ethnic vote could be considered in a sense deviant, since it went to a candidate who would have a striking appeal for Americans of immigrant background. And the election was one of a series in which peculiar circumstances existed capable of deflecting the immigrant ballot

TABLE XI

The Ten States with the Greatest Increase
in Presidential Voting, 1924 to 1928

East	Per Cent Increase	South	Per Cent Increase
New Jersey	40	Florida	50
Massachusetts	35	Louisiana	50*
Pennsylvania	30	Virginia	50
New York	25	Arkansas	30
		Alabama	30
		Georgia	28

* The population of Louisiana was 40 per cent Roman Catholic in 1928.

the Greensboro, North Carolina, *Daily News* observed a large turnout of women in its locality, November 6, 1928, p. 1. In the nation at large registration rose from twenty-nine to forty-three million. *The New York Times,* October 29, 1928, pp. 1, 2; United States Bureau of the Census: "Machine Lists of Ethnic Characteristics in the 1930 Census" (unpublished); "Registered Voters (Women), State Election, November 4, 1924, and November 6, 1928," *Boston City Document Number Eleven,* pp. 142, 152. The complete redistricting of Boston in 1925 hinders comparisons between the elections of 1924 and 1928. In the measurement of Italian female registration, precincts 1, 2, 3, 5, and 7 in ward three and precinct 5 in ward one in 1928 were compared with almost identical areas in 1924: precincts 1, 2, 3, 5, and 6 in ward five, and precinct 5 in ward two.

from its normal course: in 1920 several immigrant communities usually loyal to the Democratic party reacted to Versailles by turning to the Republican nominee; the 1924 candidacy of La Follette, which drew votes away from the major parties, attracted many of the city poor; the depression worked violence upon the politics of 1932. But in 1928 the immigrants did more than respond to the nomination of Al Smith; their presence in the Democracy effected that nomination—and the Republicans had no comparable electorate that could have won its party to a Smith. However special its context, moreover, the election of 1928 must have permanently strengthened some immigrant Democratic machines and thereby contributed to the massive party victory among immigrant-stock Americans in the depression vote of 1932. For an indication of the trend in the ethnic electorate during those years and the period immediately preceding them, at least two cities—New York and Chicago—are susceptible of close statistical analysis; within these two cities, in fact, along with Boston which has been the subject of a close study in this period, lived nearly half of America's foreign-born and their children.

Nowhere in America have immigrant communities remained more politically self-assertive than in Manhattan, where in 1920, 76.5 per cent of the white stock were themselves foreign born or the children of foreign-born parents;[7] and for a study of ethnic groupings and voting habits during the years that spanned the Versailles conference and the candidacy of Roosevelt, the pioneering census work of Walter Laidlaw, a skilled statistician employed by the New York City Department of Health, provides an excellent foundation. In an attempt to make more efficient the activity of New York's public and private social-service agencies, Laidlaw in 1920 gathered census data of richly inclusive scope on a number of territories in and around the city; and included, of course, was information on the race and national origins of the inhabitants. The Welfare Council of

---

[7] Walter Laidlaw, ed.: *Statistical Sources for Demographic Studies of Greater New York, 1920* (New York, 1922), p. xxix.

Greater New York collected similar materials for 1930. In both surveys, the data were obtained for relatively small census areas known then as sanitary districts—areas considerably smaller than assembly districts but more sizable than election districts. The information on geographic ethnic patterns obtainable from the Laidlaw and Welfare Council reports is especially trustworthy, since the investigators determined origins not upon the occasionally deceptive basis of surname, but upon personal interviews.[8]

The two surveys can therefore be of great use in the delineation of national and racial communities within the city of New York. To determine something of the nature of ethnic voting for the presidency in the twenties, the historian has to isolate on the basis of the Laidlaw and Welfare Council findings as many ethnically homogeneous sanitary districts as possible, seek out election districts lying wholly within these areas, and examine the presidential vote within those smaller sections. The 1920 ethnic figures may be used for the elections of 1916, 1920, and 1924; the 1930 data for the elections of 1928 and 1932.

Such an approach has its flaws. It does not take into account differences in the social or economic composition of the districts similar in ethnic stock. But in the early twentieth century such differences within ethnic groups were by no means so common as today, and sufficiently varied areas are ordinarily included in an examination to offset any danger of social or economic bias. Another shortcoming to our method lies in the possibility that any particular election district might represent an enclave of people ethnically divergent from those who dominate the larger

[8] Laidlaw, ed.: *Statistical Sources for Demographic Studies of Greater New York, 1920;* a summary of Laidlaw's earlier work may be found in *The New York Times,* April 1, 1923, IV, 11-12. See also Laidlaw, ed.: *Population of the City of New York, 1890–1930* (New York, 1932); Florence DuBois, ed.: *Population in Health Areas: New York City, 1930–1931,* Research Bureau, Welfare Council of New York City, Section 7 of Study 10 of the Research Bureau; *Heads of Families by Color and Nativity and Country of Birth of Foreign Born Head, by Health Areas, New York City, 1930–1934,* Research Bureau, Welfare Council of New York City, Section 9 of Study 10 of the Research Bureau.

sanitary district. Here, surnames appearing on voter registration lists—while less reliable than were the interviews employed by Laidlaw—can help to indicate whether an election district seems to correspond ethnically to the sanitary area that includes it. In the last analysis, aggregate voting studies are always hampered by the incompleteness of the data upon which they rely. Yet such figures as are within reach throw considerable light upon the politics of New York's national and racial communities.

Four immigrant groups—the German, the Irish, the Italian, and the Jewish—are sufficiently populous to warrant examination; and to these we may add the Negro, more isolated than the immigrants from native white society and headed for a major role in big-city ghetto politics. The Irish and Germans came to New York too early to count heavily as foreign-born even in the 1920 Laidlaw census; therefore it has been necessary to rely somewhat more heavily upon surnames on registration lists. The German-American vote can be followed closely. In 1916 the New York *Staats-Zeitung und Herald* declared for the Republican candidate, but its appeal went unheeded among the city's Germans. After the war they may have been motivated by what Samuel Lubell, in referring to the McCarthy era, calls the "politics of revenge" and by a desire to rid themselves of the inferior status they had acquired during the war. A vote for isolation could serve both ends; it could work vengeance upon Wilson, and it could demonstrate that German-Americans, like their fellow countrymen, wished to preserve separate the purity of the American motherland. The election issue, declared the *Staats-Zeitung*, was Wilson and the League versus Harding and Americanism. Germans in Manhattan gave Harding a spanking majority in 1920.[9]

Yet the traditional attachment held by New York's Germans for the Democratic party seems to have been only temporarily disrupted by World War I. In 1924 the Democratic German

[9] New York Bureau of Elections, *The City Record, passim;* *Staats-Zeitung und Herald,* November 1, 1916, p. 6; November 2, 1920, p. 4; *Harper's Magazine,* CCXII (April 1956), 29–35.

vote eclipsed the Republican; the percentages would probably have approached those of 1916 but for the candidacy of Robert La Follette, who had the endorsement of the *Staats-Zeitung.* La Follette was attractive to many German-Americans as an opponent of American involvement in the war, and he had a pro-

The German Vote, 1916–32: Support for Political Parties in Sanitary Districts of New York County Having a German Population of Approximately 70 Per Cent.

Year	Democratic Per Cent	Republican Per Cent	Third Party Per Cent
1916	62	38	—
1920	28	61	11 (Socialist)
1924	46	37	17 (Progressive)
1928	73	27	—
1932	80	20	—

gressive German following in the Middle West. By 1928 the Germans in New York county had arrived at a firm commitment to the Democratic party that many voters were not to attain until 1932. Possibly the local origins and popularity of Smith accounted for much of his strength among the German-Americans of New York, but his stand against prohibition increased their attachment. In addition, many Germans were Roman Catholic. The *Staats-Zeitung* supported both Smith and Roosevelt, calling the latter the "hope of America."[1]

In 1916 the Irish *World* and *Gaelic American* condemned

[1] November 3, 1924, p. 6; November 1, 1928, p. 6; October 21, 1932, p. 2; November 9, 1932, p. 6.

Wilson as an anti-Irish bigot.[2] But no widespread Irish defection from the Democracy occurred until 1920, when Wilson was excoriated by the Irish press for his part in the hated peace conference that bolstered the position of the British Empire.[3] After deserting Wilson in a predictable but not a striking

The Irish Vote, 1916–32: Support for Political Parties in Sanitary Districts of New York County Having an Irish Population of Approximately 70 Per Cent.

Year	Democratic Per Cent	Republican Per Cent	Third Party Per Cent
1916	64	36	—
1920	47	50	3 (Socialist)
1924	63	25	12 (Progressive)
1928	82	18	—
1932	81	19	—

fashion, the Irish returned to the Democratic-Tammany fold in 1924.[4] And in 1928 they gave to the Democratic party a vote higher than that of any other major nationality group—a vote that was not to be exceeded even in 1932. A prominent consideration in 1928 was Hoover's identification with England; he was denounced by the *Gaelic American* as an Anglophile.[5]

[2] Irish *World*, October 28, 1916, p. 4; *Gaelic American*, October 21, 1916, p. 4.

[3] See, for example, *Gaelic American*, October 30, 1920, p. 4. Cox said he was opposed by "a militantly anti-Wilson Catholic oligarchy." *Journey Through My Years* (New York, 1946), pp. 273-4.

[4] The newspapers declared for La Follette; Irish *World*, November 1, 1924, pp. 3-4; *Gaelic American*, October 25, 1924, p. 1.

[5] July 7, 1928, p. 1; Irish *World*, October 13, 1928, p. 4.

But John W. Davis, the Democratic candidate in 1924, had himself been Ambassador to England under Wilson and yet had won the support of the Irish. Smith's appeal, we may presume, was chiefly as a fellow religionist and fellow son of Erin. The

The Italian Vote, 1916–32: Support for Political Parties in Sanitary Districts of New York County Having an Italian Population of Approximately 85 Per Cent.

Year	Democratic Per Cent	Republican Per Cent	Third Party Per Cent
1916	63	37	—
1920	47	50	3 (Socialist)
1924	48	44	8 (Progressive)
1928	77	23	—
1932	79	21	—

depression, of course, brought its own reason for Irish working-class support of the Democrats.

The vote of the Italian Catholic bloc offers no surprises. In spite of *Il Telegrafo*'s declaration for Hughes in 1916, the Italian community supported Wilson enthusiastically. In 1920 the Italians recoiled from the hated Wilson Democracy; in 1924 they were again preponderantly Democratic. As presidential candidate, Governor Smith scored an overwhelming victory among his Italian coreligionists whose ties to the Democratic party were later strengthened by the depression years. *Il Telegrafo*, indifferent to politics since the defeat of Cox, implicitly declared both for Smith and Roosevelt.[6]

[6] November 2, 1916, p. 5; November 3, 1916, p. 5; October 25, 1928, p. 4; November 6, 1928, p. 4; November 4, 1932, p. 4; November 5, 1932, p. 6; November 7, 1932, p. 6.

The Manhattan Negro remained faithful to the Grand Old
Party until after 1928. The ties of loyalty that bound the Negro
when he cast his first vote were not broken until the depression.
In 1916 the New York *Age* vigorously condemned the southerner in the White House and charged him with wholesale dis-

*The Negro Vote, 1916–32: Support for Political Parties in
Sanitary Districts of New York County Having a Negro
Population of Approximately 95 Per Cent.*

Year	Democratic Per Cent	Republican Per Cent	Third Party Per Cent
1916	26	74	—
1920	3	94	3 (Socialist)
1924	28	69	3 (Progressive)
1928	41	59	—
1932	58	42	—

crimination in making federal appointments; the newspaper
could also have mentioned the practice of racial segregation in
the executive departments, which southern cabinet members
had introduced or strengthened. In 1920 the *Age* insisted that
"the important thing at the moment for the Negro is the destruction of the national political power of the South." The unusually
high Negro Republican vote in 1920 probably resulted from
Cox's pronouncement, which was not aimed specifically at
Negroes, that this was a "white man's country," his stated belief
that Negroes could never attain social equality in this country,
and the widely publicized stories that Harding had some Negro
ancestry. In contrast, the Republican National Committee in
1920 barred local conventions at hotels discriminating against

Negroes, the party platform strongly endorsed a federal anti-lynching law, and Harding himself spoke out for such a measure. In 1924 the *Age* endorsed Coolidge; third parties, which included anti-Negro unions, won few votes in Harlem.[7]

In 1928 the newspaper, its support thrown to Hoover, ran a picture of the "Jim Crow wire cage," a fenced-off area in which Negroes were forced to sit at the Houston convention. The paper noted the vice presidential candidate's denunciation of "Niggers" while he was governor of Arkansas; and it made much of the lynching of a Negro at Houston on the eve of the convention—the first lynching that had occurred in the city in more than fifty years. The new *Amsterdam News* also endorsed Hoover in 1928. Raskob's Democratic National Committee donated $125,000 to the Smith Colored League for proselytizing among Negroes in the large cities, but Smith himself expressed few sentiments calculated to win the Negro vote. Yet the Democrats gained impressively among the colored voters in the presidential election. The Negro vote may perhaps be explained in part by the Republicans' refusal to seat a number of Negro representatives at their Kansas City convention; the act amounted to an endorsement of "Lily White" organizations in the South. More important, Al Smith had already won the majority support of the Negroes in Manhattan's nineteenth and twenty-first assembly districts: in these areas of Harlem enough Negroes had split their tickets in 1924 to swing their districts

[7] Henry Blumenthal: "Woodrow Wilson and the Race Question," *Journal of Negro History*, XLVIII (January 1963), 1–21; Richard B. Sherman: "The Harding Administration and the Negro: An Opportunity Lost," *Journal of Negro History*, XLIX (July 1964), 151–68. A Negro leader in Ohio complained to Democratic National Chairman George White about a state Democratic pamphlet that warned of "Negro domination" in case Harding should win. Fairbank Tucker to White, December 12, 1920, George White Papers. Arthur S. Link: *Wilson: The New Freedom* (Princeton, 1956), pp. 246–53; Wesley Bagby: *The Road to Normalcy* (Baltimore, 1962), pp. 162–3; New York *Age*, October 19, 1916, p. 4; October 26, 1916, p. 4; October 20, 1920, p. 1; October 25, 1924, p. 4; *The New York Times*, June 4, 1920, p. 1; September 18, 1920, p. 14; October 15, 1920, p. 3; October 27, 1920, p. 9.

to Smith as gubernatorial candidate; and again in 1926 Smith won more of the Negro vote than did his Republican opponent. In 1932, while the *Amsterdam News* again favored Hoover, the *Age* withheld its support. Unsure itself where the hope for equality might lie, the *Age* left the decision to the economically

The Jewish Vote, 1916–32: Support for Political Parties in Sanitary Districts of New York County Having a Jewish Population of Approximately 90 Per Cent.

Year	Democratic Per Cent	Republican Per Cent	Third Party Per Cent
1916	55	45	—
1920	19	43	38 (Socialist)
1924	51	27	22 (Progressive)
1928	72	28	—
1932	82	18	—

distressed Negro voters, for whom, it would appear from the result, the depression was the paramount issue.[8]

Jewish voters in 1916 could bear in mind Wilson's appointment of Louis D. Brandeis to the Supreme Court. The first Jew to receive such an appointment, Brandeis was a leading Zionist. In addition, Jews wanted to avoid war with Germany, whose record toward the Jews contrasted favorably with that of its

[8] New York *Age*, October 13, 1928, p. 1; October 20, 1928, p. 1; October 24, 1928, p. 16; November 3, 1928, p. 1; November 5, 1932, p. 4; *Amsterdam News*, October 24, 1928, p. 6; October 2, 1932, p. 6; *The New York Times*, November 6, 1924, p. 6; November 3, 1926, p. 2; August 25, 1928, p. 4; *New Republic*, CXXVII (October 17, 1928), 392–4; Pollock: "Campaign Funds in 1928," 66; Elbert L. Tatum: *The Changed Political Thought of the Negro, 1915–1940* (New York, 1951), pp. 94–112.

great eastern rival, Russia. Aroused perhaps by the eastern European territorial settlements, the failure at Versailles to create a new Jewish homeland, and the administration's treatment of radicals, many of whom were Jewish, Jews voted against the Democrats in 1920. They gave a heavier vote to the jailed Socialist candidate Eugene Debs than to Cox; and in 1924 Robert La Follette also won considerable Jewish support. But during the twenties, urban Jews voted more and more heavily Democratic. Governor Smith's extensive employment of Jewish advisers, such as Judge Joseph Proskauer and Belle Moskowitz, helped him to win the Jewish vote. Jews, moreover, could consider Smith a fellow victim of Klan bigotry. Franklin Roosevelt —who made overtures to Jewish voters, claiming Henry Morgenthau, Jr., as his friend and neighbor among the farmers of Dutchess County—won in 1932 the overwhelming approval of Manhattan's Jews.[9]

For Chicago, population figures almost as useful as those for Manhattan reveal the voting of Germans, Jews, Poles, and Negroes between 1916 and 1932. The vote in Chicago during this period followed some of the Manhattan patterns, but it also also reacted to variations in region, religion, and degree of cultural homogeneity. Particularly noticeable is the absence of Governor Smith as a familiar and popular Democrat. Chicago's Germans adhered to the Democratic party in considerably smaller proportion than the Germans of Manhattan; the election of 1932 was perhaps the first in which they gave a majority to the national Democratic ticket, while Manhattan Germans voted Republican only once between 1916 and 1932. The comparative weakness of Roman Catholicism among Chicago Germans may in part account for the difference; and because of their location in the American heartland, Chicago's Germans may have been more isolationist than Manhattan's. In 1928 Hoover was remembered for his postwar German relief work in the face of adverse opinion at home, as well as his rejection of national

[9] Lawrence H. Fuchs: *The Political Behavior of American Jews* (Glencoe, Ill., 1956), pp. 57–69.

Chicago, 1916–32: Support for Political Parties in Sanitary Districts Having German, Jewish, Polish, and Negro Populations of 70 to 95 Per Cent.

	Democratic Per Cent	Republican Per Cent	Third Party Per Cent
1916			
German	44	56	
Jewish	57	43	
Polish	73	27	
Negro	31	69	
1920			
German	10	80	10
Jewish	28	61	11
Polish	50	45	5
Negro	6	93	1
1924			
German	18	52	30
Jewish	37	43	20
Polish	51	37	12
Negro	5	91	4
1928			
German	45	55	
Jewish	78	22	
Polish	83	17	
Negro	29	71	
1932			
German	59	41	
Jewish	85	15	
Polish	85	15	
Negro	30	70	

origins for computing immigration figures, while Smith was an unfamiliar figure.[1]

Jewish voters in Chicago failed to return to the Democratic fold in 1924, and in this they resembled Jews in the nation at large who remained Republican until 1932. Though the Chicago *Defender* did break its Republican traditions by supporting Smith in 1928, Negroes in that city were slower to become Democrats than were those of Manhattan, where Governor Smith could work his influence upon the colored minority. Initially Democratic but alienated from Wilson in 1920, the Poles gave enormous support to Smith and Roosevelt.

In Boston the first statistics on ethnic composition by sanitary district were gathered by the federal government in 1930, and they remain unpublished. The voting of Boston's Irish, who supported Smith as enthusiastically as they repudiated Wilson, is well chronicled on the ward level in J. Joseph Huthmacher's *Massachusetts People and Politics, 1919–1933* (Cambridge, 1958). Of the other ethnic groups in Boston, only the Italian is numerous enough in the government lists to assure accurate measurement. The Boston Italians showed unusual loyalty to Wilson in 1916 before deserting him in 1920. And not even in New York did they vote in more solid ranks for Al Smith in 1928.

In sum, that there was a vote cast specifically against Smith and against his social background tends to obscure the genuine assets his candidacy brought to his party. After the election a friend wrote to Roosevelt: "The Democratic Party is stronger

[1] The table on Chicago voting is based on election ward maps of the city and on Ernest W. Burgess and Charles Newcomb: *Census Data of the City of Chicago, 1920* (Chicago, 1931); *Census Data of the City of Chicago, 1930* (Chicago, 1933). Chicago *Defender*, October 20, 1928, p. 4. Harold F. Gosnell estimates the 1920 Negro vote in Chicago at 95 per cent Republican (as against 93 per cent recorded above) and declares that Hoover received 15 per cent less Negro support than Coolidge (as against 20 per cent above). *Negro Politicians: The Rise of Negro Politics in Chicago* (Chicago, 1935), pp. 28–9. Arthur W. Thurner, "The Impact of Ethnic Groups on the Democratic Party in Chicago, 1920–28," unpublished doctoral dissertation, University of Chicago, 1966.

than it has been since the Civil War."[2] Roosevelt agreed. And it could be expected that if this Protestant Democrat were nominated in 1932 he would draw back into the party the South and other areas where anti-Catholic sentiment had damaged it. At the same time, the Democratic ethnic vote, already clearly

The Italian Vote in Boston, 1916–32: Support for Political Parties in Sanitary Districts in Boston Having an Italian Population of Approximately 75 Per Cent.

Year	Democratic Per Cent	Republican Per Cent	Third Party Per Cent
1916	67	33	—
1920	43	50	7 (Socialist)
1924	45	35	20 (Progressive)
1928	95	5	—
1932	78	22	—

growing early in the decade, and now firmed and made assertive in the candidacy of Smith, would probably remain in that column in 1932, even if Smith were not renominated. The reconstruction of the party had been handsomely begun by Governor Smith; when Governor Roosevelt won the next presidential election, the party had established its strength far more soundly than ever before in the twentieth century.

[2] William F. Haywood to Roosevelt, December 11, 1928, Democratic National Committee Papers, Box 80, Colorado.

Franklin D. Roosevelt
and the Depression

The depression of 1929 offered Democrats of varying outlook the first concrete issue in many years upon which they might take common ground. Political as well as economic realities would appear at first sight to have made almost certain a new progressive course for the Democracy. As the party in power at the time of the crash, the GOP was in some degree politically identifiable with it, and would have a hard time trying to present itself as the representative of fresh departures and energies. Hoover himself, despite the notable innovations of his presidential years, simply would not think his way into certain possibilities—massive direct federal relief, for example. Conceivably, he needed more time than was to be allotted him. And if the Republicans could neither convincingly nor willingly seize the progressive standard we might expect that with something that approaches the inevitability of dialectic, the Democratic would become the party of reform.

But the reasoning here is retrospective. In fact, the politics of the thirties might have taken any number of logically definable courses. The bitterness of the previous decade need not have dissipated within the Democratic party; finding their mutual company intolerable, the leaders along with the factions for which they spoke could have found their separate ways into other political organizations more directly expressive of depression ideologies: the Republican and Socialist parties, some Dixiecrat splinter of populist hue. Or the party leadership might have taken on a hard rightist character. Al Smith, whose origins and career had made of him an ambivalent mixture of the urban progressive and the individualist conservative, was fast settling into the latter mode, and other important Democrats were of similar persuasion. In 1931 John W. Davis condemned Hoover for "following the road to socialism at a rate never before equaled in time of peace. . . ." At the Jackson and Jefferson Day dinners of 1932, Governor Cox was demanding a balanced budget and a sales tax, Davis was warning against persecution of the rich, and Smith—who did go so far as to declare for a federal bond issue to pay for unemployment relief—was implicitly labeling as a "demagogic appeal" Roosevelt's plea for the "forgotten man at the bottom of the economic pyramid." There were progressive stirrings among the congressional Democrats— at least in 1932, when the rank and file in the House broke away from the generally conservative policy its leaders had been pursuing and threw its weight behind such measures as a surtax of up to sixty-five per cent. But there was nothing to ensure that the congressional revolt could translate itself into a firm and organized movement. Had the views of Smith, Davis, and Cox prevailed within the Democratic hierarchy, the party might have crumbled under economic stress; or if a Democratic conservative had won the presidency in 1932, quite conceivably the Republicans in time of defeat, rediscovering their progressive tradition recently embodied in Theodore Roosevelt and Hoover and still maintained in Senator George Norris and his followers, would have shifted to the unoccupied left.[1]

[1] *New Republic*, LXV (December 17, 1930), 137; *The New York Times*, March 27, 1932, p. 1; Arthur Schlesinger, Jr.: *The Crisis of the Old Order* (Boston, 1957), p. 417.

The role of the Roosevelt candidacy in the rebirth of the Democratic party is therefore of a double nature; for F.D.R. gave the Democracy both a degree of harmony and a progressive cast. Both achievements owe much to his special temperament—inductive, experimental, even opportunistic rather than philosophically reformist—relishing the plasticity of the social and political materials in which he worked.

Roosevelt's progress to the White House began with his gubernatorial victory of 1928. He brought to the governorship the strenuous life of his cousin Teddy, and also a measure of T.R.'s Bull-Moose radicalism. His career as governor is not easily judged against that of his predecessor, Al Smith, since the problems of the depression demanded unprecedented response. At any rate, Roosevelt's actions in the early depression years, though episodic, showed imagination. At the Governors' Conference of 1930 he led the nation by endorsing unemployment insurance, though in the state banking crisis he acted with little foresight. An advocate of economy and retrenchment in government, he nevertheless called for two important bond issues: one to finance relief, which he at first had held to a crippling pay-as-you-go basis; the other to provide for a far-reaching reforestation program in 1931. Al Smith firmly opposed the reforestation bond; the success of the conservation referendum was in fact a victory at the polls for the incumbent governor. Roosevelt also fought earnestly for public power in a way that drew the admiration of Senator Norris. Despite his occasional hesitancy no governor was more responsive to the depression than Roosevelt, and he emerged in 1932 as the liberal in opposition to the now dominantly conservative candidacy of Al Smith.[2]

2 John J. Raskob, in a personal letter to Jouett Shouse, drew firm ideological lines: "When I think of the Democratic party being headed by such radicals as Roosevelt, Huey Long, Hearst, McAdoo, and Senators Wheeler and Dill, as against the fine, conservative talent in the party as represented by such men as you, Governor Byrd, Governor Smith, Carter Glass, John W. Davis, Governor Cox, Pierre S. duPont, Governor Ely and others . . . , it takes all one's courage and faith not to lose hope completely." July 7,

In his quest for the presidency Roosevelt had also to solve the more distinctively political problem of reconciling to a single candidacy the varied and divided elements within the Democratic party and within the larger electorate. His success was foreshadowed in his gubernatorial re-election victory of 1930 against United States Attorney Charles H. Tuttle. Not unexpectedly, that election brought him a heavy vote in the city, where he had yet to begin his attacks on the administration of Mayor Jimmy Walker and the forces of Tammany. But the upstate party organization had been a shambles, and it was there that Roosevelt had concentrated his energies. It was his intention, he said, to make "country life in every way as desirable as city life"; and he supported farm legislation and redistributed to the cities some of the tax burden formerly carried by the countryside. A Prohibition party candidate drew votes from Tuttle and helped Roosevelt to carry forty-two of the state's fifty-seven counties; he won the election with a plurality of 725,000, a record far superior to Smith's highest margin of 339,000 in 1922 and a full compensation for the title "one-half of one per cent governor" that Roosevelt had borne after his hair's breadth victory of 1928.[3]

The congressional elections of 1930 also boded well for Roosevelt or any man who should attain national Democratic leadership. In normally Democratic districts, voters who had favored Republicans in 1928 were returning to the fold—notably in southern and border states: North Carolina, Virginia, West Virginia, Maryland, Kentucky, Missouri, and Oklahoma. Outside the South, agricultural states that had reacted against

1932, Raskob Papers. Frank Freidel: *Franklin D. Roosevelt: The Triumph* (Boston, 1956), pp. 139, 186–92, 217–27, 231–3; Bernard Bellush: *Franklin D. Roosevelt as Governor of New York* (New York, 1955), *passim;* Schlesinger: *Crisis of the Old Order*, p. 111. On the reforestation amendment see also Samuel B. Hand: "Al Smith, Franklin D. Roosevelt, and the New Deal: Some Comments on Perspective," *The Historian*, XXVII (May 1965), 366–81.

[3] Franklin D. Roosevelt: *Public Papers, 1930* (Albany, 1931), pp. 700–2; *The New York Times*, November 7, 1932, p. 1; *Farm Economics*, LXX (June 1931), 1541; Bellush: *Franklin D. Roosevelt*, pp. 76–102.

Smith's alien manner and failure to formulate a program were disillusioned over Hoover's promises to alleviate the plight of the farmers; Democrats won Republican-held seats in Ohio, Indiana, Illinois, Wisconsin, and Nebraska. Finally, the districts Smith had helped to gain in urban areas in 1928 remained Democratic in 1930, and additional ones were won for the party in such localities as Chicago, northern New Jersey, southeastern Connecticut, and Pittsfield, Massachusetts. When the new Congress met in the winter of 1931, the Democrats were able to organize the House; and in the Senate, where six new Democrats were sworn in, the Republicans had an edge of only one vote.[4]

For Roosevelt the task of winning nationwide support for the presidency was an exercise in consensus. F.D.R. had first to dissociate himself sufficiently from the policies of the city faction to demonstrate that he was not the hand-picked and tractable successor of Governor Smith. "Out here," complained a Californian, "you seem to have the brand of Tammany Hall and its 'clique.'" On the issue of prohibition, Roosevelt in 1930 went damp, calling for repeal and, in the interim, for proscription of saloons and for state prohibition laws to be enforced by the federal government. After the gubernatorial election he kept quiet on the issue, subordinating it to the depression in his 1932 slogan "Bread, Not Booze": thereby he outmaneuvered Raskob, who wished to make him appear so anti-prohibitionist that southerners would promote favorite sons. To put further distance between himself and Tammany, Roosevelt called Mayor Walker on the carpet in Albany, appointed Judge Samuel Seabury to investigate the Tammany District Attorney, and supported a Republican-controlled state investigation of New York City government. And in 1932 Roosevelt decided on a southern Protestant, John Nance Garner, for the vice presidential nomination—a choice only partially offset by that of James Farley for National Chairman. In other respects, Roosevelt's program in the years preceding the presidential contest

---

[4] *Congressional Directory*, Seventieth Congress (2nd Sess., July 1930); Seventy-first Congress (1st Sess., April 1931).

was attractive to city voters: he extended workmen's compensation, promoted restraints on the injunction, attempted remedies for unemployment, and expanded the state park area. He even hedged his attack on Tammany corruption by insulting Judge Seabury and prolonging the tenure in office of Mayor Walker. Finally, Roosevelt's overtures to the older Wilsonians brought more inclusive strengths and appeals to his cause. He won over Colonel Edward House, Albert Sidney Burleson, A. Mitchell Palmer, Homer Cummings, and other men of the Wilson era. The identification with Wilson came easily to that President's Assistant Secretary of the Navy; and the support of some of the Wilsonians helped impart a liberal tone to the Roosevelt candidacy.[5]

By the time the Democrats met in Chicago to choose a presidential candidate in 1932, Roosevelt held a commanding lead among the aspirants. Though Smith and Garner had each won some important primaries, only Roosevelt had distinguished himself as a man with a positive approach to the depression. It was pointed out that his liberal rhetoric sometimes outdistanced his intentions; he only puzzled voters in May, for instance, when he suggested that the "National Income" be redistributed by means of social planning that would give more money to workers and less to owners. But set against the platitudinous statements of the urban Democrats and the confusion of the congressional party men, Roosevelt provided the hope his party and nation needed. At the convention the candidacies of Smith and Garner seriously threatened to block F.D.R.'s nomination. Had Smith given up his own ambitions and released his delegates he might have satisfied his aversion to the Governor, for many of the

[5] For a detailed account of Roosevelt's maneuvers on prohibition, there is Earland I. Carlson: "Franklin D. Roosevelt's Fight for the Presidential Nomination, 1928–1932," unpublished doctoral dissertation, University of Illinois, 1955; on Roosevelt's sometimes inept handling of his relations with Tammany, see Freidel: *Franklin D. Roosevelt: The Triumph*, p. 54; on his labor program, Bellush: *Franklin D. Roosevelt*, pp. 191–207; Casper T. Gee to F.D.R., February 19, 1929, Roosevelt Papers; Edward House to Albert Sidney Burleson, May 7, 1931, House Papers.

votes for Roosevelt were cast out of fear that Smith might win—while the Happy Warrior's own supporters would not favor the man who liked to style himself a Dutchess County farmer. But Garner and his chief backer, William Randolph Hearst, conceded the prize to F.D.R. on the fourth ballot, and Smith had to bear the ignominy of having William Gibbs McAdoo throw California's votes and the nomination to Roosevelt. McAdoo's speech before jeering galleries recalled Bryan's effort to address the convention of 1924, but this time a trump card was in hand, and McAdoo undoubtedly relished his dramatic opportunity to play it. Roosevelt flew from Albany to Chicago, bucking storms along the Great Lakes, to deliver his acceptance speech.

The brief party platform, called by one journalist "ten or fifteen percent more progressive" than the Republican, phrased its scanty remedies in a formidable language. Among other crimes, the unnamed opposition "[had] robbed millions of our people of their life savings"; and there must be a "drastic change in economic governmental policies." But that change turns out to be "an immediate and drastic reduction of governmental expenditures . . . to accomplish a saving of not less than twenty-five per cent in the cost of the Federal Government." The Farm Board was extravagant, so were government subsidies; at most, the federal government should promote "necessary and useful" public works and help impoverished states to pay their relief bills, while foreign nations should be held to the debts they owed us. Walter Lippmann noted that "the platform is the handiwork of men composing the right wing of the Roosevelt following."[6]

Neither was the campaign itself an especially articulate one, for Roosevelt had not at this time found his empirical way into a clearly progressive national policy—as he had into a program of statewide scope. Earlier in the year Hearst had prevailed upon

[6] Kirk H. Porter and Donald Bruce Johnson: *National Party Platforms, 1840–1956* (Urbana, Ill., 1956), pp. 331–3; *New Republic* LXXI (July 13, 1932), 220; Lippmann: *Interpretations, 1931–1932* (New York, 1932), p. 310.

Roosevelt to make a statement denigrating the League of Nations, and during the electioneering he practically ignored foreign policy except for attacking the debt moratorium. He also preached government economy in a way that was later to prove most embarrassing. He hedged on the tariff; he practically ignored labor; he hailed agriculture in the most general terms. Hoover called his opponent a chameleon on plaid. Only occasionally in gestures such as his meeting with the Bonus Army, or in speeches like that delivered at the Commonwealth Club in San Francisco—where he spoke of the major role in store for the national government—did Roosevelt anticipate future policies.

Still, through it all he seemed a far more sensitive humanitarian than Hoover, and the expected Democratic landslide came. As the vote in 1920 was anti-Wilson, so that in 1932 was anti-Hoover rather than pro-Roosevelt. Contemporary observers had scant reason to predict that Roosevelt would be an outstanding President, but at least he had managed, both in New York politics and in prenomination strategy, to become the representative of a party rather than a faction; and this achievement in political skill—not the least of skills for a statesman—should have been perceived as a favorable portent.

In 1932 Roosevelt won slightly over sixty per cent of the two-party vote in the nation's ten largest cities; in 1936 he would win sixty-four per cent. And in the House of Representatives, Democrats occupied seventy-five per cent of the seats in the ten largest cities in 1932 and would win ninety-seven per cent in 1936. The figures appear to demonstrate that the depression years were a time of urbanization for the Democratic party, and indeed the legislative politics and the legislative accomplishments of the party during the thirties fixed upon it a character more enduringly urban than rural: in the years since, the city has proven more faithful to the Democrats than the country. And why has this been so? Perhaps the party, thrust by the crisis into a role of emergency leadership and economic innovation, would have turned by necessity to a politics of the city where America's complex economic future, along with the majority of its electorate, would lie; and if the conservative posture of the Republicans had relatively little to attract the farmer with his own continuing burden of overproduction, it had less to attract the urban voter. But the history of the years prior to 1932 suggests that the depression merely accelerated, within the Democratic party at any rate, a process that was already well under way. The phenomenon of Smith, the rear-guard politics of the Klan, the drama of the 1924 convention and the 1928 presidential campaign all demonstrate at least impressionistically the increasing strength of the urban Democracy, and the increasing significance of its immigrant-stock component; the congressional vote beginning in 1922, and the presidential returns of 1928, chart the trend with some precision.

Yet in 1932 Roosevelt won almost as large a portion of the hinterland as the metropolis. For his total popular vote was fifty-nine per cent. Indeed, the Roosevelt coalition of 1932 included elements comparable to those in the Wilson coalition of 1916. In 1932 Roosevelt's candidacy sealed together in common cause farmers and laborers, natives and foreign stock, country and city. The revolution is traceable to many sources: the victories of Smith among the immigrants and their children, the political craft of Roosevelt, the dilemmas and bad fortune of the Republican administration, and the crucible of the depression— which substituted for the divisions of culture and ancestry the common identity of the dispossessed. The victory of Roosevelt in 1932 was only a step toward the more lasting conquest of the electorate. But it was the new President who saw the revolution through and fulfilled the wishes of his old friend Josephus Daniels: "I am ambitious that your administration shall be followed by a repetition of the strengthening of the Democratic party so that it will not henceforth be dependent upon the southern states and three or four pivotal states, but that it shall be, as in the early days of the Republic, the dominant party in all parts of the country."[7]

[7] Daniels to Roosevelt, November 10, 1932, Roosevelt Papers.

APPENDIX

Homogeneous Election Districts
Used in Voting Samples for Chapter VIII

(AD = assembly district; ED = election district; Pcts = precincts)
I. Manhattan
   A. The German Vote
      1916: AD 23; ED 9, 11–21.
      1920: AD 16; ED 4, 5, 25–35, 37, 40, 46.
      1924: AD 16; ED 2–5, 25–33, 38.
      1928: AD 16; ED 1–8, 16–19, 22–29, 31–40.
      1932: AD 16; ED 1–7, 12, 14, 16–20, 23–30, 32–40.

   B. The Irish Vote
      1916: AD 11; ED 6, 11–16. AD 14; ED 20, 21.
            AD 16; ED 20. AD 23; ED 16. AD 27; ED 17, 22.
      1920: AD 5; ED 16, 18, 19, 24–27. AD 11; ED 31, 33.
            AD 12; ED 28, 29, 31–33.
      1924: AD 5; ED 16, 18, 19, 23–26. AD 12; ED 28, 31–33, 51.
      1928: AD 5; ED 29–31, 33, 34, 36.
      1932: AD 5; ED 31, 33, 35, 36, 38.

   C. The Italian Vote
      1916: AD 1, ED 17, 18. AD 2; ED 5–8. AD 3; ED 2, 3, 7, 8, 11–13.
            11–13. AD 5; ED 2–4.
      1920: AD 1; ED 14–16. AD 2; ED 17, 20, 21. AD 10; ED 16.
      1924: AD 1; ED 15–17, 24, 26. AD 2; ED 23, 28, 30.
            AD 10; ED 18, 19, 21, 22.
      1928: AD 1; ED 2–8. AD 2; ED 14, 16–19, 23, 24.
            AD 4; ED 1, 3. AD 6; ED 6–10, 12–14, 16–20.
      1932: AD 1; ED 1–7. AD 2; ED 2–5, 8. AD 4; ED 1, 3, 4, 10.
            AD 6; ED 6–12, 14–18.

D. The Negro Vote

    1916: AD 21; ED 20, 22, 26–28. AD 23; ED 1–5. AD 30; ED 25–30.

    1920: AD 19; ED 36, 38–43. AD 21; ED 21, 23, 24.

    1924: AD 19; ED 39–43. AD 21; ED 17, 18, 21–30, 32, 33.

    1928: AD 13; ED 22, 23, 28, 30. AD 19; ED 16, 18, 20, 23, 24.

           AD 21; ED 12–14, 19–22.

    1932: AD 13; ED 16–23, 25–30, 32.

E. The Jewish Vote

    1916: AD 2; ED 16, 18. AD 4; ED 6–11, 13, 15.

           AD 6; ED 3–7. AD 8; ED 6. AD 18; ED 16, 19–24.

           AD 26; ED 9, 11.

    1920: AD 1; ED 1–5. AD 4; ED 4, 9–11, 14–17.

           AD 6; ED 1–4, 6, 7. AD 14; ED 25–26, 31.

           AD 15; ED 47–50. AD 17; ED 1, 2.

    1924: AD 1; ED 1–5. AD 4; ED 8–12, 17–20. AD 6; ED 1–8.

    1928: AD 1; ED 2–8. AD 2; ED 5, 6. AD 4; ED 1, 3.

           AD 6; ED 6–10, 12–14, 16–20.

    1932: AD 1; ED 1–7. AD 2; ED 2–5, 8. AD 4; ED 1, 3, 4, 10.

           AD 6; ED 6–12, 14–18.

II. Chicago

A. The German Vote

    1916: Ward 24; Pcts 11–17.

    1920: Ward 24; Pcts 13–19.

    1924: Ward 45; Pcts 9–19.

    1928: Ward 45; Pcts 9–19. Ward 47; Pcts 22–26.

    1932: Ward 45; Pcts 1, 10–13, 15, 34–43, 45, 50.

B. The Jewish Vote

    1916: Ward 12; Pcts 45–47. Ward 15; Pcts 1–18.

           Ward 20; Pcts 4–12.

    1920: Ward 10; Pcts 2–5. Ward 11; Pcts 6–8. Ward 12; Pcts 41–47.

           Ward 14; Pcts 1–16, 18, 44–50, 52.

    1924: Ward 20; Pcts 3–9. Ward 24; Pcts 3–10, 13–23.

           Ward 26: Pcts 7, 9, 11–16, 23. Ward 34; Pcts 8–16.

    1928: Ward 24; Pcts 15, 16, 18–24, 30. Ward 29; Pct 15.

    1932: Ward 24; Pcts 19–22, 24–29, 33, 35–39.

C. The Polish Vote

    1916: Ward 8; Pcts 9, 18–20. Ward 16; Pcts 15–24.

    1920: Ward 8; Pcts 9, 18–20. Ward 17; Pcts 1–7.

    1924: Ward 31; Pcts 1–7. Ward 33; Pcts 12–19.

    1928: Ward 31; Pcts 1–7, 18, 19. Ward 33; Pcts 13–22.

    1932: Ward 26; Pcts 16, 17, 19–23, 25, 27, 28. Ward 32; Pcts 39–47.

D. The Negro Vote

    1916: Ward 2; Pcts 17, 20, 22–30, 34, 55–59, 62–74.

    1920: Ward 2; Pcts 20–35, 50–74.

    1924: Ward 2; Pcts 20, 24–37, 49, 50, 54–58. Ward 3; Pcts 1–17.

    1928: Ward 2; all Pcts. Ward 3; Pcts 1–70. Ward 4; Pcts 12–42.

    1932: Ward 2; all Pcts. Ward 3; Pcts 1–40, 64–69.
           Ward 4; Pcts 44–66.

III. Boston

A. The Italian Vote

    1916: Ward 1; Pcts 1, 2. Ward 2; Pcts 1–7. Ward 5; Pcts 1, 2.

    1920: Ward 1; Pcts 1, 2. Ward 2; Pcts 1–7. Ward 5; Pcts 1.

    1924: Ward 1; Pcts 1, 2. Ward 2; Pcts 1–7. Ward 5; Pcts 1, 2.

    1928: Ward 1; Pcts 2, 4–6, 12. Ward 3; Pcts 1, 2.

    1932: Ward 1; Pcts 2, 4–6, 12. Ward 3; Pcts 1, 2.

BIBLIOGRAPHY

I. MANUSCRIPTS

American Civil Liberties Union, Princeton University Library.

Chandler P. Anderson, Library of Congress.

Association Against the Prohibition Amendment, Library of Congress.

Josiah W. Bailey, Duke University Library.

Newton D. Baker, Library of Congress and Western Reserve University Library.

Ray Stannard Baker, Library of Congress.

William Watts Ball, Duke University Library.

William B. Bankhead, Department of Archives and History, State of Alabama.

Alben W. Barkley, University of Kentucky Library.

Bernard Baruch, Princeton University Library.

William E. Borah, Library of Congress.

Gutzon Borglum, Library of Congress.

William Bruce, University of Virginia Library.

Charles W. Bryan, Nebraska State Historical Society.

William Jennings Bryan, Library of Congress and Nebraska State Historical Society.

Albert S. Burleson, Library of Congress.

Nicholas Murray Butler, Columbia University Library.

Warren A. Candler, Emory University Library.

James Cannon, Jr., Duke University Library.

John H. Clarke, Western Reserve University Library.

William Bourke Cockran, New York Public Library.

Tom Connally, Library of Congress.

Royal Copeland, Michigan Historical Collections, University of Michigan.

George Creel, Library of Congress.

James M. Curley Scrapbooks, College of the Holy Cross Library.

Bronson Cutting, Library of Congress.

Josephus Daniels, Library of Congress.

Chester C. Davis, Western Historical Manuscripts Collection, University of Missouri Library.

John W. Davis, Yale University Library.
Democratic National Committee Papers, 1929–1933, Franklin D. Roosevelt Library.
Mary Dewson, Franklin D. Roosevelt Library.
Nathaniel B. Dial, Duke University Library.
Edward A. Dickson, University of California Library (Los Angeles).
William E. Dodd, Library of Congress.
Robert L. Doughton, Southern Historical Collection, University of North Carolina.
Woodbridge Ferris, Michigan Historical Collections, University of Michigan.
Henry Ford, Ford Motor Company Archives.
Carter Glass, University of Virginia Library.
Samuel Gompers, New York Public Library.
Thomas Gore, University of Oklahoma Library.
Theodore Green, Library of Congress.
Thomas Gregory, Library of Congress.
Charles S. Hamlin, Library of Congress.
Frank A. Hampton, Duke University Library.
Byron Patton Harrison, The Mississippi Collection, University of Mississippi Library.
Will H. Hays, Indiana State Library.
James Thomas Heflin, Howard College Library.
Gilbert Hitchcock, Library of Congress.
Herbert Hoover, Herbert Hoover Presidential Library.
Edward House, Yale University Library.
David Houston, National Archives.
Louis Howe, Franklin D. Roosevelt Library
Cordell Hull, Library of Congress.
Arthur M. Hyde, Western Historical Manuscripts Collection, University of Missouri.
William M. Jardine, Library of Congress.
Hiram Johnson, Bancroft Library, University of California.
Edwin P. Kilroe, Tammany Hall Collection, Columbia University Library.
Franklin K. Lane, Library of Congress.
Robert Lansing, Library of Congress.
League of Women Voters, Library of Congress.
Breckinridge Long, Library of Congress.
Thomas B. Love, Dallas Historical Society.
Norman Mack, Buffalo Historical Society.
Thomas R. Marshall, Indiana State Library.
William Gibbs McAdoo, Library of Congress.

Vance McCormick, Yale University Library.

Kenneth D. McKellar, Memphis Public Library.

Charles McNary, Library of Congress.

George Fort Milton, Library of Congress.

Meredith Nicholson, Indiana State Library.

Peter Norbeck, University of South Dakota Library.

George W. Norris, Library of Congress and Nebraska Historical Society.

Lee Overman, Southern Historical Collection, University of North Carolina.

Robert L. Owen, Library of Congress.

Alexander Mitchell Palmer, Library of Congress and National Archives.

George Peek, Western Historical Manuscripts Collection, University of Missouri.

James D. Phelan, Bancroft Library, University of California.

Gifford Pinchot, Library of Congress.

Key Pittman, Library of Congress.

Louis Post, Library of Congress.

Chester D. Pugley, Duke University Library.

Henry Rainey, Library of Congress.

Samuel Ralston, Indiana University Library.

Joseph E. Ransdell, Louisiana State University Library.

John J. Raskob, Eleutherian Mills Historical Library.

Donald R. Richberg, Chicago Historical Society.

Franklin D. Roosevelt, Franklin D. Roosevelt Library.

Jared Y. Sanders, Louisiana State University Library.

Jouett Shouse, University of Kentucky Library.

Furnifold M. Simmons, Duke University Library.

Alfred E. Smith, New York State Library.

Augustus O. Stanley, University of Kentucky Library.

Mark Sullivan, Herbert Hoover Institute on War, Revolution, and Peace.

Claude A. Swanson, Duke University Library and University of Virginia Library.

Thomas Taggart, Indiana State Library.

Elmer Thomas, University of Oklahoma Library and Franklin D. Roosevelt Library.

Joe Tumulty, Library of Congress.

Lawrence D. Tyson, University of North Carolina Library.

Oscar W. Underwood, Department of Archives and History, State of Alabama.

Lillian Wald, New York Public Library.

David I. Walsh, College of the Holy Cross Library.

Frank P. Walsh, New York Public Library.

Thomas J. Walsh, Library of Congress.
Lindsey Warren, University of North Carolina Library.
James Watson, Indiana State Library.
Tom Watson, University of North Carolina Library.
Henry Watterson, Library of Congress.
George White, The Ohio Historical Society.
William Allen White, Library of Congress.
John Sharp Williams, Library of Congress.
William B. Wilson, Historical Society of Pennsylvania.
Woodrow Wilson, Library of Congress.
Robert Woolley, Library of Congress.

II. *BOOKS: Primary Sources*

Baker, Ray Stannard: *Woodrow Wilson, Life and Letters.* 8 vols. New York, 1931.
Barkley, Alben: *That Reminds Me—*. Garden City, N.Y., 1954.
Behind the Scenes in Politics. Anonymous. New York, 1924.
Bowers, Claude: *My Life.* New York, 1962.
Burgess, Ernest W., and Charles Newcomb: *Census Data of the City of Chicago, 1920.* Chicago, 1931.
———: *Census Data of the City of Chicago, 1930.* Chicago, 1933.
Campaign Book of the Democratic Party, Candidates and Issues in 1928. New York, 1928.
Campaign Book of the Democratic Party, Candidates and Issues in 1932. New York, 1932.
Cannon, James: *Bishop Cannon's Own Story,* ed. Richard L. Watson, Jr. Durham, N.C., 1955.
Colby, Lewis Sells: *I'll Take the Democrats.* New York, 1964.
Connally, Tom, and Alfred Steinberg: *My Name is Tom Connally.* New York, 1954.
Coolidge, Calvin: *The Autobiography of Calvin Coolidge.* New York, 1929.
Cox, James M.: *Journey Through My Years.* New York, 1946.
Creel, George: *How We Advertized America.* New York, 1920.
———: *Rebel at Large.* New York, 1947.
———: *The War, the World, and Wilson.* New York, 1920.
Daniels, Josephus: *The Cabinet Diaries of Josephus Daniels, 1913–1921,* ed. E. David Cronon. Lincoln, Neb., 1963.
———: *The Wilson Era: Years of War and After, 1917–1923.* Chapel Hill, N.C., 1946.

Darrow, Clarence: *The Story of My Life.* New York, 1932.

Davis, Julia: *Legacy of Love.* New York, 1961.

Dawes, Charles G.: *Notes as Vice-President, 1927–1928.* Boston, 1935.

The Democratic Campaign Book, 1924. New York, 1924.

The Democratic Text Book, 1916. New York, 1916.

The Democratic Text Book, 1920. New York, 1920.

Farley, James A.: *Jim Farley's Story.* New York, 1948.

Flynn, Edward J.: *You're the Boss.* New York, 1947.

Gerard, James W.: *My First Eighty-Three Years in America.* New York, 1951.

Gompers, Samuel: *Seventy Years of Life and Labor.* Vol. II. New York, 1925.

Guzman, Jessie P. *et al.,* eds.: *The Negro Yearbook, 1952.* New York, 1952.

Harris, Joseph P.: *Registration of Voters in the United States.* Washington, D.C., 1929.

Hays, Will H.: *Memoirs.* Garden City, N.Y., 1955.

Hoover, Herbert: *The Memoirs of Herbert Hoover.* Vol. I. *Years of Adventure, 1874–1920;* Vol. II. *The Cabinet and the Presidency, 1920–1933.* New York, 1952.

————: *The New Day, Campaign Speeches of Herbert Hoover, 1928.* Stanford, 1928.

Houston, David F.: *Eight Years with Wilson's Cabinet, 1913–1920.* Vol. II. New York, 1926.

Howe, Frederic C.: *The Confessions of a Reformer.* New York, 1925.

Hull, Cordell: *Memoirs.* Vol. I. New York, 1948.

Ickes, Harold L.: *The Autobiography of a Curmudgeon.* New York, 1943.

Laidlaw, Walter, ed.: *Population of the City of New York, 1890–1930.* New York, 1932.

————: *Statistical Sources for Demographic Studies of Greater New York, 1920.* New York, 1922.

Lane, Franklin K.: *The Letters of Franklin K. Lane, Personal and Political,* eds. Anne W. Lane and Louis H. Wall. Boston, 1922.

Le Brun, George: *It's Time to Tell.* New York, 1962.

Lodge, Henry Cabot: *The Senate and the League of Nations.* New York, 1925.

March, Peyton C.: *The Nation at War.* Garden City, N.Y., 1932.

Marshall, Thomas R.: *Recollections of Thomas R. Marshall: A Hoosier Salad.* Indianapolis, 1925.

McAdoo, Eleanor Wilson: *The Woodrow Wilsons.* New York, 1937.

McAdoo, William Gibbs: *Crowded Years.* Boston, 1931.

Norris, George W.: *Fighting Liberal: The Autobiography of George W. Norris.* New York, 1945.

Official Report of the Proceedings of the Democratic National Convention ... [of] ... *1920*. Indianapolis, 1920.

Official Report of the Proceedings of the Democratic National Convention ... [of] ... *1924*. Indianapolis, 1925.

Official Report of the Proceedings of the Democratic National Convention ... [of] ... *1928*. Indianapolis, 1928.

Percy, William Alexander: *Lanterns on the Levee*. New York, 1941.

Petersen, Svend: *A Statistical History of the American Presidential Elections*. New York, 1963.

Porter, Kirk H., ed.: *National Party Platforms, 1840–1960*. Urbana, Ill., 1961.

Proskauer, Joseph M.: *A Segment of My Years*. New York, 1950.

Quint, Howard H., and Robert H. Ferrell, eds.: *Talkative President: The Off-the-Record Press Conferences of Calvin Coolidge*. Amherst, Mass., 1964.

Robinson, Edgar E.: *The Presidential Vote, 1896–1932*. Stanford, 1934.

Roosevelt, Eleanor: *The Autobiography of Eleanor Roosevelt*. New York, 1961.

Roosevelt, Elliott, ed.: *Roosevelt, Franklin D.: His Personal Letters: 1905–1928*. Vol. II. New York, 1948. *His Personal Letters: 1928–1945*. Vol. III. New York, 1950.

Roper, Daniel C.: *Fifty Years of Public Life*. Durham, N.C., 1941.

Simmons, Furnifold M.: *Memoirs and Addresses*, ed. J. Fred Rippy. Durham, N.C., 1936.

Smith, Alfred E.: *Campaign Addresses of Governor Alfred E. Smith*. Washington, D.C., 1929.

———: *Up to Now*. New York, 1929.

Steffens, Lincoln: *The Autobiography of Lincoln Steffens*. New York, 1931.

———: *The Letters of Lincoln Steffens*, eds. Ella Winter and Granville Hicks. 2 vols. New York, 1938.

Stevens, Doris: *Jailed for Freedom*. New York, 1920.

Syrett, Harold C., ed.: *The Gentleman and the Tiger: The Autobiography of George B. McClellan, Jr*. Philadelphia, 1956.

Thompson, Warren S.: *Population: The Growth of Metropolitan Districts in the United States: 1900–1940*. Washington, D.C., 1947.

Tumulty, Joseph P.: *Woodrow Wilson As I Knew Him*. New York, 1921.

Underwood, Oscar W.: *Drifting Sands of Party Politics*. New York, 1928.

United States Bureau of the Census: *Fifteenth Census, 1930*. Washington, D.C., 1933.

———: *Fourteenth Census, 1920*. Washington, D.C., 1923.

―――: *Historical Statistics of the United States, Colonial Times to 1957.* Washington, D.C., 1960.

―――: *Religious Bodies, 1926.* Vol. I. Washington, D.C., 1930.

―――: *Religious Bodies, 1926.* Vol. II. Washington, D.C., 1929.

―――: *Thirteenth Census, 1910.* Washington, D.C., 1913.

―――: *Twelfth Census, 1900.* Washington, D.C., 1903.

United States Department of Agriculture: *Second Annual Report.* Federal Farm Loan Board. Washington, D.C., 1918.

United States Department of Agriculture: *Yearbook of Agriculture, 1920.* Washington, D.C., 1921.

United States Department of Agriculture: *Yearbook of Agriculture, 1928.* Washington, D.C., 1929.

United States Department of Labor: *Annual Report of the Commissioner of Immigration, 1920.* Washington, D.C., 1921.

Watson, James E.: *As I Knew Them.* Indianapolis, 1936.

Wheeler, Burton K., and Paul F. Healy: *Yankee from the West.* New York, 1962.

White, William Allen: *The Autobiography of William Allen White.* New York, 1946.

―――: *Politics: The Citizen's Business.* New York, 1924.

―――: *Selected Letters of William Allen White, 1899–1943,* ed. Walter Johnson. New York, 1947.

Wilson, Edith Bolling: *My Memoir.* Indianapolis, 1939.

Wilson, Woodrow: *War and Peace: Presidential Messages, Addresses, and Public Papers (1917–1924),* eds. Ray Stannard Baker and William E. Dodd. 2 Vols. New York, 1927.

III. *BOOKS: Secondary Sources*

Aaron, Daniel, ed.: *America in Crisis.* New York, 1952.

Acheson, Sam Hanna: *Joe Bailey: The Last Democrat.* New York, 1932.

Adams, Frank C.: *Texas Democracy.* Austin, Tex., 1937.

Adler, Selig: *The Isolationist Impulse: Its Twentieth-Century Reaction.* New York, 1957.

Agar, Herbert: *Pursuit of Happiness: The Story of American Democracy.* Boston, 1938.

Alexander, Charles C.: *The Ku Klux Klan in the Southwest.* Lexington, Ky., 1965.

Allen, Frederick Lewis: *Only Yesterday.* New York, 1931.

Allen, William Harvey: *Al Smith's Tammany Hall: Champion Political Viper.* New York, 1928.

Anderson, William H.: *The Church in Action Against the Saloon.* Westerville, Ohio, 1910.

Angle, Paul M.: *Bloody Williamson.* New York, 1952.

Asbury, Herbert: *The Great Illusion: An Informal History of Prohibition.* Garden City, N.Y., 1950.

Bagby, Wesley: *The Road to Normalcy.* Baltimore, 1962.

Bailey, Thomas A.: *Woodrow Wilson and the Great Betrayal.* New York, 1945.

———: *Woodrow Wilson and the Lost Peace.* New York, 1944.

Bain, Richard C.: *Convention Decisions and Voting Records.* Washington, D.C., 1960.

Barnes, Harry Elmer: *Prohibition Versus Civilization.* New York, 1932.

Bartlett, Ruhl J.: *The League to Enforce Peace.* Chapel Hill, N.C., 1944.

Baruch, Bernard M.: *Baruch: The Public Years.* New York, 1960.

———, and John M. Hancock: *War and Postwar Adjustment Policies.* Washington, D.C., 1944.

Bates, J. Leonard: *The Origins of Teapot Dome: Progressives, Parties, and Petroleum, 1909-1921.* Urbana, Ill., 1963.

Bean, Louis: *Ballot Behavior: A Study of Presidential Elections.* Washington, D.C., 1940.

———: *How to Predict Elections.* New York, 1948.

Beasley, Norman, and Rixey Smith: *Carter Glass.* New York, 1939.

Bell, Herbert C. F.: *Woodrow Wilson and the People.* Garden City, N.Y., 1945.

Bellush, Bernard: *Franklin D. Roosevelt as Governor of New York State.* New York, 1955.

Benedict, Murray R.: *Farm Policies in the United States, 1790-1950.* New York, 1953.

Benson, Lee: *The Concept of Jacksonian Democracy: New York as a Test Case.* Princeton, 1961.

Bent, Silas: *Strange Bedfellows.* New York, 1928.

Berelson, Bernard, et al.: *Voting; A Study of Opinion Formation in a Presidential Campaign.* Chicago, 1954.

Berman, Edward: *Labor Disputes and the President of the United States.* New York, 1924.

Bernstein, Irving: *The Lean Years: A History of the American Worker, 1920-1933.* Boston, 1960.

Berridge, William A.: *Cycles of Unemployment in the United States, 1903-1922.* Boston, 1923.

Binkley, Wilfred E.: *American Political Parties: Their Natural History.* 3rd edn. New York, 1958.

Blum, John M.: *Joe Tumulty and the Wilson Era.* Boston, 1951.

————: *Woodrow Wilson and the Politics of Morality*. Boston, 1956.

Bone, Hugh: *American Politics and the Party System*. New York, 1949.

————: *Party Committees and National Politics*. Seattle, 1958.

Booth, Edgar Allen: *The Mad Mullah of America*. Columbus, 1927.

Booth, Edward Townsend: *God Made the Country*. New York, 1946.

Bornet, Vaughn D.: *Labor Politics in a Democratic Republic: Moderation, Division, and Disruption in the Presidential Election of 1928*. Washington, D.C., 1964.

Boulding, Kenneth: *The Image*. Ann Arbor, Mich., 1956.

Bowden, Robert D.: *Boies Penrose*. New York, 1937.

Bowers, Claude G.: *Beveridge and the Progressive Era*. Cambridge, Mass., 1932.

Bowers, David F., ed.: *Foreign Influences in American Life*. Princeton, 1944.

Broderick, Francis L.: *Right Reverend New Dealer, John A. Ryan*. New York, 1963.

Brody, David: *Labor in Crisis: The Steel Strike of 1919*. Philadelphia, 1965.

Brooks, Robert C.: *Political Parties and Electoral Problems*. 3rd edn. New York, 1933.

Brown, William Burlie: *The People's Choice: The Presidential Image in Campaign Biography*. Baton Rouge, 1960.

Bryce, James: *The American Commonwealth*. Vol. II. New York, 1895.

Burdick, Eugene, and Arthur J. Brodbeck, eds.: *American Voting Behavior*. Glencoe, Ill., 1959.

Burnham, Walter Dean: *Presidential Ballots, 1836–1892*. Baltimore, 1955.

Burns, James M.: *The Deadlock of Democracy: Four-Party Politics in America*. Englewood Cliffs, N.J., 1963.

————: *John Kennedy: A Political Profile*. New York, 1961.

Butler, Robert A.: *So They Framed Stephenson*. Huntington, Ind., 1940.

Campbell, Angus, *et al.*: *The American Voter*. New York, 1960.

————: *Elections and the Political Order*. New York, 1966.

————: *The Voter Decides*. Evanston, Ill., 1954.

Campbell, Christiana M.: *The Farm Bureau: A Study of the Making of National Farm Policy, 1933–1940*. Urbana, Ill., 1962.

Capper, Arthur: *The Agricultural Bloc*. New York, 1922.

Carroll, Mollie R.: *Labor and Politics: The Attitude of the AF of L Toward Legislation and Politics*. New York, 1923.

Carter, Paul A.: *The Decline and Revival of the Social Gospel; Social and Political Liberalism in American Protestant Churches, 1920–1940*. Ithaca, N.Y., 1956.

Cash, Wilbur: *The Mind of the South*. New York, 1941.

Cash, William T.: *History of the Democratic Party in Florida.* Tallahassee, Fla., 1936.

Catt, Carrie C., and Nettie R. Shuler: *Woman Suffrage and Politics: The Inner Story of the Suffrage Movement.* New York, 1923.

Chaffee, Zechariah, Jr.: *Free Speech in the United States.* Cambridge, Mass., 1941.

Chalmers, David M.: *Hooded Americanism: The First Century of the Ku Klux Klan, 1865–1965.* New York, 1965.

Chambers, Clarke A.: *Seedtime of Reform: American Social Service and Social Action, 1918–1933.* Minneapolis, 1963.

Chambers, William N.: *The Democrats, 1789–1964.* Princeton, 1964.

Child, Clifton J. *The German-Americans in Politics, 1914–1917.* Madison, Wisc., 1939.

Churchill, Winston S.: *The Aftermath.* London, 1929.

Claghorn, Kate H.: *The Immigrant's Day in Court.* New York, 1923.

Clark, Norman H.: *The Dry Years: Prohibition and Social Change in Washington.* Seattle, 1965.

Cleveland, Frederic A., and Joseph Schafer, eds.: *Democracy in Reconstruction.* Boston, 1919.

Coben, Stanley: *A. Mitchell Palmer: Politician.* New York, 1963.

Cohn, David L.: *The Fabulous Democrats.* New York, 1956.

Coit, Margaret L.: *Mr. Baruch.* Boston, 1957.

Coletta, Paolo E.: *William Jennings Bryan.* Vol. I. *Political Evangelist, 1860–1908.* Lincoln, Neb., 1964.

The Commonweal: Catholicism in America. New York, 1953.

Connable, Alfred, and Edward Silberfarb: *Tigers of Tammany: Nine Men Who Ran New York.* New York, 1967.

Cook, Sherwin L.: *Torchlight Parade: Our Presidential Pageant.* New York, 1929.

Cotter, Cornelius P., and Bernard C. Hennessy: *Politics Without Power: The National Party Committees.* New York, 1964.

Cramer, Clarence H.: *Newton D. Baker.* Cleveland, 1961.

Cross, Robert D.: *The Emergence of Liberal Catholicism in America.* Cambridge, Mass., 1958.

Crowell, Benedict, and Robert Forrest Wilson: *Demobilization: Our Industrial and Military Demobilization After the Armistice, 1918–1920.* New Haven, 1921.

Cummings, Homer, and Carl MacFarland: *Federal Justice.* New York, 1937.

Dabney, Virginius: *Below the Potomac: A Book About the New South.* New York, 1942.

————: *Dry Messiah, The Life of Bishop Cannon.* New York, 1949.

———: *Liberalism in the South*. Chapel Hill, N.C., 1932.

Daniels, Jonathan: *The End of Innocence*. Philadelphia, 1954.

Daniels, Roger: *The Politics of Prejudice: The Anti-Japanese Movement in California and the Struggle for Japanese Exclusion*. Berkeley, 1962.

David, Paul T., *et al.*: The Politics of National Party Conventions. Washington, D.C., 1960.

Denison, John D. *Iowa Democracy*. Vol. I. Iowa City, 1939.

Dickinson, Thomas H.: *The Portrait of a Man as Governor*. New York, 1928.

Dobyns, Fletcher: *The Amazing Story of Repeal*. Chicago, 1940.

———: *The Underworld of American Politics*. New York, 1932.

Dodd, William E.: *Woodrow Wilson and His Work*. New York, 1922.

Dos Passos, John: *U.S.A.* Vol. II. *Nineteen Nineteen*. New York, 1930.

Douglas, Paul H.: *The Coming of a New Party*. New York, 1932.

Duffield, Marcus: *King Legion*. New York, 1931.

Dunn, Robert W., ed.: *The Palmer Raids*. New York, 1948.

Dunnington, Miles W.: *Thomas J. Walsh, Independent Democrat in the Wilson Years*. Chicago, 1940.

Durden, Robert F.: *The Climax of Populism*. Lexington, Ky., 1965.

Eaton, Herbert A.: *Presidential Timber: A History of Nominating Conventions, 1868–1960*. New York, 1964.

Ellis, David M. *et al.*: *A Short History of New York State*. Ithaca, N.Y., 1957.

Ellis, John Tracy: *American Catholicism*. Chicago, 1956.

Ewing, Cortez A.: *Presidential Elections from Abraham Lincoln to Franklin D. Roosevelt*. Norman, Okla., 1940.

Fenno, Richard F., Jr.: *The President's Cabinet*. New York, 1959.

Fenton, John H.: *The Catholic Vote*. New Orleans, 1960.

———: *Politics in the Border States*. New Orleans, 1957.

Field, Carter: *Bernard Baruch*. New York, 1944.

Fite, Gilbert C.: *George N. Peek and the Fight for Farm Parity*. Norman, Okla., 1954.

Fleming, Denna F.: *The Treaty Veto of the American Senate*. New York, 1930.

———: *The United States and the League of Nations, 1918–1920*. New York, 1932.

Flexner, Eleanor: *Century of Struggle: The Woman's Rights Movement in the United States*. Cambridge, Mass., 1959.

Freidel, Frank: *Franklin D. Roosevelt: The Ordeal*. Boston, 1954.

———: *Franklin D. Roosevelt: The Triumph*. Boston, 1956.

Friedman, Elisha M., ed.: *American Problems of Reconstruction*. New York, 1918.

Frost, Stanley, and Milton Elrod: *The Challenge of the Klan.* Indianapolis, 1924.

Fry, Henry P.: *The Modern Ku Klux Klan.* Boston, 1922.

Fuchs, Lawrence H.: *The Political Behavior of American Jews.* Glencoe, Ill., 1956.

Fuller, Edgar I.: *The Visible of the Invisible Empire.* Denver, 1925.

Furniss, Norman F.: *The Fundamentalist Controversy, 1918–1931.* New Haven, 1954.

Garraty, John: *Henry Cabot Lodge.* New York, 1953.

———: *Right-Hand Man: The Life of George W. Perkins.* New York, 1960.

———: *Woodrow Wilson.* New York, 1956.

Garrett, Garet: *The Wild Wheel.* New York, 1952.

Garrison, Winfred E.: *Catholicism and the American Mind.* Chicago, 1928.

Gerson, Louis L. *The Hyphenate in Recent American Politics and Diplomacy.* Lawrence, Kan., 1964.

Gibson, Florence E.: *The Attitude of the New York Irish Toward State and National Affairs, 1848–1892.* New York, 1951.

Gilbert, Clinton W.: *You Takes Your Choice.* New York, 1924.

Gist, Noel P.: *Secret Societies.* Columbia, Mo., 1940.

Glad, Paul W.: *McKinley, Bryan, and the People.* Philadelphia, 1964.

———: *The Trumpet Soundeth: William Jennings Bryan and His Democracy, 1896–1912.* Lincoln, Neb., 1960.

Glass, Carter, Jr., and Robert C. Glass: *Virginia Democracy.* Springfield, Ill., 1937.

Goldman, Eric F.: *Rendezvous With Destiny.* New York, 1952.

Gosnell, Harold F.: *Getting Out the Vote.* Chicago, 1927.

———: *Machine Politics: Chicago Model.* Chicago, 1937.

———: *Negro Politicians: The Rise of Negro Politics in Chicago.* Chicago, 1935.

Gossett, Thomas F.: *Race: The History of an Idea in America.* Dallas, 1963.

Graham, Frank: *Al Smith: American.* New York, 1945.

Grant, Madison: *The Passing of the Great Race.* New York, 1916.

Grantham, Dewey W., Jr.: *The Democratic South.* Athens, Ga., 1963.

———: *Hoke Smith and the Politics of the New South.* Baton Rouge, 1958.

Grassmuck, George L.: *Sectional Biases in Congress on Foreign Policy.* Baltimore, 1951.

Greer, Thomas H.: *What Roosevelt Thought: The Social and Political Ideas of Franklin D. Roosevelt.* East Lansing, Mich., 1958.

Gunther, John: *Roosevelt in Retrospect.* New York, 1950.

Gusfield, Joseph R.: *Symbolic Crusade: Status Politics and the American Temperance Movement*. Urbana, Ill., 1963.

Hagedorn, Herman: *Leonard Wood*. Vol. II. New York, 1931.

Handlin, Oscar: *Al Smith and His America*. Boston, 1958.

———: *The American People in the Twentieth Century*. Cambridge, Mass., 1954.

———: *The Uprooted*. Boston, 1951.

Hapgood, Norman, ed.: *Professional Patriots*. New York, 1928.

———, and Henry Moskowitz: *Up From the City Streets*. New York, 1927.

Harbaugh, William Henry: *Power and Responsibility: The Life and Times of Theodore Roosevelt*. New York, 1961.

Harris, Warren G.: *Herbert Hoover and the Great Depression*. New York, 1959.

Havard, William C., and Loren P. Beth: *The Politics of Mis-representation; Rural-Urban Conflict in the Florida Legislature*. Baton Rouge, 1962.

Hays, Samuel P.: *The Response to Industrialism, 1885–1914*. Chicago, 1957.

Hennessy, Michael E.: *Four Decades of Massachusetts Politics, 1890–1935*. Norwood, Mass., 1935.

Herrick, Genevieve Forbes, and John Origin Herrick: *The Life of William Jennings Bryan*. Chicago, 1925.

Herring, Pendleton E.: *The Politics of Democracy*. New York, 1940.

Hibben, Paxton: *The Peerless Leader: William Jennings Bryan*. New York, 1929.

Hicks, John D.: *Republican Ascendancy, 1921–1933*. New York, 1960.

———, and Theodore Saloutos: *Agricultural Discontent in the Middle West, 1900–1939*. Madison, Wisc., 1951.

High, Stanley: *The Church in Politics*. New York, 1930.

Higham, John: *Strangers in the Land*. New Brunswick, N.J., 1955.

Hinton, Harold B.: *Cordell Hull*. New York, 1942.

Hirsch, Mark D.: *William C. Whitney, Modern Warwick*. New York, 1948.

Hofstadter, Richard: *The Age of Reform: From Bryan to F.D.R.* New York, 1955.

———: *The American Political Tradition and the Men Who Made It*. New York, 1948.

———: *Anti-Intellectualism in American Life*. New York, 1963.

Holcombe, Arthur: *The New Party Politics*. New York, 1933.

———: *The Political Parties of Today*. 2nd edn. New York, 1925.

———: *State Government in the United States*. 2nd edn. New York, 1926.

Hollingsworth, J. Rogers: *The Whirligig of Politics: The Democracy of Cleveland and Bryan.* Chicago, 1963.

Holt, W. Stull: *Treaties Defeated by the Senate.* Baltimore, 1933.

Hoover, Herbert: *The Ordeal of Woodrow Wilson.* New York, 1958.

Howe, Frederic C.: *The Confessions of a Reformer.* New York, 1925.

Howe, M. A. DeWolfe, ed.: *John Jay Chapman and His Letters.* Cambridge, Mass., 1937.

Hoyt, Edwin P.: *Jumbos and Jackasses.* Garden City, 1960.

Hubbard, Preston J.: *Origins of the TVA: The Muscle Shoals Controversy, 1920–1932.* Nashville, 1961.

Humes, D. Joy: *Oswald Garrison Villard, Liberal of the 1920's.* Syracuse, 1960.

Huntley, Theodore A.: *The Life of John W. Davis.* New York, 1924.

Hutchinson, William T.: *Lowden of Illinois.* Vol. II. Chicago, 1957.

Huthmacher, J. Joseph. *Massachusetts People and Politics, 1919–1933.* Cambridge, Mass., 1959.

Hyman, Herbert: *Political Socialization.* Glencoe, Ill., 1959.

Inglehart, Frederick M.: *King Alcohol Dethroned.* New York, 1917.

Ise, John: *The United States Oil Policy.* New Haven, 1926.

Israel, Fred L.: *Nevada's Key Pittman.* Lincoln, Neb., 1963.

Jefferson, Charles E.: *Roman Catholicism and the Ku Klux Klan.* New York, 1925.

Jefferson, Thomas: *Notes on Virginia,* ed. William Peden. Chapel Hill, N.C., 1954.

Johnson, Claudius O.: *Borah of Idaho.* New York, 1936.

Johnson, Donald: *The Challenge to American Freedoms: World War I and the Rise of the American Civil Liberties Union.* Lexington, Ky., 1963.

Johnson, Walter: *William Allen White's America.* New York, 1947.

Johnson, Willis F.: *George Harvey.* Boston, 1929.

Jones, Richard S.: *A History of the American Legion.* Indianapolis, 1946.

Jones, Stanley L.: *The Presidential Election of 1896.* Madison, Wisc., 1964.

Jones, Winfield: *Knights of the Ku Klux Klan.* New York, 1941.

Kane, John J.: *Catholic-Protestant Conflicts in America.* Chicago, 1955.

Karson, Marc: *American Labor Unions and Politics, 1900–1918.* Carbondale, Ill., 1958.

Keller, Morton: *In Defense of Yesterday: James M. Beck and the Politics of Conservatism, 1861–1936.* New York, 1958.

Kent, Frank R.: *The Democratic Party: A History.* New York, 1928.

———: *The Great Game of Politics.* New York, 1935.

Kerwin, Jerome G.: *Federal Water-Power Legislation.* New York, 1926.

Key, V. O., Jr.: *Politics, Parties, and Pressure Groups.* 4th edn. New York, 1958.

———: *A Primer of Statistics for Political Scientists.* New York, 1954.

———: *Southern Politics in State and Nation.* New York, 1949.

Kile, Orville M.: *The Farm Bureau Through Three Decades.* Baltimore, 1948.

Kilpatrick, Carroll, ed.: *Roosevelt and Daniels: A Friendship in Politics.* Chapel Hill, N.C., 1952.

Kilroe, Edwin P., *et al.*: *The Story of Tammany.* New York, 1924.

King, Judson: *The Conservation Fight: From Theodore Roosevelt to the Tennessee Valley Authority.* Washington, D.C., 1959.

Kinzer, Donald L.: *An Episode in Anti-Catholicism: The American Protective Association.* Seattle, 1964.

Komarovsky, Mirra, ed.: *Common Frontiers of the Social Sciences.* Glencoe, Ill., 1957.

La Follette, Belle C., and Fola La Follette: *La Follette.* 2 vols. New York, 1953.

Lally, Francis J.: *The Catholic Church in a Changing America.* Boston, 1962.

Lane, Robert E.: *Political Life.* Rev. edn. New York, 1965.

Lasch, Christopher: *The American Liberals and the Russian Revolution.* New York, 1962.

Lasswell, Harold: *Psychopathology and Politics.* Chicago, 1930.

Latham, Earl, ed.: *The Philosophy and Policies of Woodrow Wilson.* Chicago, 1958.

Lee, Henry W.: *How Dry We Were: Prohibition Revisited.* New York, 1963.

Lee, Robert, and Martin E. Marty, eds.: *Religion and Social Conflict.* New York, 1964.

Lenski, Gerhard: *The Religious Factor.* Garden City, N.Y., 1961.

Leuchtenburg, William: *Franklin D. Roosevelt and the New Deal, 1932–1940.* New York, 1963.

———: *The Perils of Prosperity, 1914–1932.* Chicago, 1958.

Levine, Edward M.: *The Irish and Irish Politicians: A Study of Cultural and Social Alienation.* Notre Dame, Ind., 1966.

Levine, Lawrence: *Defender of the Faith: William Jennings Bryan; The Last Decade, 1915–1925.* New York, 1965.

Lewinson, Paul: *Race, Class, Party: A History of Negro Suffrage and White Politics in the South.* New York, 1932.

Lief, Alfred: *Democracy's Norris.* New York, 1939.

Lindley, Ernest K.: *The Roosevelt Revolution.* New York, 1933.

Link, Arthur S.: *Wilson: Confusions and Crises, 1915–1916*. Princeton, 1964.
———: *Wilson: Campaigns for Progressivism and Peace*. Princeton, 1965.
———: *Wilson the Diplomatist: A Look at His Major Foreign Policies*. 2nd edn. Chicago, 1963.
———: *Wilson: The New Freedom*. Princeton, 1956.
———: *Wilson: The Road to the White House*. Princeton, 1947.
———: *Woodrow Wilson*. New York, 1963.
———: *Woodrow Wilson and the Progressive Era, 1910–1917*. New York, 1954.
———, and Bruce Catton: *American Epoch*. 2nd edn. New York, 1963.
Lippincott, Isaac: *Problems of Reconstruction*. New York, 1919.
Lippmann, Walter: *Interpretations, 1931–1932*. New York, 1932.
———: *Men of Destiny*. New York, 1927.
Lipset, Seymour M.: *Political Man; The Social Bases of Politics*. Garden City, N.Y., 1960.
Littleton, Martin W.: *The Democratic Party of the State of New York*. Vol. II. New York, 1905.
Livermore, Seward W.: *Politics Is Adjourned: Woodrow Wilson and the War Congress, 1916–1918*. Middletown, Conn., 1966.
Lombardi, John: *Labor's Voice in the Cabinet: A History of the Department of Labor from Its Origin to 1921*. New York, 1942.
Loucks, Emerson H.: *The Ku Klux Klan in Pennsylvania*. New York, 1936.
Lowitt, Richard: *George W. Norris: The Making of a Progressive, 1861–1912*. Syracuse, 1963.
Lubell, Samuel: *The Future of American Politics*. New York, 1952.
———: *The Revolt of the Moderates*. New York, 1956.
Lynd, Robert S., and Helen Merrell Lynd: *Middletown: A Study in Contemporary American Culture*. New York, 1929.
Lyons, Eugene: *Herbert Hoover*. Garden City, N.Y., 1964.
MacKay, Kenneth C.: *The Progressive Movement of 1924*. New York, 1947.
MacKaye, Milton: *The Tin Box Parade: A Handbook for Larceny*. New York, 1934.
Manchester, William: *H. L. Mencken: Disturber of the Peace*. New York, 1950.
Mann, Arthur. *La Guardia: A Fighter Against His Times, 1882–1933*. Philadelphia, 1959.
———: *La Guardia Comes to Power*. Philadelphia, 1965.
Marshall, Charles C.: *The Roman Catholic Church in the Modern State*. New York, 1928.
Mason, Alpheus T.: *Brandeis, A Free Man's Life*. New York, 1946.

Maury, Reuben: *The Wars of the Godly*. New York, 1928.

Maxey, Chester C.: *Urban Democracy*. Boston, 1929.

May, Ernest R.: *The World War and American Isolation, 1914–1917*. Cambridge, Mass., 1959.

Mayer, George H.: *The Republican Party, 1854–1964*. New York, 1964.

McAdoo, William Gibbs: *The Challenge: Liquor and Lawlessness Versus Constitutional Government*. New York, 1928.

McBain, Howard Lee: *Prohibition, Legal and Illegal*. New York, 1928.

McConnell, Grant: *The Decline of Agrarian Democracy*. Berkeley, 1953.

McCoy, Donald R: *Calvin Coolidge: Quiet President*. New York, 1967.

McDougall, William: *Ethics and Some Modern World Problems*. New York, 1924.

———: *Is America Safe for Democracy?* New York, 1921.

McGovney, Dudley O.: *The American Suffrage Medley*. Chicago, 1949.

McGrath, James H.: *The Power of the People*. New York, 1948.

McGurrin, James: *Bourke Cockran*. New York, 1948.

McKay, Claude: *Harlem: Negro Metropolis*. New York, 1940.

McKean, Dayton D.: *The Boss: The Hague Machine in Action*. Boston, 1940.

McKenna, Marian C.: *Borah*. Ann Arbor, Mich., 1961.

McLoughlin, William G., Jr.: *Billy Sunday Was His Real Name*. Chicago, 1955.

McMaster, John Bach: *The United States in the World War, 1918–1920*. New York, 1920.

Mecklin, John M.: *The Ku Klux Klan: A Study of the American Mind*. New York, 1924.

Mencken, H. L.: *A Carnival of Buncombe*, ed. Malcolm Moos. Baltimore, 1956.

———: *Making a President*. New York, 1932.

———: *Prejudices: First Series, 1919; Second Series, 1920; Third Series, 1922; Fourth Series, 1924; Fifth Series, 1926; Sixth Series, 1927*. New York.

Meredith, Ellis, ed.: *Democracy at the Crossroads: A Symposium*. New York, 1932.

Meriwether, Lee: *Jim Reed, 'Senatorial Immortal.'* Webster Groves, Mo., 1948.

Merriam, Charles E.: *Chicago: A More Intimate View of Urban Politics*. New York, 1929.

———: *Four American Party Leaders*. New York, 1926.

———, and Harold F. Gosnell: *Non Voting: Causes and Methods of Control*. Chicago, 1924.

Merz, Charles: *The Dry Decade*. New York, 1931.

———: *And Then Came Ford*. Garden City, N.Y., 1929.

Meyer, Donald B.: *The Protestant Search for Political Realism*. Berkeley, 1960.

Michie, Allan, and Frank Ryhlick: *Dixie Demagogues*. New York, 1939.

Miller, Robert M.: *American Protestantism and Social Issues, 1919–1939*. Chapel Hill, N.C., 1958.

Mims, Edwin: *The Advancing South: Stories of Progress and Reaction*. New York, 1926.

Minor, Henry A.: *The Story of the Democratic Party*. New York, 1928.

Mitgang, Herbert: *The Man Who Rode the Tiger*. New York, 1963.

Mock, James R., and Cedric Larson: *Words That Won the War: The Story of the Committee on Public Information, 1917–1919*. Princeton, 1939.

———, and Evangeline Thurber: *Report on Demobilization*. Norman, Okla., 1944.

Monteval, Marion: *The Klan Inside Out*. Claremore, Okla., 1924.

Moore, Edmund A.: *A Catholic Runs for President: The Campaign of 1928*. New York, 1956.

Moos, Malcolm: *The Republicans*. New York, 1956.

Morgan, H. Wayne, ed.: *The Gilded Age: A Reappraisal*. Syracuse, 1963.

Morris, Richard B.: *Encyclopedia of American History*. 2nd rev. edn. New York, 1965.

Morrison, Joseph L.: *Josephus Daniels: The Small-d Democrat*. New York, 1967.

Moses, Robert: *A Tribute to Governor Smith*. New York, 1962.

Mowry, George E.: *The Era of Theodore Roosevelt, 1900–1912*. New York, 1958.

———: *Theodore Roosevelt and the Progressive Movement*. Madison, Wisc., 1946.

———: *The Urban Nation, 1920–1960*. New York, 1965.

Mullen, Arthur F.: *Western Democrat*. New York, 1940.

Munro, William B.: *Personality in Politics*. New York, 1934.

Murphy, John C.: *An Analysis of the Attitudes of American Catholics Toward the Immigrant and the Negro, 1825–1925*. Washington, D.C., 1940.

Murray, Robert K.: *Red Scare: A Study in National Hysteria, 1919–1920*. Minneapolis, 1955.

Myers, Gustavus: *The History of Tammany Hall*. 2nd edn. New York, 1917.

———: *History of Bigotry in the United States*. New York, 1943.

Myers, William S.: *The Republican Party: A History*. New York, 1931.

Myrdal, Gunnar.: *An American Dilemma: The Negro Problem and Modern Democracy.* New York, 1942.

Nations, Gilbert O.: *The Political Career of Alfred E. Smith.* Washington, D.C., 1928.

Nelson, William H., ed.: *Theory and Practice in American Politics.* Chicago, 1964.

Neuberger, Richard L., and Stephen B. Kahn: *Integrity: The Life of George W. Norris.* New York, 1937.

Nevins, Allan: *Henry White: Thirty Years of American Diplomacy.* New York, 1930.

———: *Herbert H. Lehman and His Era.* New York, 1963.

———, and Frank E. Hill: *Ford, Expansion and Challenge, 1915–1932.* New York, 1957.

Noggle, Burl: *Teapot Dome: Oil and Politics in the 1920's.* Baton Rouge, 1962.

Northrop, William B., and John B. Northrop: *The Insolence of Office: The Story of the Seabury Investigations.* New York, 1932.

Nye, Russel B.: *Midwestern Progressive Politics.* East Lansing, Mich., 1951.

O'Connor, Harvey: *Mellon's Millions.* New York, 1933.

Odegard, Peter H.: *Pressure Politics.* New York, 1928.

———, ed.: *Religion and Politics.* New York, 1960.

Ogburn, William F., ed.: *Social Changes in 1928.* Chicago, 1929.

O'Keane, Josephine: *Thomas J. Walsh.* Francestown, N.H., 1955.

Ostrander, Gilman: *The Prohibition Movement in California, 1848–1933.* Berkeley, 1957.

Overacker, Louise, and Victor J. West: *Money in Elections, 1920–1928.* New York, 1932.

Palmer, Frederic: *Newton D. Baker: America at War.* Vol. II. New York, 1931.

Panunzio, Constantine: *The Deportation Cases of 1919–1920.* New York, 1932.

Paul, Randolph: *Taxation in the United States.* Boston, 1954.

Paxson, Frederic L.: *The Great Demobilization and Other Essays.* Madison, Wisc., 1941.

———: *Postwar Years: Normalcy, 1918–1923.* Berkeley, 1948.

Peck, Mary Gray: *Carrie Chapman Catt.* New York, 1944.

Peel, Roy V.: *The Political Clubs of New York City.* New York, 1935.

Peel, Roy V., and Thomas C. Donnelly: *The 1928 Campaign: An Analysis.* New York, 1931.

———: *The 1932 Campaign: An Analysis.* New York, 1935.

Penniman, Howard R.: *Sait's American Parties and Elections.* 5th edn. New York, 1952.

Perkins, Frances: *The Roosevelt I Knew.* New York, 1946.

Perlman, Selig, and Philip Taft: *History of Labor in the United States, 1896–1932.* New York, 1935.

Petersen, H. C., and Gilbert C. Fite: *Opponents of War, 1917–1918.* Madison, Wisc., 1957.

Pike, James A.: *A Roman Catholic in the White House.* New York, 1960.

Pinchot, Gifford: *The Power Monopoly: Its Makeup and Its Menace.* Milford, Pa., 1928.

Pollock, James Kerr, and Samuel Eldersveld: *Michigan Politics in Transition.* Ann Arbor, Mich., 1942.

Pollock, Norman: *The Populist Response to Industrial America: Midwestern Populist Thought.* Cambridge, Mass., 1962.

Pomper, Gerald: *Nominating the President: The Politics of Convention Choice.* Evanston, Ill., 1963.

Porter, Kirk H., and Donald Bruce Johnson: *National Party Platforms, 1840–1956.* Urbana, Ill., 1956.

Post, Louis: *The Deportations Delirium of Nineteen Twenty.* Chicago, 1923.

Preston, William, Jr.: *Aliens and Dissenters: Federal Suppression of Radicals, 1903–1933.* Cambridge, Mass., 1963.

Pringle, Henry F.: *Alfred E. Smith: A Critical Study.* New York, 1927.

Pritchett, C. Herman: *The Tennessee Valley Authority: A Study in Public Administration.* Chapel Hill, N.C., 1943.

Puryear, Elmer: *Democratic Party Dissension in North Carolina, 1928–1934.* Chapel Hill, N.C., 1962.

Pusey, Merlo J.: *Charles Evans Hughes.* 2 vols. New York, 1951.

Randel, William Peirce: *The Ku Klux Klan: A Century of Infamy.* Philadelphia, 1965.

Rank, S. E.: *Prices of Farm Products in New York State, 1841–1935.* Ithaca, N.Y., 1936.

Raper, Arthur F.: *The Tragedy of Lynching.* Chapel Hill, N.C., 1933.

Rauschenbusch, Stephen: *High Power Propaganda.* New York, 1928.

Rayback, Joseph G.: *A History of American Labor.* New York, 1959.

Rice, Arnold S.: *The Ku Klux Klan in American Politics.* Washington, D.C., 1962.

Rice, Stuart A.: *Farmers and Workers in American Politics.* Washington, D.C., 1942.

———: *Quantitative Methods in Politics.* New York, 1928.

Richards, William C.: *The Last Billionaire: Henry Ford.* New York, 1948.

Richter, Edward J., and Berton Dulce: *Religion and the Presidency: A Recurring American Problem.* New York, 1962.

Rischin, Moses: *The Promised City: New York's Jews, 1870–1914.* Cambridge, Mass., 1962.

Roberts, Edward F.: *Ireland in America.* New York, 1931.

Robertson, William J.: *The Changing South.* New York, 1927.

Robinson, Claude F.: *Straw Votes.* New York, 1932.

Rodman, Bella, and Philip Sterling: *Fiorello La Guardia.* New York, 1962.

Rollins, Alfred B., Jr.: *Roosevelt and Howe.* New York, 1962.

Romasco, Albert U.: *The Poverty of Abundance: Hoover, the Nation, the Depression.* New York, 1965.

Root, Grace C.: *Woman and Repeal.* New York, 1934.

Roseboom, Eugene H.: *A History of Presidential Elections.* New York, 1957.

Ross, Edward A.: *The Old World in the New.* New York, 1913.

Ryan, John A.: *Social Doctrine in Action.* New York, 1941.

Ryan, John A. and Moorhouse F. X. Millar: *The State and the Church.* New York, 1922.

Salter, John Thomas: *Boss Rule: Portraits in City Politics.* New York, 1935.

Samuelson, Paul A., and Everett E. Hagen: *After the War—1918–1920: Military and Economic Demobilization of the United States.* National Resources Planning Board. Washington, D.C., 1943.

Scammon, Richard M.: *America at the Polls: A Handbook of American Presidential Election Statistics, 1920–1964.* Pittsburgh, 1965.

Scheiber, Harry: *The Wilson Administration and Civil Liberties, 1917–1921.* Ithaca, N.Y., 1960.

Schiavo, Giovanni E.: *The Italians in Chicago.* Chicago, 1928.

Schlesinger, Arthur, Jr.: *The Age of Roosevelt.* Vol. I. *Crisis of the Old Order, 1919–1933.* Boston, 1957.

Schriftgiesser, Karl: *This Was Normalcy.* Boston, 1948.

Schroeder, Theodore: *Al Smith, the Pope, and the Presidency.* Cos Cob, Conn., 1928.

Seller, James B.: *The Prohibition Movement in Alabama, 1703–1943.* Chapel Hill, N.C., 1943.

Seymour, Charles: *Woodrow Wilson and the World War.* New Haven, 1921.

Shannon, William V.: *The American Irish.* New York, 1963.

Shideler, James H.: *Farm Crisis, 1919–1923.* Berkeley, 1957.

Shuler, Antoinette, and Carrie Chapman Catt: *Woman Suffrage and Politics.* New York, 1926.

Siegfried, André: *America Comes of Age.* New York, 1927.

Silva, Ruth C.: *Rum, Religion, and Votes: 1928 Re-examined.* University Park, Pa., 1962.

Simmons, William J. *The Klan Unmasked.* Atlanta, 1923.

Sinclair, Andrew. *The Available Man: The Life Behind the Masks of Warren Gamaliel Harding.* New York, 1965.

——: *The Better Half: The Emancipation of the American Woman.* New York, 1965.

——: *Prohibition: The Era of Excess.* Boston, 1962.

Sinclair, Upton B.: *The Flivver King: A Story of Ford-America.* Pasadena, Calif., 1937.

Slosson, Preston William: *The Great Crusade and After, 1914–1928.* New York, 1930.

Smith, Alfred E.: *The Citizen and His Government.* New York, 1935.

Smith, Daniel M.: *The Great Departure: The United States and World War I, 1914–1920.* New York, 1965.

Smith, Emily W., and Daniel Hawthorne: *The Happy Warrior.* New York, 1950.

Smith, Gene: *When the Cheering Stopped: The Last Years of Woodrow Wilson.* New York, 1964.

Smith, Mortimer: *William J. Gaynor, Mayor of New York.* Chicago, 1951.

Smith, Rembert: *Politics in a Protestant Church.* Atlanta, 1930.

Socolofsky, Homer E.: *Arthur Capper.* Lawrence, Kan., 1962.

Soule, George H.: *Economic Forces in American History.* New York, 1952.

——: *Prosperity Decade.* New York, 1947.

Sparrow, John C.: *History of Personnel Demobilization in the United States Army.* Washington, D.C., 1951. (Mimeographed.)

Speranza, Gino: *Race or Nation.* Indianapolis, 1925.

Stanwood, Edward: *A History of the Presidency.* Boston, 1898.

Stephenson, George M.: *A History of American Immigration, 1820–1924.* Boston, 1926.

Steuart, Justin: *Wayne Wheeler, Dry Boss.* New York, 1928.

Stiles, Lela: *The Man Behind Roosevelt.* Cleveland, 1954.

——: *It Costs To Be President.* New York, 1936.

Stoddard, Henry L.: *Presidential Sweepstakes: The Story of Political Conventions and Campaigns.* New York, 1948.

Stokes, Anson Phelps: *Church and State in the United States.* Vol. II. New York, 1950.

Stokes, Thomas L.: *Chip Off My Shoulder.* Princeton, 1940.

Stone, Irving: *They Also Ran.* Garden City, N.Y., 1943.

Stromberg, Roland: *Republicanism Reappraised.* Washington, D.C., 1952.

Stuart, William H.: *The Twenty Incredible Years.* Chicago, 1935.

Sullivan, Mark: *Our Times, The United States: 1900–1925.* 6 vols. New York, 1926–35.

Surface, Frank M.: *The Grain Trade During the World War.* New York, 1928.

Sward, Keith: *The Legend of Henry Ford.* New York, 1948.

Synon, Mary: *McAdoo: The Man and His Times.* Indianapolis, 1924.

Taft, Philip: *The AF of L from the Death of Gompers to the Merger.* New York, 1959.

———: *The AF of L in the Time of Gompers.* New York, 1957.

Tannenbaum, Frank: *Darker Phases of the South.* New York, 1924.

Tatum, Elbert L.: *The Changed Political Though of the Negro, 1915–1940.* New York, 1951.

Taylor, Mack: *Alfred E. Smith: A Psychoanalytical Study.* Fort Worth, 1928.

Thomas, Norman, and Paul Blanshard: *What's the Matter with New York: A National Problem.* New York, 1932.

Timberlake, James H.: *Prohibition and the Progressive Movement, 1900–1920.* Cambridge, Mass., 1963.

Timmons, Bascom N.: *Garner of Texas.* New York, 1948.

———: *Jesse H. Jones: The Man and the Statesman.* New York, 1956.

———: *Portrait of an American: Charles G. Dawes.* New York, 1953.

Tucker, Ray T.: *The Mirrors of 1932.* New York, 1931.

Van Devander, Charles W.: *The Big Bosses.* New York, 1944.

Vinson, John Chalmers: *Referendum for Isolation.* Athens, Ga., 1961.

Wahlke, John C., and Heinz Eulau, eds.: *Legislative Behavior.* Glencoe, Ill., 1959.

Wall, Joseph: *Henry Watterson, Unreconstructed Rebel.* New York, 1956.

Wallace, Henry: *Our Debt and Duty to the Farmer.* New York, 1925.

Wallis, J. H.: *The Politician.* New York, 1935.

Walsh, Thomas J., Lindsay Rogers, and John Dickson: *The Future of Party Government.* Winter Park, Fla., 1929.

Walworth, Arthur: *Woodrow Wilson.* Vol. II. *World Prophet.* New York, 1958.

Warren, Harris G.: *Herbert Hoover and the Great Depression.* New York, 1959.

Wayman, Dorthy G.: *David I. Walsh: Citizen-Patriot.* Milwaukee, 1952.

Wecter, Dixon: *The Hero in America.* New York, 1941.

———: *When Johnny Comes Marching Home.* Cambridge, Mass., 1944.

Weeks, Oliver D.: *The Democratic Victory of 1932.* Dallas, 1933.

Werner, Morris R.: *Bryan.* New York, 1929.

———: *Tammany Hall*. Garden City, N.Y., 1928.

Werner, Morris R., and John Starr: *Teapot Dome*. New York, 1959.

White, Alma B.: *Heroes of the Fiery Cross*. Zarephath, N.J., 1928.

———: *The Ku Klux Klan in Prophecy*. Zarephath, N.J., 1925.

White, Morton, and Lucia White: *The Intellectual Versus the City: From Thomas Jefferson to Frank Lloyd Wright*. Cambridge, Mass., 1962.

White, Theodore H.: *The Making of the President, 1960*. New York, 1961.

White, Walter: *A Man Called White*. New York, 1948.

White, William Alanson: *Thoughts of a Psychologist on the War and After*. New York, 1919.

White, William Allen: *Masks in a Pageant*. New York, 1928.

———: *A Puritan in Babylon: The Story of Calvin Coolidge*. New York, 1938.

Whitener, Daniel Jay: *Prohibition in North Carolina, 1715–1945*. Chapel Hill, N.C., 1945.

Wiebe, Robert: *Businessmen and Reform*. Cambridge, Mass., 1962.

Willebrandt, Mabel Walker: *The Inside of Prohibition*. Indianapolis, 1929.

Williams, Michael: *Shadow of the Pope*. New York, 1932.

Winter, Paul: *What Price Tolerance?* Hewlitt, N.Y., 1928.

Wittke, Carl: *German-Americans and the World War*. Columbus, 1936.

———: *The Irish in America*. Baton Rouge, 1956.

Woddy, C. H.: *The Case of Frank L. Smith*. Chicago, 1930.

Wolfe, Harold: *Herbert Hoover*. New York, 1956.

Zink, Harold: *City Bosses in the United States*. Durham, N.C., 1930.

Zinn, Howard: *La Guardia in Congress*. Ithaca, N.Y., 1958.

Zucker, Norman L.: *George W. Norris: Gentle Knight of American Democracy*. Urbana, Ill., 1966.

IV. SCHOLARLY ARTICLES

Abrams, Richard M.: "Woodrow Wilson and the Southern Congressmen, 1913–1916," *Journal of Southern History*, XXII (November 1956), 417–37.

Acheson, Sam: "Al Smith and the Solid South," *Southwest Review*, XIII (October 1927), 119–22.

Adler, Selig: "The Congressional Election of 1918," *South Atlantic Quarterly*, XXXVI (October 1937), 447–65.

———: "Isolationism Since 1914," *American Scholar*, XXI (Summer 1952), 335–44.

Alexander, Charles C.: "Defeat, Decline, Disintegration: The Ku Klux Klan in Arkansas, 1924 and After," *Arkansas Historical Quarterly,* XXII (Winter 1963), 311–31.

——: "Kleagles and Cash: The Ku Klux Klan as a Business Organization, 1915–1930," *Business History Review,* XXIX (Autumn 1965), 348–67.

——: "The Ku Klux Klan in Texas, 1920–1930," *The Historian of the University of Texas,* I (1962), 21–43.

——: "Secrecy Bids for Power: The Ku Klux Klan in Texas Politics in the 1920's," *Mid-America,* XLVI (January 1964), 3–28.

——: "White Robes in Politics: The Ku Klux Klan in Arkansas, 1922–1924," *Arkansas Historical Quarterly,* XXII (Fall 1963), 195–214.

——: "White-Robed Reformers: The Ku Klux Klan Comes to Arkansas, 1921–1923," *Arkansas Historical Quarterly,* XXII (Spring 1963), 8–23.

Allan, Howard W.: "Isolationism and German-Americans," *Journal of the Illinois State Historical Society,* LVI (Summer 1964), 321–39.

Allen, Lee: "The Democratic Presidential Primary Election of 1924 in Texas," *Southwestern Historical Quarterly,* LVI (April 1958), 474–93.

——: "The McAdoo Campaign for the Presidential Nomination in 1924," *Journal of Southern History,* XXIX (May 1963), 211–38.

——: "The 1924 Underwood Campaign in Alabama," *Alabama Review,* IX (July 1956), 176–87.

——: "The Underwood Presidential Movement of 1924," *Alabama Review,* XV (April 1962), 83–99.

Bagby, Wesley M.: "William Gibbs McAdoo and the 1920 Democratic Presidential Nomination," *East Tennessee Historical Society Publication,* XXXI (1959), 43–58.

——: "Woodrow Wilson, a Third Term, and the Solemn Referendum," *American Historical Review,* LX (April 1955), 567–75.

Baggaley, Andrew R.: "Religious Influences on Wisconsin Voting, 1928–1960," *American Political Science Review,* LVI (March 1962), 66–70.

Barclay, Thomas S.: "The Publicity Division of the Democratic Party, 1929–1930," *American Political Science Review,* XXV (Fall 1931), 68–73.

Bates, J. Leonard: "The Teapot Dome Scandal and the Election of 1924," *American Historical Review,* LX (January 1955), 303–22.

Berman, Daniel M.: "Hugo Black, Southerner," *American University Law Review,* XXI (1961), 35–42.

Billington, Ray A.: "The Origins of Middle Western Isolationism," *Political Science Quarterly,* LX (March 1945), 44–64.

Blum, John: "Nativism, Anti-Radicalism and the Foreign Scare, 1917–1920," *Midwest Journal,* III (1950–51), 46–53.

Blumenthal, Henry: "Woodrow Wilson and the Race Question," *Journal of Negro History,* XLVIII (January 1963), 1–21.

Bohn, Frank: "The Ku Klux Klan Interpreted," *American Journal of Sociology,* XXX (January 1925), 385–407.

Borg, Walter T.: "Food Administration Experiment with Hogs, 1917–1919," *Journal of Farm Economics,* XXV (May 1943), 444–57.

Brown, D. A.: "Historical Prices of Farm Products of States: A Bibliography," *Agricultural History,* XXXVI (July 1962), 169–70.

Burner, David B.: "The Breakup of the Wilson Coalition of 1916," *Mid-America,* XLV (January 1963), 18–35.

———: "The Democratic Party in the Election of 1924," *Mid-America,* XLVI (April 1964), 92–113.

———: "The Brown Derby Campaign," *New York History,* XLVI (October 1965), 356–80.

Burnham, Walter Dean: "The Changing Shape of the American Political Universe," *American Political Science Review,* LIX (March 1965), 7–28.

Carleton, William G.: "Isolationism and the Middle West," *Mississippi Valley Historical Review,* XXXIII (December 1946), 377–90.

———: "A New Look at Woodrow Wilson," *Virginia Quarterly Review,* XXXVIII (Autumn 1962), 545–66.

———: "The Popish Plot of 1928: Smith-Hoover Presidential Campaign," *The Forum,* CXII (September 1949), 141–7.

Carlson, Earland I.: "Franklin D. Roosevelt's Post-Mortem of the 1928 Election," *Midwest Journal of Political Science,* VIII (August 1964), 298–308.

Carter, Paul A.: "The Campaign of 1928 Re-examined," *Wisconsin Magazine of History,* XLVI (Summer 1963), 263–72.

———: "The Other Catholic Candidate: The 1928 Presidential Bid of Thomas J. Walsh," *Pacific Northwest Quarterly,* LV (January 1964), 1–8.

Casey, Ralph D.: "Scripps-Howard Newspapers in the 1928 Presidential Campaign," *Journalism Quarterly,* VII (September 1930), 207–31.

Chalmers, David: "The Ku Klux Klan in the Sunshine State: The 1920's," *Florida Historical Quarterly,* XLII (January 1964), 209–15.

Christenson, Alice M.: "Agricultural Pressure and Governmental Response, 1919–1929," *Agricultural History,* XI (January 1937), 33–42.

Coben, Stanley: "A Study in Nativism: The American Red Scare of 1919–1920," *Political Science Quarterly,* LXXIX (March 1964), 52–75.

Converse, Philip *et al.*: "Stability and Change in 1960: A Reinstating Election," *American Political Science Review*, LV (June 1961), 269–80.

Corwin, Edward S.: "Woodrow Wilson and the Presidency," *Virginia Law Review*, XLII (October 1956), 761–83.

Darling, H. Maurice: "Who Kept the United States Out of the League of Nations?" *Canadian Historical Review*, X (Spring 1929), 196–211.

David, Henry: "Labor and Politics After World War I: 1919–1924," *Labor and Nation*, I (February–March 1946), 27–32.

Davis, James H.: "Colorado Under the Klan," *Colorado Magazine*, XLII (Spring 1965), 93–115.

Degler, Carl N.: "A Century of the Klans: A Review Article," *Journal of Southern History*, XXXI (November 1965), 435–43.

———: "American Political Parties and the Rise of the City: An Interpretation," *Journal of American History*, LI (June 1964), 41–59.

———: "The Great Reversal: The Republican Party's First Century," *South Atlantic Quarterly*, LXV (Winter 1966), 1–11.

———: "The Ordeal of Herbert Hoover," *Yale Review*, LII (Summer 1963), 563–83.

Diamond, William: "Urban and Rural Voting in 1896," *American Historical Review*, XLVI (January 1941), 281–305.

Dimock, Marshall E.: "Woodrow Wilson as a Legislative Leader," *Journal of Politics*, XIX (February 1957), 3–19.

Doherty, Herbert J., Jr.: "Florida and the Presidential Election of 1928," *Florida Historical Quarterly*, XXVI (October 1947), 174–86.

Edelman, Murray: "Symbols and Political Quiescence," *American Political Science Review*, LIV (September 1960), 695–704.

Eldersveld, Samuel J.: "The Influence of Metropolitan Party Pluralities in Presidential Elections Since 1920," *American Political Science Review*, XLIII (December 1949), 1189–1206.

Farris, Charles D.: "Prohibition as a Political Issue," *Journal of Politics*, XXIII (August 1961), 507–25.

Fite, Gilbert: "The Agricultural Issue in the Presidential Campaign of 1928," *Mississippi Valley Historical Review*, XXXVII (March 1951), 653–72.

Fletcher, Ralph, and Mildred Fletcher: "Consistency in Party Voting, 1896–1932," *Social Forces*, XV (1936), 281–5.

Gosnell, Harold F., and Norman Gill: "Analysis of the 1932 Presidential Vote in Chicago," *American Political Science Review*, XXIX (December 1935), 967–84.

Grantham, Dewey W., Jr.: "The Southern Senators and the League of Nations," *North Carolina Historical Review*, XXVI (April 1949), 187–205.

Greer, Scott: "Catholic Voters and the Democratic Party," *Public Opinion Quarterly*, XXV (Winter 1961), 611–25.

Hand, Samuel B.: "Al Smith, Franklin D. Roosevelt, and the New Deal: Some Comments on Perspective," *The Historian*, XXVII (May 1965), 366–81.

Hanneman, Max: "Das Deutschtum in den Vereigten Staaten," *Zu Petermans Milteilungen. Erganzungbund.* CCXXIV (1936), Tafel 9.

Hattery, John W.: "The Presidential Election Campaigns of 1928 and 1960: A Comparison of *The Christian Century* and *America*," *A Journal of Church and State*, IX (Winter 1967), 36–50.

Hennings, Robert E.: "California Democratic Politics in the Period of Republican Ascendance," *Pacific Historical Review*, XXXI (August 1962), 667–80.

Hicks, John D.: "Some Parallels with Populism in the Twentieth Century," *Special Education*, VIII (November 1944), 297–301.

Hines, Tom S., Jr.: "Mississippi and the Repeal of Prohibition," *Journal of Mississippi History*, XXIV (January 1962), 1–39.

Hofstadter, Richard: "Could a Protestant Have Beaten Hoover in 1928?" *The Reporter*, XXII (March 17, 1960), 31–3.

Howenstine, E. Jay, Jr.: "Demobilization After the First World War," *Quarterly Journal of Economy*, LVIII (November 1943), 91–105.

———: "Lessons of World War I," *Annals of the American Academy of Political and Social Science*, CCXXXVIII (April 1945), 180–7.

———: "Public Works Program After World War I," *Journal of Political Economy*, LI (December 1943), 523–37.

Humphreys, Sexson E.: "The Nomination of the Democratic Candidate in 1924," *Indiana Magazine of History*, XXXI (March 1935), 1–9.

Hutchmacher, J. Joseph: "Charles Evans Hughes and Charles Francis Murphy: The Metamorphosis of Progressivism," *New York History*, XLVI (June 1965), 25–40.

———: "Urban Liberalism and the Age of Reform," *Mississippi Valley Historical Review*, XLIX (September 1962), 231–41.

Jackson, Charles O.: "William J. Simmons: A Career in Ku Kluxism," *Georgia Historical Quarterly*, L (December 1966), 351–65.

Johnson, Donald: "The Political Career of A. Mitchell Palmer," *Pennsylvania History*, XXV (October 1958), 345–70.

Johnson, Hildegard B.: "The Location of German Immigrants in the Middle West," *Annals of the American Association of Geographers*, XLI (March 1951), 1–41.

Kelley, Darwin N.: "The McNary-Haugen Bills, 1924–1928," *Agricultural History*, XIV (October 1940), 170–80.

Kelley, Donald B.: "Deep South Dilemma: The Mississippi Press in the

Presidential Election of 1928," *Journal of Mississippi History*, XXV (April 1963), 63–92.

Kerr, Thomas J., IV: "German-Americans and Neutrality in the 1916 Election," *Mid-America*, XLIII (April 1961), 95–105.

Key, V. O., Jr.: "The Future of the Democratic Party," *Virginia Quarterly Review*, XXVIII (Spring 1952), 161–75.

———: "Secular Realignment and the Party System," *Journal of Politics*, XXI (May 1959), 198–210.

———: "A Theory of Critical Elections," *Journal of Politics*, XVII (February 1955), 3–18.

Kirschner, Don S.: "Conflicts and Politics in the 1920's," *Mid-America*, XLVIII (October, 1966), 219–33.

Kutler, Stanley I.: "Labor, the Clayton Act, and the Supreme Court," *Labor History*, III (Winter 1962), 19–38.

Leary, William M., Jr.: "Woodrow Wilson, Irish Americans and the Election of 1916," *Journal of American History*, LIV (June 1967), 57–72.

Link, Arthur S.: "The Enigma of Woodrow Wilson," *American Mercury*, LXV (September 1947), 303–13.

———: "The Federal Reserve Policy and the Agricultural Depression of 1920–21," *Agricultural History*, XX (July 1946), 166–75.

———: "The Middle West and the Coming of World War I," *Ohio Archaeological and Historical Quarterly*, LXII (April 1953), 109–21.

———: "The South and the 'New Freedom': An Interpretation," *American Scholar*, XX (Summer 1951), 314–24.

———: "What Happened to the Progressive Movement in the 1920's?" *American Historical Review*, LXIV (July 1959), 833–51.

———: "Woodrow Wilson and the Democratic Party," *Review of Politics*, XVIII (April 1956), 145–56.

Lippmann, Walter: "Our Predicament Under the Eighteenth Amendment," *Harper's*, CLIV (July 1926), 51–60.

———: "Reconstruction of the Democratic Party," *Yale Review*, XVIII (September 1928), 18–27.

———: "The Setting for John W. Davis," *Atlantic Monthly*, CXXIV (October 1924), 530–5.

———: "Two Leading Democratic Candidates," *New Republic*, XXIII (June 2, 1920), 10–11.

———: "The Wetness of Al Smith," *Harper's*, XLVI (January 1928), 133–9.

Lipset, Seymour Martin: "Some Statistics on Bigotry in Voting," *Commentary*, XXX (October 1960), 286–90.

Livermore, Seward: "The Sectional Issue in the 1918 Congressional Election," *Mississippi Valley Historical Review*, XXXV (June 1948), 29–60.

Lubell, Samuel: "The Politics of Revenge," *Harper's*, CCVI (April 1956), 29–36.

——: "Who Votes Isolationist and Why?" *Harper's*, CCII (April 1951), 29–36.

Margulies, Herbert F.: "The Election of 1920 in Wisconsin: The Return to 'Normalcy' Reappraised," *Wisconsin Magazine of History*, XLI (Autumn 1957), 15–22.

——: "Recent Opinion on the Decline of the Progressive Movement," *Mid-America*, XLV (October 1963), 250–68.

McKinney, Madge W.: "Religion and Elections," *Public Opinion Quarterly*, VIII (Spring 1944), 110–14.

Merriam, Charles E., and Norman N. Gill: "An Analysis of the 1932 Presidential Vote in Chicago," *American Political Science Review*, XXIX (December 1933), 967–84.

Merritt, Richard L.: "Woodrow Wilson and the 'Great and Solemn Referendum,' 1920," *Review of Politics*, XXVII (January 1965), 78–194.

Miller, Robert M.: "A Footnote to the Role of the Protestant Churches in the Election of 1928," *Church History*, XXV (June 1956), 145–59.

——: "A Note on the Relation Between the Protestant Churches and the Revival of the Ku Klux Klan," *Journal of Southern History*, XXII (August 1956), 355–68.

Murphy, Paul L.: "Normalcy, Intolerance, and the American Character," *Virginia Quarterly Review*, XL (Summer 1964), 445–59.

——: "Sources and Nature of Intolerance in the 1920's," *Journal of American History*, LI (June 1964), 60–76.

Nash, Gerald D.: "Herbert Hoover and the Origins of the Reconstruction Finance Corporation," *Mississippi Valley Historical Review*, XLVI (December 1959), 455–68.

Neal, Nevin E.: "The Smith-Robinson Arkansas Campaign of 1928," *Arkansas Historical Quarterly*, XIX (Spring 1960), 3–11.

Niebuhr, H. Richard: "Fundamentalism," *Encyclopaedia of Social Sciences*, eds. E. R. A. Seligman and Alvin Johnson. New York, 1937. III, 527.

Noggle, Burl: "Conservation in Politics: A Study of Teapot Dome," *Mississippi Valley Historical Review*, XLIV (September 1957), 237–60.

Ogburn, William F., and Nell S. Talbot: "A Measurement of the Factors in the Presidential Election of 1928," *Social Forces*, VIII (December 1929), 178–85.

Osgood, Robert E.: "Woodrow Wilson, Collective Security, and the Lessons of History," *Confluence*, V (Winter 1957), 341–54.

Pollock, James K., Jr.: "Campaign Funds in 1928," *American Political Science Review*, XXIII (February 1929), 59–69.

Posner, Russell: "California's Role in the Nomination of Franklin D. Roosevelt," *California Historical Society Quarterly*, XXXIX (Winter 1960), 120–40.

Rankin, Robert S.: "The Future of the Democratic Party," *South Atlantic Quarterly*, XXVIII (July 1929), 225–35.

Reagan, Hugh D.: "Race as a Factor in the Presidential Election of 1928 in Alabama," *Alabama Review*, XIX (January 1966), 5–19.

Rice, Stuart A.: "Differential Changes of Political Preference Under Campaign Stimulation," *Journal of Abnormal and Social Psychology*, XXI (October–December 1926), 297–303.

Rice, Stuart A., and Malcolm M. Willey: "American Women's Ineffective Use of the Vote," *Current History*, XX (July 1924), 641–7.

———: "A Sex Cleavage in the Presidential Election of 1920," *Journal of the American Statistical Association*, XIX (December 1928), 519–20.

Richa, Karel Denis: "Liberalism Frustrated: The League for Independent Political Action, 1928–1933," *Mid-America*, XLVIII (January 1966), 19–28.

Robinson, Edgar E.: "The Decline of the Democratic Party," *American Journal of Sociology*, XX (November 1914), 331–4.

Rollins, Alfred B., Jr.: "Franklin Roosevelt's Introduction to Labor," *Labor History*, III (Winter 1962), 3–18.

———: "Young F.D.R. and the Moral Crusaders," *New York History*, XXXII (January 1956), 3–16.

———: "Young F.D.R. as the Farmer's Friend," *New York History*, XLIII (April 1962), 186–98.

Rothschild, Donald S.: "F.D.R.: Leader in a Time of Drift," *Colby Library Quarterly*, V (September 1960), 143–50.

Sayre, Wallace S.: "Personnel of the Republican and Democratic National Committees," *American Political Science Review*, XXVI (April 1932), 360–3.

Schruben, Francis W.: "William Jennings Bryan, Reformer," *Social Studies*, LV (January 1964), 12–17.

Schwarz, Jordan A.: "Al Smith in the Thirties," *New York History*, XLV (October 1964), 316–30.

———: "John Nance Garner and the Sales Tax Rebellion of 1932," *Journal of Southern History*, XXX (May 1964), 162–80.

Scott, Anne Firor: "A Progressive Wind from the South," *Journal of Southern History*, XXIX (February 1963), 53–70.

Sherman, Richard B.: "The Harding Administration and the Negro: An Opportunity Lost," *Journal of Negro History*, XLIX (July 1964), 151–68.

———: "Republicans and Negroes: The Lessons of Normalcy," *Phylon*, XXVII (Spring 1966), 63–79.

Shideler, James H.: "The La Follette Progressive Party Campaign of 1924," *Wisconsin Magazine of History*, XXXIII (June 1950), 444–57.

———: "The Disintegration of the Progressive Party Movement of 1924," *The Historian*, XIII (Spring 1951), 189–201.

Smith, John S.: "Organized Labor and Government in the Wilson Era; Some Conclusions," *Labor History*, III (Fall 1962), 265–86.

Smylie, James H.: "The Roman Catholic Church, the State, and Al Smith," *Church History*, XXIX (September 1960), 321–43.

Snodgrass, Katharine: "Price Fluctuations in the Woolen Industry," *Annals of the American Academy of Political and Social Science*, LXXXIX (May 1920), 55–60.

Stratton, David H.: "Behind Teapot Dome: Some Personal Insights," *Business History Review*, XXXI (Winter 1957), 385–402.

———: "Splattered with Oil: William G. McAdoo and the 1924 Democratic Presidential Nomination," *Southwestern Social Science Quarterly*, XLIV (June 1963), 62–75.

Taft, Philip: "The Federal Trials of the IWW," *Labor History*, III (Winter 1962), 57–91.

Taner, Ralph M.: "Senator Tom Heflin as Story Teller," *Alabama Review*, XV (January 1962), 54–60.

Tindall, George B.: "Business Progressivism: Southern Politics in the Twenties," *South Atlantic Quarterly*, LXII (Winter 1963), 92–106.

Toy, Eckard V., Jr.: "The KKK in Tillamook, Oregon," *Pacific Historical Quarterly*, LIII (April 1962), 60–4.

Wallace, Anthony F. C.: "Revitalization Movements," *American Anthropologist*, LVIII (March 1956), 264–81.

Warth, Robert D.: "The Palmer Raids," *South Atlantic Quarterly*, XLVIII (January 1949), 1–23.

Watson, Richard A.: "Religion and Politics in Mid-America: Presidential Voting in Missouri, 1928 and 1960," *Midcontinent American Studies Journal*, V (Spring 1964), 33–55.

Watson, Richard L., Jr.: "A Political Leader Bolts—F. M. Simmons in the Presidential Election of 1928," *North Carolina Historical Review*, XXXVII (October 1960), 516–43.

Weeks, O. Douglas: "The Election of 1928," *Southwest Political and Social Science Quarterly*, IX (December 1928), 337–48.

Wesser, Robert F.: "Charles Evans Hughes and the Urban Sources of

Political Progressivism," *New York Historical Society Quarterly,* L (October 1966), 365–400.

Wimer, Kurt: "Woodrow Wilson and a Third Term," *Pennsylvania History,* XXIX (April 1962), 193–211.

———: "Woodrow Wilson Tries Conciliation: An Effort That Failed," *The Historian,* XXV (August 1963), 419–38.

Wolfinger, Raymond E.: "The Development and Persistence of Ethnic Voting," *American Political Science Review,* LIX (December 1965), 896–908.

Woodward, C. Vann: "The Populist Heritage and the Intellectual," *American Scholar,* XXIX (Winter 1960), 55–72.

V. *SERIALS*

A. MAGAZINES

America
The American Federationist
The American Mercury
The Atlantic Monthly
Christian Register
Collier's
The Commoner
The Commonweal
Congressional Digest
The Literary Digest
The Nation
The New Republic
The North American Review
The Outlook
Progressive Farmer
Review of Reviews [American]
The Saturday Evening Post
The Survey
Time
Wallace's Farmer
World's Work
Yale Review

B. NEWSPAPERS

Atlanta *Constitution*
Boston *Herald*
Chicago *Daily Tribune*
Denver *Post*

Los Angeles *Times*
The New York Times
New York *World*
St. Louis *Post-Dispatch*
C. GOVERNMENT PUBLICATIONS
Congressional Record
Monthly Labor Review

VI. *ORAL HISTORY COLLECTION,* Columbia University

Will W. Alexander, 1952
William H. Anderson, 1950
Martin C. Ansorge, 1949
William S. Bennet, 1951
Robert S. Binkerd, 1949
Hobart S. Bird, 1949
Claude Bowers, 1954
John W. Davis, 1954
Samuel Dickstein, 1950
Edward Flynn, 1950
Joseph A. Gavagan, 1950
James W. Gerard, 1950
Florence Harriman, 1950
Marvin Jones, 1953
Samuel Koenig, 1950
Jeremiah T. Mahoney, 1949
Geoffrey Parsons, 1949
Herbert Pell, 1951
Lindsay Rogers, 1958
George Rublee, 1951
William Schieffelin, 1949
Francis R. Stoddard, 1949
Louis Taber, 1952
Eva Valesh, 1954
Lawrence Veiller, 1949
James Wadsworth, 1952

VII. *PERSONAL INTERVIEWS*

Charles W. Berry, March 25, 1963
Warren Kiplinger, September 8, 1964
Joseph M. Proskauer, January 8, 1963

VIII. *UNPUBLISHED DOCTORAL DISSERTATIONS*

Adrian, Frederick W.: "The Political Significance of the Prohibition Party." The Ohio State University, 1942.

Allen, Lee: "The Underwood Presidential Movement of 1924." University of Pennsylvania, 1955.

Almond, Gabriel: "Plutocracy and Politics in New York City." University of Chicago, 1938.

Avin, Benjamin H.: "The Ku Klux Klan, 1915–1925: A Study in Religious Intolerance." Georgetown University, 1952.

Bates, James L.: "Senator Walsh of Montana, 1918–1924: A Liberal Under Pressure." University of North Carolina, 1952.

Bean, Walton E.: "George Creel and His Critics: A Study of the Attacks on the Committee of Public Information, 1917–1919." University of California (Berkeley), 1941.

Boothe, Leon E.: "Woodrow Wilson's Cold War: The President, The Public, and the League Fight, 1919–1920." University of Illinois, 1966.

Carlson, Earland I.: "Franklin D. Roosevelt's Fight for the Presidential Nomination, 1928–1932." University of Illinois, 1955.

Casey, Ralph D.: "Campaign Techniques in 1928." University of Wisconsin, 1929.

Chatham, Marie: "The Role of the National Party Chairman from Hanna to Farley." University of Maryland, 1953.

Chinn, Ronald E.: "Democratic Party Politics in California, 1920–1956." University of California (Berkeley), 1958.

Christensen, Alice M.: "Agricultural Pressure and Government Response in the United States, 1919–1929." University of California (Berkeley), 1937.

Clark, Norman H.: "Liquor Reform and Social Change: A History of the Prohibition Movement in the State of Washington." University of Washington, 1964.

Cuddy, Joseph E.: "Irish-America and National Isolation, 1914–20." State University of New York (Buffalo), 1965.

Dalrymple, Gordon: "The Repeal of the Eighteenth Amendment." Vanderbilt University, 1951.

Davis, John A.: "The Ku Klux Klan in Indiana," Northwestern University, 1966.

Delmatier, Royce D.: "The Rebirth of the Democratic Party in California, 1928–1938." University of California (Berkeley), 1955.

Deskins, Stuart C.: "The Presidential Election of 1928 in North Carolina." University of North Carolina, 1945.

Dohn, Norman H.: "The History of the Anti-Saloon League." The Ohio State University, 1959.

Eldersveld, Samuel J.: "A Study of Urban Electoral Trends in Michigan, 1920–1940." University of Michigan, 1946.

Eldot, Paula: "Alfred E. Smith, Reforming Governor." Yale University, 1961.

Feldman, Martin I.: "An Abstract of the Political Thought of Alfred E. Smith." New York University, 1963.

Ferguson, Jenniellen W.: "Presidential Election Trends in the United States, 1900–1950: A Statistical Study." University of California (Los Angeles), 1956.

Fite, Gilbert C.: "Peter Norbeck: Prairie Statesman." University of Missouri, 1945.

Flynt, James W.: "Duncan Upshaw Fletcher: Florida's Reluctant Progressive." Florida State University, 1965.

Gold, David: "The Influence of Religious Affiliation on Voting Behavior." University of Chicago, 1953.

Goodman, T. William: "The Presidential Campaign of 1920." The Ohio State University, 1951.

Gravell, Grady J.: "A Rhetorical Study of Franklin D. Roosevelt's 1920 Campaign." Louisiana State University, 1963.

Greenlee, Howard S.: "The Republican Party in Division and Reunion, 1913–1920." University of Chicago, 1950.

Hanks, Raymond J.: "The Democratic Party in 1920: The Rupture of the Wilsonian Synthesis." University of Chicago, 1960.

Harrell, Kenneth E. "The Ku Klux Klan in Louisiana, 1920–1930." Louisiana State University, 1966.

Harris, Arvil E.: "Organized Labor in Party Politics, 1906–1932." State University of Iowa, 1936.

Heckman, Dayton E.: "Prohibition Passes: The Story of the Association Against the Prohibition Amendment." The Ohio State University, 1939.

Henderson, Bancroft: "The Democratic National Committee." University of Minnesota, 1958.

Jamison, Edward A.: "Irish-Americans, the Irish Question and Irish Diplomacy, 1895–1921." 2 vols. Harvard University, 1944.

Jennings, David H.: "President Wilson's Tour in September, 1919: A Study of Forces Operating During the League of Nations Fight." The Ohio State University, 1958.

Johnson, Dorothy E.: "Organized Women and National Legislation, 1920–1941." Western Reserve University, 1960.

Jones, Bartlett C.: "The Debate Over National Prohibition, 1920–1933." Emory University, 1961.

Jones, Dallas Lee: "The Wilson Administration and Organized Labor, 1912–1919." Cornell University, 1954.

Kendrick, Jack E.: "The League of Nations and the Republican Senate, 1918–1921." University of North Carolina, 1953.

Kirschner, Don S.: "Conflict in the Corn Belt: Rural Response to Urbanization, 1919–1929." State University of Iowa, 1964.

Manning, Eugene A.: "Old Bob La Follette: Champion of the People." University of Wisconsin, 1966.

McCleiren, Beryl F.: "The Southern Baptist State Newspapers and the Religious Issue During the Presidential Campaigns of 1928 and 1960." Southern Illinois University, 1964.

Milner, Cooper: "The Public Life of Cordell Hull." Vanderbilt University, 1960.

Mitchell, Frank: "Embattled Democrats: Missouri Democratic Politics, 1919–1932." University of Missouri, 1964.

Morsell, John A.: "The Political Behavior of Negroes in New York City." Columbia University, 1950.

Nathan, Meyer J.: "The Presidential Election of 1916 in the Middle West." Princeton University, 1966.

Neal, Nevin E.: "A Biography of Joseph T. Robinson." University of Oklahoma, 1957.

Nugent, Gloria W.: "James A. Farley and the Politics of Victory: 1928–1936." 2 vols. University of Southern California, 1966.

Olsen, Keith: "Franklin K. Lane: A Biography." University of Wisconsin, 1964.

Paone, Rocco M.: "The Presidential Election of 1920." Georgetown University, 1949.

Patterson, Robert E.: "Gilbert M. Hitchcock: A Study of Two Careers." University of Colorado, 1940.

Payne, John W.: "David Franklin Houston: A Biography." University of Texas, 1953.

Reagan, Hugh D.: "The Presidential Campaign of 1928 in Alabama." University of Texas, 1961.

Rofinot, Henry L.: "Normalcy and the Farmer: Agricultural Policy Under Harding and Coolidge, 1920–1928." Columbia University, 1958.

Rollins, Alfred B., Jr.: "The Political Education of Franklin Roosevelt, His Career in New York Politics: 1909–1928." 2 vols. Harvard University, 1953.

Ruetten, Richard T.: "Burton K. Wheeler of Montana." University of Oregon, 1961.

Schapsmeier, Frederick T.: "The Political Philosophy of Walter Lippmann: A Half Century of Thought and Commentary." University of Southern California, 1965.

Schofield, Kent M.: "The Figure of Herbert Hoover in the 1928 Campaign." University of California (Riverside), 1966.

Shideler, James: "The Neo-Progressives: Reform Politics in the United States, 1920–1925." University of California (Berkeley), 1945.

Silbert, Edward M.: "Support for Reform Among Congressional Democrats, 1897–1913." University of Florida, 1966.

Silver, Paul L.: "Wilsonians and the New Deal." University of Pennsylvania, 1964.

Silveri, Louis D.: "The Political Education of Alfred E. Smith: The Assembly Years, 1904–1915." St. John's University, 1964.

Skolnik, Richard.: "The Crystallization of Reform in New York City, 1890–1917." Yale University, 1964.

Smith, John S.: "Organized Labor and Government in the Wilson Era, 1913–1921." Catholic University, 1963.

Smith, William David: "Alfred E. Smith and John F. Kennedy: The Religious Issue During the Presidential Campaigns of 1928 and 1960." Southern Illinois University, 1964.

Springen, Donald K.: "A Rhetorical Analysis of the Speaking of Senator Oscar Underwood in His 1924 Campaign for the Democratic Presidential Nomination." State University of Iowa, 1962.

Stillings, Edwin J.: "Turnout and Electoral Trends, 1870–1950." University of Chicago, 1953.

Thurner, Arthur W.: "The Impact of Ethnic Groups on the Democratic Party in Chicago, 1920–1928." University of Chicago, 1966.

Watts, James F., Jr.: "The Public Life of Breckinridge Long, 1916–1944." University of Missouri, 1964.

Weaver, Norman F.: "The Knights of the Ku Klux Klan in Wisconsin, Indiana, Ohio, and Michigan." University of Wisconsin, 1954.

INDEX

A NOTE ABOUT THE AUTHOR

DAVID BURNER was born in Cornwall, New York, in 1937. He was graduated from Hamilton College in 1958 and received his Ph.D. from Columbia University in 1965. He has taught at Colby College, Hunter College, and Oakland University and is now associate professor of history at the State University of New York in Stony Brook, Long Island. Mr. Burner is married and has one daughter.

A NOTE ON THE TYPE

The text of this book was set on the Linotype in Janson, a recutting made direct from type cast from matrices long thought to have been made by the Dutchman Anton Janson, who was a practicing type founder in Leipzig during the years 1668–87. However, it has been conclusively demonstrated that these types are actually the work of Nicholas Kis (1650–1702), a Hungarian, who most probably learned his trade from the master Dutch type founder Kirk Voskens. The type is an excellent example of the influential and sturdy Dutch types that prevailed in England up to the time William Caslon developed his own incomparable designs from these Dutch faces.

The book was composed, printed and bound by The Book Press Incorporated, Brattleboro, Vermont. Typography and binding design by Betty Anderson.